EVERYTHING

SOUP
COOKBOOK

300 mouthwatering recipes— from heartwarming chicken noodle to sumptuous lobster bisque

B. J. Hanson

Adams Media Corporation
Avon, Massachusetts

EDITORIAL
Publishing Director: Gary M. Krebs
Managing Editor: Kate McBride
Copy Chief: Laura MacLaughlin
Acquisitions Editor: Bethany Brown
Development Editor: Michael Paydos

PRODUCTION
Production Director: Susan Beale
Production Manager: Michelle Roy Kelly
Series Designer: Daria Perreault, Colleen Cunningham
Cover Design: Paul Beatrice, Frank Rivera
Layout and Graphics: Brooke Camfield,
Colleen Cunningham, Rachael Eiben,
Michelle Roy Kelly, Daria Perreault

An Everything® Series Book.
Everything® is a registered trademark of Adams Media Corporation.

Published by Adams Media Corporation
57 Littlefield Street, Avon, MA 02322 U.S.A.
www.adamsmedia.com

ISBN: 1-58062-556-8
Printed in the United States of America.

J I H G F E D C B A

Library of Congress Cataloging-in-Publication Data
Hanson, B.J.
The everything soup cookbook / B.J. Hanson.
p. cm. -- (Everything series)
ISBN 1-58062-556-8
1. Soups. I. Title. II. Series.
TX757 .H36 2002
641.8'13–dc21

2002008440

Illustrations by Barry Littmann.
This book is available at quantity discounts for bulk purchases.
For information, call 1-800-872-5627.

Visit the entire Everything® series at everything.com

Contents

Introduction

Why soup? Soup entices the senses as it simmers, warm and fragrant. Served, it tastes sumptuous. And it is just as vivid in food value: vitamins in ample variety, proteins from grand grains to tasty meats, fiber from vegetables to fruits to nuts, everything. The beauty of soup lies in the way it can introduce or anchor a meal. A small cup is an appetizer. Or a bowl can buttress a sandwich, a small platter of cheeses or nuts or fruit slices, a salad, a plate of rolls, a warm cottage loaf.

Different Soup Families

The following are a few of the different categories of soups. Most varieties are based on texture, ingredients, and, very commonly, thickness. By understanding the different varieties of soup, you will have a better understanding of what a recipe will be like before you even make it!

BISQUE—A soup made with vegetables, fish, or shellfish that is thick, smooth in texture, and opaque (this is usually done by pureeing vegetables or adding cream).

BOUILLABAISSE—On the French Mediterranean coast, a list of specific fish/shellfish, garlic, and spices creates the classic bouillabaisse ("bool-ya-base") (classic stewed with saffron). Most people define it most flexibly, to contain a good variety of different kinds of fish/shellfish.

BOUILLON—A clear, thin broth.

CHOWDER—A thick, chunky soup made with potatoes. There are a large variety of chowders that can include vegetables, seafood, chicken or virtually any other ingredient.

CONSOMMÉ—A very clear soup or stock.

GAZPACHO—A vegetable soup served cold, often made with tomatoes as a key ingredient.

GUMBO—These are soups filled to the gills with a variety of seafood, vegetables, and meat chunks of all kinds, thick broths, and sometimes Creole seasonings (filé and/or okra).

PANADE—Soups thickened with bread, either diced pieces or rounds placed on the bottom of the individual soup bowls.

POTAGE—A French word for soup in general, now used to refer to especially hearty soups.

STEW—A very thick soup based on chunks of meat or occasionally fish.

STOCK—Basically a broth, but sometimes used to refer to broths made using meat bones that have been preroasted.

Basic Soup-Making Equipment

The one crucial piece of equipment you'll need for whipping up some soup is a nice big soup pot. A minimum of two gallons in size will ensure that you'll be able to make most soup recipes in this book and won't have to worry about boilovers. The ideal choice of material for an all-purpose soup pot is stainless steel with an aluminum core or an aluminum disc on the bottom (aluminum helps ensure even heating). All-aluminum pots are not a good choice—aluminum will react to acidic liquids which can create off-colored and off-tasting soups.

Some other things you will want or need to make and serve your favorite soups include:

- Ladles
- Tureen or large serving dish
- Bowls, crocks, soup cups, and soup spoons
- Blender, food processor, hand-held immersion blender, or food mill
- Basic set of cutlery
- A saute pan (you can often just saute in your soup pot before you add liquids as well)

Simmering Broths

Basic Beef Broth

Yields 10 cups

Before freezing or refrigerating the broth, cool it to room temperature by immersing it in a bath of cold water.

1 medium potato
3 large carrots
1 large onion
2 stalks celery, including leaves
1 large tomato (optional)
½ pound lean beef trimmings
4 pounds beef soup bones

8–10 whole black peppercorns
5 sprigs fresh parsley
1 bay leaf
1 tablespoon salt
3 cloves garlic
13 cups cold water

1. Preheat oven to 450 degrees. Clean the potato and carrots thoroughly (do not peel). Chop the potato, carrots, onion, celery, tomato. Cut the beef into medium-sized chunks (around the size of a golf ball).
2. Place the beef bones, onion, and carrots on a baking sheet and bake for 30 minutes or until bones begin to brown. In the meantime, place all the other ingredients *except* ½ cup water into a soup pot. Put the pot on medium heat; do not let the broth boil.
3. Remove the baking sheet and allow it to cool. Place the bones and vegetables in the soup pot and turn the heat up to high. Pour the remaining ½ cup water onto the baking sheet and swish it around for a few seconds; drain the water into the soup pot.
4. Bring to a boil and then simmer for 4 hours, covered. Strain the mixture through a cheesecloth-lined colander into another pot. Freezes well.

Safe Handling of Broth

Bacteria can begin to grow on broth quickly, so it is important to handle it with care. Strain the broth and discard all solids as soon as the stock is done cooking. If the broth is not going to be used immediately, chill it to room temperature by immersing it in a bath of ice water; then refrigerate or freeze it promptly. Always cool broths to room temperature before refrigerating or freezing them. Hot broth can take up to a day to cool in the refrigerator, allowing bacteria to form.

Basic Chicken Broth

*3 pounds chicken (whole **or** parts)*
16 cups (1 gallon) cold water
1 teaspoon salt
1 pound onions, coarsely chopped
½ pound celery, coarsely chopped
2 whole cloves

½ pound carrots, coarsely chopped (cleaned but not peeled)
2 cloves garlic, sliced in half
1 bay leaf
½ teaspoon black peppercorns
½ teaspoon fresh thyme
3–4 sprigs of parsley

> **Yields 12 cups**
>
> This broth can be kept in the fridge for 2 to 3 days and will be ready for immediate use.
>
> ∾

1. Wash the chicken under cold running water. Place it in a soup pot with the water and bring to a gentle boil. Simmer for 1 hour, frequently skimming off the fat that rises to the top.
2. Add salt, onions, carrots, and celery and continue to simmer for an additional 1½ hours.
3. Add the remaining ingredients and simmer for another 30 minutes. When finished, remove the pot from the heat and cool immediately. Chicken stock is highly susceptible to spoilage, so the temperature needs to be reduced quickly. This can be done by setting the pot in the sink in 5 to 6 inches of cool water.
4. When cool enough to handle, strain the soup through a sieve or colander into another pot or large container. Straining a second time through cheesecloth will get you a much clearer broth.

Buying Garlic

When buying fresh garlic, look for heads that are plump, firm, and heavy for their size. Any green shoots or spouts indicate that the garlic is old and will have an off flavor. Store whole bulbs in an open plastic bag in the vegetable drawer of your refrigerator. Markets now carry a variety of processed garlic options, from peeled cloves to fully chopped pastes. They are a great convenience, but buy these in the smallest containers possible, since they lose their fresh taste and become stale very quickly.

Dashi

Yields 4 cups

This traditional Japanese clear broth is used extensively for soups, sauces, and as a delicate seasoning.

*1 piece kelp (kombu), about
    5 inches square*
5 cups cold water

*⅓ cup dried bonito flakes (also
    called smoked fish flakes)*

1. Place the kelp and cold water in a soup pot; bring to a boil. Remove from heat and stir in the bonito flakes. Let it stand for 2 to 3 minutes.
2. Using a slotted spoon or tongs, remove the kelp and discard. Strain the broth into a new container. Use it now, in any Japanese-inspired soup, or cool it to room temperature by immersing it in a bath of cold water, then refrigerate immediately. (This broth does not freeze well.)

Basic Vegetable Broth

Yields 5–6 cups

Feel free to make additions, subtractions, and substitutions in your vegetable broth. Leeks, spinach, turnips, mushrooms, and tomatoes are all good choices.

*4 large onions, peeled and
    quartered*
*6 large carrots, peeled and
    quartered*
*3 large stalks celery, peeled
    and quartered*
1 medium potato, peeled

1 cup cabbage, cut into eighths
5–6 peppercorns
1 bay leaf
3 sprigs of thyme
3 sprigs of parsley
8 cups cold water
Salt

1. Place all the ingredients in a large soup pot. Bring to a boil, then immediately reduce to a simmer. Cook for 1 hour.
2. Allow the pot to cool, uncovered, off the heat for an hour or so. Strain the soup through a sieve or colander; then squeeze the solid ingredients so that the extra broth is collected (squeezing inside a cheesecloth works really well). Strain again through cheesecloth for clearer broth. Salt to taste. Freezes well.

Potato and Vegetable Broth

3 baking potatoes
1 large leek
6 carrots
6 stalks of celery
3 medium zucchini
4 large onions
½ pound fresh mushrooms
  (any kind)
1 whole head of garlic

10 peppercorns
8 sprigs fresh thyme
  (**or** 1 tablespoon dried)
8 sprigs fresh flat-leaf parsley
3 bay leaves

Yields 8 cups

If broth is not going to be used immediately, cool it to room temperature by immersing the pot in a bath of cold water; refrigerate or freeze promptly.

ᘒ

1. Without peeling them, clean, then chop the potatoes, leek (white light green parts only), carrots, celery, and zucchini. Quarter the onions and mushrooms; do not discard any parts. Slice off the very top of the garlic head, just enough to expose the tops of the cloves.
2. Place all the ingredients in a soup pot. Add enough cold water to cover the vegetables; then add more water until its level is about 6 inches higher.
3. Bring to a boil, then reduce to a simmer. Cook for about 1¾ hours. Squeeze the liquid out of the vegetables, adding the liquid to the broth. Strain.

Broth—the Foundation of Soups

Many soups start off with a broth, or stock. Broths are basically the liquid remnants of boiled meat, poultry, seafood, and/or vegetables along with some seasonings. The finished product is often robust and rich in flavor. Broths are also used in a lot of sauces and other dishes. In supermarkets, broths can be bought in the form of cubes, powder, or liquid in cans or jars.

Fish Broth

Yields 6–8 cups

The recipe works best with a low-oil fish, like cod. Avoid oily fishes such as tuna, salmon, or mackerel.

2 onions
½ head of celery
4 pounds fish heads and bones
1 bay leaf
6 sprigs parsley
3 sprigs of thyme
Pepper

1. Chop the onions and celery. Rinse off the fish parts; then place them in a large pot and cover amply with cold water. Add all remaining ingredients.
2. Bring to a boil, then reduce to a simmer; simmer uncovered for 30 minutes. Strain and discard all solids. If broth is not going to be used immediately, allow it to cool to room temperature by immersing it in a bath of cold water; then refrigerate it promptly.

Vegetable Broth with Apple

Yields 8 cups

Depending on how intense you want the flavor in this broth, you can gently simmer it down to taste.

4 medium onions
2 apples, cored
3 large carrots
3 parsnips
6 leeks
3 celery stalks
2 whole heads garlic
4 shallots
3¼-inch piece ginger
½ bunch thyme
½ bunch chervil
½ bunch parsley
2 bay leaves
1 tablespoon peppercorns
24 cups cold water

1. Core the onions and apples. Chop the carrots, parsnips, leeks, and celery into large pieces. Leave the garlic heads, shallots, and ginger unpeeled.
2. In a very large soup pot, combine all the ingredients. Bring to a boil, then reduce to a simmer. Cook for 2 hours.
3. Let cool slightly. Squeeze the liquid from the vegetables into the soup pot. Strain and discard solids. Re-boil and simmer for another hour.

Scotch Broth

*1½ pounds lamb bones, rinsed
(shoulders are fine)*
8 cups cold water
3 leeks, thoroughly cleaned
*2 large onions, peeled and
quartered*
½ bunch celery, chopped
3 carrots, peeled and chopped
2 bay leaves

¼ bunch of parsley stems
3 sprigs of thyme
½ cup pearl barley
Salt and pepper

Yields 5 cups

Next time you use
parsley, freeze the
stems. That way, you'll
have them handy for
your Scotch Broth.

1. Trim all visible fat from the lamb bones and cut or break them into
   the smallest pieces you can. Place the bones and vegetables in the
   water in a soup pot. Bring to a boil, then reduce to a simmer.
   Simmer for approximately 4 hours, skimming off the scum that rises to
   the top several times with a large spoon.
2. Stir in the barley and herbs. Bring to a boil again and reduce to a
   simmer for 1 hour, adding a bit more cold water as necessary to
   cover the bones.
3. Skim off the fat and season with salt and pepper. Strain, discarding all
   solids. (To store the broth for later use, cool it to room temperature
   by immersing the cooking pot in a bath of cold water; then refrigerate
   or freeze promptly.)

Roasted Vegetable Broth

Yields 4 cups

A bouquet garni is a small bag of mixed fresh herbs that often includes sprigs of parsley and thyme and a bay leaf.

1 teaspoon olive oil
1 bouquet garni
½ pound (8 ounces) mushrooms
4 carrots, peeled and chopped
8 cloves garlic, peeled
2 onions, peeled and quartered
½ head of celery, chopped
1 turnip, peeled and quartered
7 cups cold water
Salt to taste

1. Preheat oven to 400 degrees. Using the olive oil, lightly grease a baking pan that has sides. Prepare the bouquet garni using the fresh herbs of your choice. (A traditional bouquet with a few red pepper flakes added is a nice complement to the flavor of this broth.)
2. Place all the vegetables in the oven and roast for 1 hour, turning them over a couple of times.
3. Place the roasted vegetables in soup pot. Pour 1 cup of the water into the baking pan and use a wooden spoon to scrape up the remaining bits of roasted vegetables. Add this to the soup pot.
4. Pour the remaining 6 cups of water over the mixture and add the herb bag. Bring to a boil and reduce to a simmer for 1 to 1½ hours.
5. Strain, squeezing the liquid from all the solid ingredients. Discard the bouquet garni and all solids.

Bag o' Spices

A small bag of mixed fresh herbs, called a bouquet garni (or sachet d'épices), is often used in broth and soup recipes. A traditional bouquet garni includes a thyme sprig, parsley stems, and a bay leaf. To make a bouquet garni, simply place the fresh herbs of your choice on a four-inch square of cheesecloth and fold the sides up around the herbs to make a pouch, securing it closed with a piece of string. This bundle is then dropped into the broth or soup and left in throughout the cooking process to release the herbs' flavors. When the broth or soup is done cooking, this bag of spices is easily removed and discarded. You can also use a leek leaf in place of the cheesecloth; simply wrap the herbs in the leaf and tie a string tightly around the bundle.

Giblet Broth

2 tablespoons butter
Neck and giblets from an
   18-pound turkey
1 cup chopped onion
2 leeks, chopped
1½ cups chopped carrots
½ cup chopped celery
1 cup dry white wine

5 cups cold water
½ bunch parsley sprigs
1–2 teaspoons thyme
2 bay leaves
2 cloves
5 whole black peppercorns
Salt to taste

Yields 3–4 cups

If the broth is not going to be used immediately, cool it to room temperature by immersing the pot in a bath of ice water, then refrigerate or freeze promptly.

1. In a soup pot, heat the butter. Add the neck, giblets, and vegetables; sauté for 10 minutes. Pour in the wine, and let it reduce for 1 minute. Add the water. Bring to a boil and simmer for 30 minutes.
2. Add all the remaining ingredients to the pot. Bring to a boil again, then reduce to a simmer. Cook for 1 hour. Strain.

Mushroom Broth

2 pounds fresh mushrooms
   (a mix of varieties is nice)
½ bunch celery
½ pound carrots

3 large onions
3 cups cold water
Basic Chicken Broth (page 3)
1 tablespoon sherry

Yields 6 cups

If you are fresh out of chicken broth—not to worry! This recipe works well with beef broth, too.

1. Dice the mushrooms, celery, carrots, and onions. Place all of the vegetables in a soup pot with 3 cups of water. Bring to a boil, then reduce to a simmer and cook for 45 minutes. Strain.
2. Add enough chicken (or beef) broth to make a total of 6 cups of liquid. Reheat thoroughly. Add the sherry just before using the broth.

Lobster Broth

Yields 8 cups

Chill as quickly as possible if not using both immediately. After it has cooled, cover it tightly and refrigerate.

1 or 2 whole lobsters (about 2 pounds total; more is fine)
12 cups water
1 cup dry white wine
3 yellow onions, chopped
5 stalks celery, chopped
1 pound mushrooms (any type)
4 cloves garlic, minced or crushed

½ bunch of parsley
4 sprigs thyme
2 bay leaves
¼ teaspoon fennel
1 teaspoon peppercorns

1. Split the lobsters from front to back and remove the little sacs from behind the eyes of each lobster; discard the sacs. Break the lobster into pieces to make everything fit into the soup pot.
2. Cover the lobster pieces with the water and bring to a boil. Using a ladle, skim off and discard the white scum that accumulates on the top of the water.
3. Reduce the heat. Add all the remaining ingredients; cook for 1 hour, pouring in a bit more water as necessary to keep the shells covered.
4. Check flavor and seasonings, allowing the liquid to reduce and concentrate for 20 minutes longer if you desire a stronger flavor. Strain and discard all solids.

Veal Broth

2½ pounds veal bones
   (meaty ones)
6 cups cold water
2 cups chopped onions
1 cup chopped carrots
1 cup chopped celery

1 parsnip, chopped
1 bay leaf
½ bunch of parsley
5 sprigs of thyme
1 teaspoon peppercorns

Yields 3 cups

Refrigerate the broth overnight. The next day, skim off and discard the fat layer from the top.

---

1. Preheat oven to 450 degrees. Cut or break the veal bones into several pieces. Put into a baking dish with sides, in a single layer. Roast for 30 minutes. Add the vegetables and roast for 30 more minutes. Remove from the oven.

2. Using a slotted spoon, transfer the bones and vegetables to a soup pot. Pour 1 cup of the water into the baking dish and use a wooden spoon to loosen any cooked-on bits from the bottom of the dish; add this to the soup pot, along with the remaining 5 cups of water. Bring to a boil and simmer for 3 to 4 hours, uncovered. Add the herbs and simmer 1 hour longer.

3. Strain the mixture and cool it to room temperature by immersing the pot in a bath of ice water.

Taking Stock

Adventurous cooks who get into diverse cuisines look to broths that provide an appropriate palette on which to build their dishes. By adding one or two ingredients to the Basic Vegetable Broth recipe (page 4), you can make many stocks with just that one recipe. For Chinese stock, add one thinly sliced two-inch piece of fresh ginger and two sliced garlic cloves (in addition to the original five the recipe calls for). For Vietnamese stock, add one star anise and one chopped stalk of lemongrass (or ¼ cup dried). When making stocks for Mexican foods, add one ancho chili pod and one cinnamon stick. For Middle Eastern dishes, a stock with the zest of one lemon adds another dimension.

Wild Mushroom Broth

Yields 4 cups

Reconstitute dried mushrooms 20 to 30 minutes before cooking time.

1 ounce dried wild mushrooms
   (porcini, morels, or any kind)
2 pounds white button
   mushrooms
½ pound (8 ounces) fresh
   shiitake mushrooms
4 shallots, peeled and quartered
¼ head of celery, chopped
1 bay leaf
4 sprigs of parsley
1 sprig fresh thyme
   (**or** 1 tablespoon dried)
½ teaspoon black peppercorns

Without trimming or slicing them, place all the mushrooms in a soup pot. Add the seasonings and enough cold water to cover all the ingredients. Bring to a boil, then reduce to a simmer. Cook for 2 hours. Squeeze the liquid from the mushrooms, adding that to the liquid in the pot. Discard the mushroom solids.

Thai Broth

Yields 6 cups

Check with your guests before serving this broth made with fresh cilantro. Some people dislike the flavor of this herb.

2 small Thai chilies, seeded
3 cloves garlic
2 shallots
1¼-inch piece of ginger
4 kaffir lime leaves
5-inch piece of lemongrass
6 cups Basic Chicken Broth
   (see page 3)
1 scallion
¼ cup cilantro
3 tablespoons tamarind paste in
   ½ cup hot water (**or** use
   the juice from 2 limes)
¼ cup Thai fish sauce (nam pla)
White pepper to taste

1. Chop the chilies, garlic, shallots, and ginger. Thinly slice the lime leaves and the lemongrass. Place these ingredients in a soup pot with the broth. Bring to a boil, then reduce to a simmer and cook for 30 minutes.
2. Finely chop the scallion and the cilantro. Add them to the soup pot, along with all the remaining ingredients; simmer for 2 more minutes. Strain, discarding all solids.

Red Wine Broth

1 medium carrot
1 medium-sized yellow onion
1 small turnip
2 cloves garlic
1 pound raw meat (beef or
  pork is best)

1 bouquet garni (see "Bag o'
  Spices" on page 8)
2 tablespoons butter
*4 cups other meat broth **or***
  cold water
3 cups dry red wine

> **Yields 4 cups**
>
> Other veggies and herbs may be substituted. Try parsnips, fennel, ginger, basil, or tarragon.
>
>

1. Chop the carrot, onion, turnip, and garlic. Trim the fat from the meat and cut the meat it into ½-inch cubes. Prepare the bouquet garni using your choice of fresh herbs. (A traditional bouquet garni with a few black peppercorns added complements this recipe well.)

2. In a soup pot, melt the butter. Add the meat and the vegetables and cook on low heat for 20 minutes until they are all completely browned. Add the ½ cup of broth or water and ½ cup of the red wine. Boil the mixture until the soup pot is almost completely dry and virtually all liquids have evaporated.

3. Add the rest of the red wine, broth, and the bouquet garni. Bring to a boil, then reduce to a simmer and cook for about 2 hours. Skim off the impurities with a spoon several times during this period. (Feel free to add cold water at this point to adjust the strength of the broth.) Strain and discard all solids. If the stock is not going to be used immediately, cool it to room temperature by immersing the pot in a bath of cold water before refrigerating.

Water Temperature

To maintain the clarity of your broth, always use cold water; adding hot water to broth will produce a less desirable, cloudy final product.

Asian Pork Broth

Yields 8–10 cups

Don't have any pork spare ribs handy? Substitute pork chops and still ensure a tasty broth.

2 pounds pork spare ribs
3 leeks
12 cups cold water
1 bunch celery, chopped

8 black peppercorns
1-inch piece ginger root
2 teaspoon soy sauce

1. Separate the spare ribs. Chop the leeks coarsely (white and light green parts only).
2. In a soup pot combine the pork, leeks and, water. Bring to a boil, then reduce to a simmer; cook for 1 ¾ hours, skimming off the impurities and the fat regularly.
3. Add the peppercorns, unpeeled ginger root, and soy sauce. Simmer for ½ hour. Discard all solids. Strain the broth thoroughly. Use some; freeze some. (Before freezing or refrigerating the broth, cool it to room temperature by immersing the pot in a bath of cold water.)

Soybean Broth

Yields 3 cups

Mung bean sprouts can be substituted for soybeans and sprouts, but they aren't as flavorful.

½ pound (8 ounces) soybean sprouts
2 cloves garlic
2 scallions

2 tablespoon soy sauce
2 teaspoon sesame oil
Red pepper threads

1. Cut the small threads from the sprouts and discard the threads. Place the sprouts in water to cover, bring to a boil, and reduce to a simmer; cook for 7 minutes. Meanwhile, mince the garlic and diagonally slice the scallions into small pieces.
2. When the sprouts have steamed, add the garlic, soy sauce, sesame oil, the white parts of the scallions, and salt to taste. Pour in 3 cups of cold water and bring to a boil; reduce to a simmer and cook for 15 minutes. Garnish with the green parts of the scallions and the red pepper threads in the individual bowls.

CHAPTER 2
Seafood Soups

Shrimp and Butternut Squash Soup

2 tablespoons fresh-squeezed lime juice
6 tablespoons fresh-squeezed orange juice
1 ½ teaspoon ground coriander, divided
¼ teaspoon red pepper flakes
3 tablespoons vegetable oil, divided

½ pound (8 ounces) large shrimp
2 medium butternut squash
4 cups (1 quart) chicken broth
1 cup cream
2 teaspoon grated orange rind
4 teaspoons minced cilantro
Salt and pepper

1. Combine the lime juice, orange juice, ½ teaspoon of the coriander, the red pepper flakes, and 1 tablespoon of the vegetable oil in a large bowl and whisk thoroughly. Peel and devein the shrimp, then slice in half lengthwise. Toss together. Refrigerate this marinade for 2 hours.
2. While the shrimp is marinating, preheat the oven to 425 degrees. Cut the squash into quarters and remove the seeds, leaving the skin on. Using a large roasting pan, place the squash pieces face down and add enough water to cover the bottom of the pan, about ⅛ of an inch deep. Cover the pan loosely with foil; bake for 50 minutes.
3. Allow the squash to cool, then remove the skin. Using a blender, blend half the squash with about half the chicken broth. Pour the mixture into a soup pot. Prepare the other half of the squash the same way. Stir in the cream, orange rind, and remaining coriander. Cover and warm gently on a low heat.
4. In a large saucepan, heat the remaining oil. Drain the marinade from the shrimp. Place the shrimp in the pan and cook for 1 minute on each side.
5. Pour the squash base into serving bowls. Top with the shrimp, then the cilantro.

Shellfish Chowder

2 (6½-ounce) cans chopped
  clams
3 ounces salt pork
1 onion
1 pound red potatoes
2 tablespoons flour
1 cup water
2 tablespoons chopped dill

1 bay leaf
10 ounces scallops
3½ cups milk
¼ teaspoon white pepper

Serves 6–8

You can substitute 1½ pounds of fresh clams for each 6½-ounce can. Boil them in just enough water to cover for 10 minutes and reserve the liquid (discard the shells).

1. For this early American-style recipe, drain the clams, reserving the liquid. Dice the salt pork and the onion. Dice the potatoes into ½-inch cubes, peels on.
2. In a large saucepan, sauté the salt pork in its own fat over medium heat for 7 minutes. With a slotted spoon, remove the pork pieces to drain on paper towels. Discard all but 2 tablespoons of the fat.
3. Using this fat, sauté the onion for 3 minutes; then allow it to cool slightly. Add the flour to coat. Pour in the water and add the potatoes, dill, and bay leaf. Bring to a boil, then reduce to a simmer and cook for 15 minutes. Add the clam liquid and the scallops; cook for 6 minutes. Add the clams and simmer for 1 minute.
4. Stir in the milk and white pepper and serve.

Brothy vs. Thick Chowders
While generations of canned soups have conditioned us to believe that chowder is, by definition, a thick, pasty soup, some of the most delicious handmade versions of these chunky soups feature a thin, though rich, broth.

Saffroned Fish Soup

Serves 6

If you have bought the fish whole, add the fish heads, too, for a more full-bodied and authentic broth, removing the heads at the end.

2 pounds Spanish onions
2½ pounds tomatoes
6 cloves garlic
¾ teaspoon saffron threads
3 tablespoons olive oil
1 teaspoon thyme
1 teaspoon fennel seeds
2 bay leaves
Black pepper
4 cups water

2 pounds firm fish, such as sea bass, snapper, pike, or trout
1 cup dry white wine
¼ cup mayonnaise
¼ cup plain nonfat yogurt
¼ teaspoon red pepper
12 small slices French bread
½ pound halibut **or** monkfish fillets
¾ cup grated Swiss cheese

1. For a Provençal delight, slice the onions, quarter the tomatoes and squeeze out seeds, then cut the flesh into large chunks. Finely chop the garlic. Break the saffron threads with a small knife.
2. Using a soup pot, heat the oil. Sauté the onions on medium for 3 minutes. Add the tomatoes, ⅔ of the garlic, the thyme, fennel, bay leaves, black pepper to taste, and half of the saffron. Sauté for 5 more minutes.
3. Cut the 2 pounds of fish into slices 1–2 inches wide. Add them to the soup pot along with the water and the wine. Bring the mixture to a boil, reduce to a medium heat, and cook for 25 minutes, stirring often.
4. Meanwhile, mash the rest of the garlic slightly. Place it in a bowl with the other half of the saffron, the mayonnaise, yogurt, and red pepper; mix well and refrigerate, covered. Toast the bread slices.
5. Strain the soup, squeezing the liquid from all the vegetable ingredients and discarding the fish heads if you have used them.
6. Cut the fillets into 1-inch cubes and stir them into the soup. Bring to a simmer and cook for 5 minutes; be careful not to overcook the fish. (Overcooking will cause the fish to lose its flavor.)
7. In 6 individual soup bowls, pour the soup and top with the cheese. Float 2 slices of the French bread on each bowl, spread with the chilled mayonnaise mixture.

Salmon Chowder

20 scallions (**or** 2 cups of any
    type of onion, chopped)
¼ pound (4 ounces) bacon
2 shallots
1 teaspoon thyme **or** summer
    savory (fresh, if possible)
1 teaspoon tarragon
    (fresh, if possible)
2 pounds potatoes
    (any kind but red)

3 pounds salmon
4 tablespoons butter
2 bay leaves
4 cups Fish Broth **or**
    Basic Chicken Broth (see
    recipes on pages 6 and 3)
1½ cups cream
Salt and pepper
Fresh chopped dill (optional)

Serves 4–6

To substitute fresh herbs for dried, double the amount called for and add them 5 minutes before the soup is ready.

∾

1. Trim the scallions and cut into 1-inch pieces. Dice the bacon. Finely dice the shallots and herbs. Slice the potatoes into ⅛-inch-thick slices. Remove the skin and bones from the salmon and cut into 3-inch chunks.
2. In a soup pot, sauté the bacon to a golden brown in its own fat. Discard all but 1 tablespoon of the fat, leaving that much in the pot along with the bacon. Add the butter, scallions, shallots, and bay leaves, and cook for 2 minutes.
3. Add the potatoes and the broth, supplementing the mixture with enough water to cover the potatoes, if necessary. Bring to a boil, reduce to medium, and cook for 10 minutes only.
4. With the back of a spoon, mash some of the potatoes against the side of the pot and stir to thicken the mixture. Add the salmon and cook for 10 minutes. Allow the soup to cool slightly, then stir in the cream and add salt and pepper to taste. Garnish with chopped dill, if desired.

Common Fresh Herbs

Most supermarkets now carry a variety of fresh herbs including thyme, chives, rosemary, sage, and oregano. But even if they don't, you can almost always find fresh Italian (flat-leaf) parsley, the best kind for cooking. Dill and cilantro are now quite common, and I recently saw fresh flash-frozen herbs in the freezer section of a store.

Crab Chowder

2 pounds fresh crabs **or** 12 ounces canned crabmeat

6 cups milk

1 bay leaf

1 pinch of saffron

2 leeks

1 stalk celery

2 small red potatoes

2 whole artichokes, cooked (**or** 2 artichoke hearts, canned or frozen)

1 cup water

2 tablespoons lemon juice

1 pinch of cayenne pepper

1 tablespoon chervil (optional)

1. If using fresh crab, boil in water for 3 to 6 minutes, depending upon the size. Remove the meat with a nutcracker and cut into large dice.
2. Combine the milk, bay leaf, and saffron in a soup pot. Over medium heat, bring to a boil; add the crab and cover. Take off heat, keeping it covered, and let it stand.
3. Finely dice the white part of the leeks, the celery, and the potatoes. Remove the leaves and the center choke from the artichoke and dice the bottom (the heart).
4. In a saucepan, melt the butter and add all the vegetables, the water, and the lemon juice. Bring to a boil, reduce to medium heat, cover the pan, and cook for 10 minutes. Take the cover off, turn the heat up, and cook until the liquids have evaporated. Turn the heat down to the lowest setting.
5. Add the fish and milk mixture along with the cayenne. Stir and warm thoroughly, but slowly. Garnish with the chervil.

Clam Chowder

8 pounds fresh clams
   (cherrystones, littlenecks,
   butters, or quahogs)
¼ pound (4 ounces) bacon
10 cloves garlic
3 scallions
4 tablespoons butter
2 teaspoons thyme

2 teaspoons dill
1 bay leaf
2 pounds potatoes
1½ cups cream
Salt and pepper
Flat-leaf parsley, chopped
   (optional)

Serves 6

Before chopping the clams, be sure to remove the skin around the neck of the clam.

1. Clean the clams thoroughly. Cover them barely with cold water in a large pot, and cover the pot tightly with a lid. Bring to a boil, remove from the heat quickly, and let stand covered for 10 minutes, or until the shells open.
2. Remove the clams from their shells and cool. Discard the shells, but reserve the cooking liquid, straining it through cheesecloth. Cut the clams into ½-inch dice and refrigerate. Clean the soup pot.
3. Cut the bacon into ⅛-inch pieces. Place in soup pot over low heat. Cook over medium heat until golden brown. Discard all but 1 tablespoon of the bacon grease, leaving the rest of the fat and the bacon in the pan.
4. Peel the garlic cloves and cut the cloves in half, lengthwise. Chop the scallions coarsely, including half of the green parts.
5. Add the butter, vegetables, and herbs to the pot and sauté for 5 minutes.
6. Dice the potatoes into a ½-inch cubes. Add them to the pot along with all of the reserved clam broth. Bring to a boil, reduce to medium, and cook for 15 minutes. Adjust the thickness of the broth by mashing some of the potatoes against the side of the pot with a wooden spoon. Stir for 1 minute. Remove from the heat.
7. Stir in the chopped clams and cream, and add salt and pepper to taste. Garnish with the parsley.

Lobster Chowder

Serves 6

To thicken the chowder, mash some of the potatoes against the side of the soup pot before adding the lobster, stirring for 1 minute.

3-4 fresh whole lobsters
3 ears corn
10 medium shallots
1½ pounds potatoes
¼ pound (4 ounces) bacon
4 tablespoons butter
1 teaspoon dill
⅛ teaspoon cayenne pepper
1½ cups milk
2 small green onions (green parts only), thinly sliced (optional)

1. Boil the lobsters in a large pot half-full of salted water for exactly 4 minutes. Remove the pot from the heat and set it aside to cool, then remove the meat from the tails and claws and dice into large cubes. Refrigerate the meat and save the shells.
2. Remove the innards from the inside of the shells. Place the shells in a pot and add enough water to cover. Bring to a boil, then reduce to a simmer and cook for 1½ hours. Strain the broth and discard the shells.
3. While the broth is cooking, husk the corn. Using a sharp knife, cut the kernels off the cobs. Peel and coarsely chop the shallots. Cut the potatoes into ¾-inch cubes. Chop the bacon into small chunks.
4. Using a soup pot, cook the bacon pieces on low heat until the fat begins to collect in the pot. Turn the heat up to medium and cook the bacon until it is golden brown. Discard all but 1 tablespoon of the bacon grease, keeping the rest of the fat and the bacon in the pot.
5. Add the butter, shallots, and dill to the soup pot. Sauté for 6 minutes, stirring now and then. Add the cayenne.
6. When the lobster broth is ready, add it to the soup pot with the bacon, along with the potatoes and the corn kernels. Add cold water to cover all ingredients. Bring to a boil and simmer for 12 minutes. To thicken the chowder, mash some of the potatoes against the side of the soup pot just before adding the lobster, stirring for 1 minute, to thicken the mixture a bit.
7. Add the lobster pieces, and simmer for 8 minutes. Cool slightly, then stir in the milk. Garnish with green onions.

Shrimp and Spinach Soup

1 large garlic head
1 pound (16 ounces) medium-
   sized uncooked shrimp
4 cups white rice, cooked
½ teaspoon lemon rind
1½ teaspoon lemon juice

4 cups Basic Vegetable Broth
   or Basic Chicken Broth (see
   recipes on page 4 and 3)
Salt and pepper
4 cups finely chopped spinach
   (stems removed)

Serves 4

If possible, get all of
the ingredients fresh.
This recipe will benefit
greatly from this extra
effort.

1. Roast the garlic first: Preheat the oven to 350 degrees. Cut off and discard the very top of the garlic head. Place the garlic (top up) in a small baking dish with a lid, and drizzle some olive oil over the garlic. Cover and cook for 35 to 45 minutes. Allow to cool. Squeeze out the roasted garlic pulp, discarding the rest.
2. Bring water to a boil in a large saucepan. When the water boils, reduce to a simmer and add the shrimp (shells on). Cook, uncovered, for about 3 minutes, or until the shrimp turns pink. Remove the shells and the veins from the shrimp. Cut the shrimp in half and reserve.
3. In a mixing bowl, mix the rice, the lemon rind, and the lemon juice.
4. In a soup pot, bring the broth to a boil. Season with salt and pepper if desired.
5. Place a large scoop of the rice mixture in 4 individual soup bowls. Top with the spinach, then the shrimp, and then the roasted garlic. Pour the broth around this.

Orzo

Orzo is a type of pasta shaped like a grain of rice. It has a delicate flavor and consistency that result in a totally new dish when substituted for larger pasta or rice. However, it tends to get mushy, so add it later in the cooking process than you would pasta or rice.

Gumbo

Serves 6–8

When preparing your gumbo, makes sure there are no shells or cartilage in the crabmeat.

1 pound (16 ounces) medium-sized uncooked shrimp
12 cups water
3 bay leaves
2 stalks celery, chopped
3 cups sliced okra
1 large green bell pepper
1 large onion
4 cloves garlic
1 (28-ounce) can tomatoes
4 tablespoons oil

Salt (about ¾ to 1 teaspoon)
½ teaspoon pepper
½ teaspoon cayenne pepper
1 teaspoon dried thyme
1 pound (16 ounces) lump crabmeat
24 oysters, shucked, liquid reserved

1. Peel and devein the shrimp, reserving the shells. Place the shells in a large soup pot with the bay leaves and half of the celery. Add the water, bring to a boil, reduce to a simmer, and cook for 30 minutes.
2. Meanwhile, slice the okra into ¼-inch rounds, dice the green pepper and onion, and mince the garlic. Drain the tomatoes and chop them coarsely.
3. In a large skillet, heat 2 tablespoons of the oil and sauté the okra (on low to medium heat) for 20 minutes, stirring it constantly.
4. In another skillet, heat the remaining oil on medium and sauté the garlic, onion, green pepper, tomatoes, and the remaining celery with the salt and black pepper for about 5 minutes.
5. Strain the shrimp broth into a soup pot, discarding the shells. Add all the sautéed vegetables the cayenne pepper, and the thyme to the pot. Bring to a boil, reduce to a simmer, and cook for 30 minutes. Add the shrimp and crabmeat and simmer for 10 more minutes. Take it off the heat.
6. Stir the oysters and their liquid into the mixture. Cover and let it sit 5–10 minutes, or until the edges of the oysters begin to curl, before serving.

Swedish Shrimp Bisque

*3½ pounds fresh, raw, white-
     fleshed fish fillets **or** whole
     fish (preferably halibut or
     cod)*
3 onions
1 carrot, peeled
4 stalks celery
1 tomato
4 cloves garlic
3 tablespoons butter, divided
10 sprigs fresh dill

8 cups water
1 teaspoon lemon juice
2 bay leaves
10 black peppercorns
*1 pound (16 ounces) raw
     shrimp, unpeeled*
3 tablespoons flour
2 egg yolks
½ teaspoon salt, optional
¼ cup chopped fresh chives
½ cup cream

Serves 8

If you are using a whole fish, double-check to make sure you have removed all of the bones.

---

1. If you are using whole fish, trim the fish a bit, but retain the heads, bones, and skin if you like. Chop the onions, carrot, celery, tomato (discard the tomato seeds), and garlic.
2. In a soup pot, warm 1 tablespoon of the butter. Sauté the onions and garlic on medium heat for 3 minutes. Add all the other vegetables, the fish, dill, and water. Bring to a boil over medium heat, skimming off the impurities with a slotted spoon until no more form. Add the lemon, bay leaves, and peppercorns. Simmer for 30 minutes.
3. Add the shrimp and simmer for 5 minutes. Remove the shrimp, peel and devein them, and refrigerate.
4. Simmer the soup mixture for 30 more minutes. Strain, squeezing the liquid out off all ingredients, and discard all solids.
5. In a large saucepan, melt the remaining 2 tablespoons of butter and whisk in the flour. Gradually stir in 6 cups of the soup mixture. Simmer for 3 minutes. Meanwhile, beat the egg yolks slightly in a small bowl.
6. Stir the chives, egg, and cream into the mixture. Add the shrimp (whole or cut lengthwise). Serve.

Lobster Bisque

2 medium-sized fresh lobsters
4 stalks celery
2 cloves garlic
1 onion
2½ cups Fish Broth **or** Basic
    Chicken Broth (see recipes
    on pages 6 and 3)
2 bay leaves
6 black peppercorns

4 tablespoons butter
4 tablespoons flour
1 dash of nutmeg
1 cup cream
4 tablespoons sherry
Dill sprigs (optional)

1. Using a large soup pot, fill it about ⅔ of the way up with water. Bring to a boil. Pick up the first lobster by its back. Remove the claw plugs and drop the lobster, headfirst, into the pot. Let it cook for 6 minutes. Do the same for the other lobster. Set them aside to cool a bit.

2. Chop the celery and garlic coarsely. Slice the onion. Remove the lobster meat from the tails, claws, and body. Discard other inner parts. Crush the shells.

3. Place the shells, the broth, the vegetables, bay leaves, and peppercorns in a soup pot. Bring to a boil, then reduce to medium heat and cook for 45 minutes. Remove from the heat, strain, and discard all solids.

4. In a small saucepan, melt the butter and whisk in the flour. Cook for 2 minutes, stirring constantly. This mixture is called a *roux*. Add the nutmeg.

5. Stir the roux into the main broth mixture. In a small saucepan, heat the cream separately and thoroughly, but do not let it boil. Meanwhile, dice the lobster meat.

6. Place the roux-broth mixture back on low heat and simmer for 2 minutes. Add the cream and lobster; stir. Serve garnished with the dill.

Fish and Squid Soup

½ pound (8 ounces) whole
　squid (calamari)
¾ pound (12 ounces) monkfish
　fillets
1 pound (16 ounces) cod fillets
4 tablespoons olive oil
2 tablespoons minced garlic
1¾ cups finely diced onion
1½ cups finely diced leeks
　(white and light green
　parts only)
2 cups cubed tomatoes

½ teaspoon saffron threads
3 tablespoon tomato paste
½ cup dry white wine
1 teaspoon thyme
1 teaspoon fennel seeds,
　crushed
Black pepper to taste
4 cups water
2 hot dried red peppers
½ cup finely chopped parsley
　(optional)

> **Serves 4**
>
> Unless you're familiar
> with cleaning fresh
> squid, purchase it
> cleaned and ready to
> cook from your fish
> market.
>
>

1. Cut the squid's central body into ½-inch pieces. Cut the tentacles into bite-sized pieces. Cut the rest into 1½-inch chunks. Cut the monkfish and cod into 1½-inch cubes.
2. In a soup pot, heat the oil. Add the garlic and onion, stirring constantly for 3 minutes. Add the leeks, tomato cubes, saffron, tomato paste, wine, thyme, fennel, and black pepper. Pour in the water. Bring everything to a boil.
3. Add the squid and monkfish pieces and 1 of the red peppers; simmer for 15 minutes. Add the cod and the other red pepper, bring back to a boil, and cook for 5 minutes. Discard the peppers. Garnish with the parsley before serving.

ℰ Cooking with Fish

Fresh seafood should be used within one day of purchase. Check the smell. There should be no fishy odor. The flesh should be firm and the eyes on a whole fish should be clear.

Mussels and Wine Soup

Serves 6

Place up to ten peppercorns at a time on a flat, hard surface. Using a small saucepot or small skillet, apply pressure with the heel of your hand to break the seeds.

48 mussels
5 cloves garlic
5 black peppercorns
2 tablespoons oil

2 cups light Rhine wine
½ cup water

1. Wash the mussels and clean the shells well with cold water. Slice the garlic cloves and crack the peppercorns.
2. In a soup pot, heat the oil. Sauté the garlic on medium heat for 2 minutes. Add the wine, water, peppercorns, and mussels. Bring to a boil, cover, reduce heat, and shake the pot until the shells open.
3. Place a colander over a bowl and pour the mixture through the colander to collect the liquid in the bowl below. Pull off the top shells and the beards of the mussels and discard these. Keep the mussels, on the half shell, warm in a bowl.
4. Using a clean pot, strain the broth again using cheesecloth or a fine sieve. Bring back to a boil. Into each soup bowl, place some of the mussels. Pour broth over them and serve.

Cooking with Shellfish

To prevent eating spoiled shellfish, discard all mussels or clams that are open before cooking. Discard all that are closed after cooking.

Catfish Soup

2 pounds catfish fillets
2 onions
2 stalks celery
2 cups chopped tomatoes
4 cloves garlic
5 tablespoons minced parsley
½ of a lemon
6 tablespoons olive oil
½ cup flour
½ can tomato paste
½ cup full-bodied red wine

4 cups Fish Broth (see recipe
  on page 6) **or** water
1 generous pinch of thyme
1 generous pinch pf basil
1 pinch of cayenne pepper
Cooked rice (optional)
Fresh chopped green herb of
  your choice (optional)

Serves 8–10

Cooked rice can be
frozen for up to six
months. Make twice
what you need and
freeze the rest in an
airtight container.

---

1. Cut the catfish fillets into 2-inch-thick pieces. Chop the onions, celery, and tomatoes. Mince the garlic and parsley. Cut the lemon into several slices.
2. In a soup pot, warm the oil. Whisk in the flour, stirring well on low heat. Cook it on medium for several minutes, until brown.
3. Add the onions, celery, garlic, and parsley to the flour mixture. Cook 3–4 minutes. Add the tomatoes, tomato paste, wine, broth (or water), lemon slices, and all the seasonings. Simmer for 1 hour, stirring occasionally.
4. Place the catfish pieces in a single layer in the pot. Bring to a boil, reduce to a simmer, and cook for 20 minutes.
5. Serve over the cooked rice and garnished with a sprinkle of any green herb.

Sea Bass and Shrimp Soup

8 cups water (**or** 4 cups water and 4 cups dry white wine)
1 onion, quartered
1 carrot, chopped
6 tablespoons chopped flat-leaf parsley
5 cloves garlic
5 black peppercorns
1 bay leaf
1½ pounds tomatoes
½ pound (8 ounces) shrimp
2 pounds sea bass fillets
5 tablespoons olive oil
6–8 slices toasted Italian bread

1. Pour the water (and wine, if using) into a soup pot; add the onion, carrot, 3 tablespoons of the parsley, 2 of the whole garlic cloves, the black peppercorns, and the bay leaf. Boil, uncovered, for 20 minutes. (This mixture is called *court bouillon*.)
2. While the court bouillon is cooking, mince the remaining 3 garlic cloves. Coarsely chop the tomatoes. Peel the shrimp and remove their veins, discarding everything but the shrimp themselves.
3. When the court bouillon is done cooking, remove it from the heat. Add the sea bass, cover, and simmer for 12 to 16 minutes, making sure not to let the liquid boil. (Be careful not to overcook the fish. It should be simmered for about 6 to 8 minutes per pound.)
4. Meanwhile, heat the olive oil in a large saucepan and simmer the minced garlic, the remaining 3 tablespoons of parsley, and the tomatoes for 6 minutes. Add the shrimp and cook for another 3 minutes, adding a little warmed water (or dry white wine) if you need more liquid.
4. When the sea bass is ready, remove it from the pot using a slotted spoon; cover the fish to keep it warm. Strain the court bouillon, discarding the solids. Keep it on low heat.
5. Add the sea bass to the shrimp mixture, stirring it very carefully. Rewarm. Add 3 cups of the strained court bouillon to the fish-shrimp mixture. Keep the remaining court bouillon on low heat.
6. Place a piece of the Italian bread in the bottom of each individual soup bowl. Ladle the court bouillon over the bread, then ladle the fish-shrimp mixture over that.

English Cod Chowder

1¼ pound cod pieces
2 onions
1 carrot
2 stalks celery
½ pound potatoes
1 bouquet garni (see "Bag o' Spices" on page 8)

2 tablespoons butter
2 tablespoons olive oil
1 teaspoon curry powder
3 tablespoons dry white wine
2 tablespoons corn flour
¼ cup milk
¼ cup cream

Serves 6

If you don't have any cream on hand, increase the milk to ½ cup and add an additional 2 table-spoons of butter.

---

1. Remove the skin from the cod and cut the fish into small pieces. Thinly slice the onions, carrot, and celery. Peel and dice the potatoes. Prepare the bouquet garni using your choice of fresh herbs.

2. In a soup pot, warm the butter and the oil. Add the onions, carrot, and celery, and sauté on medium heat for 5 minutes. Stir in the curry and cook for 1 minute. As that is cooking, boil 3½ cups of water in a separate pot.

3. Add the water, bouquet garni, and fish pieces to the main soup pot with the vegetables. Bring to a boil, reduce to a simmer, and cook for 5 minutes.

4. With a slotted spoon, and using a small, clean bowl, remove about a dozen of the neatest-looking fish pieces. Add some of the hot broth to cover them. Cover the bowl itself to keep it warm.

5. In the main soup pot, turn up the heat a bit and cook the mixture, uncovered, until its volume is reduced—15 minutes of reduction should be fine. Discard the bouquet garni and cool this mixture slightly; then place it in a blender or food processor and purée. Put it back into the pot, add the wine, and begin reheating it.

6. Meanwhile, whisk the corn flour into a couple of tablespoons of the milk; then add all the milk. Pour this mixture into the main soup pot, stirring constantly. Remove from heat, add the fish mixture to the pot, and stir in the cream. Serve.

Scallop Soup

1 large onion
½ pound carrots
1¾ pounds potatoes
3 tablespoons chopped parsley
8 tablespoons butter, divided
15 large scallops
1 sprig thyme
1 tablespoon dill
½ cup dry white wine
4½ cups Fish Broth (see recipe on page 6)
1 cup whole milk
1 pinch of cayenne pepper

1. Finely chop the onion and carrots. Peel and dice the potatoes. Chop the parsley.
2. In a soup pot, melt 6 tablespoons of the butter. Chop the other 2 tablespoons into small pieces and refrigerate. Sauté the onions and carrots on low for 10 minutes.
3. Add the scallops, thyme, dill, parsley, wine, and broth to the pot. Bring to a boil, reduce to a simmer, and cook for 10 minutes. Meanwhile warm a large bowl.
4. With a slotted spoon, remove the scallops, placing them in the heated bowl. Cover it.
5. Add the potatoes to the soup pot. Bring to a boil, reduce to a simmer, and cook for 15 minutes. Remove the thyme sprigs. Cool slightly. In a blender or food processor, purée the potato mixture.
6. Rewarm the soup gently, adding the milk gradually. Add the scallops, the chilled bits of butter, and sprinkle with the cayenne pepper.

Using Bouillon Cubes

Bouillon cubes will work in place of broth when necessary. When using them instead of homemade broth, be sure to add a little extra of the aromatic vegetables such as onion, celery, and carrots. You may also want to choose the low- or lower-salt variety so you can have more control over how salty your soup will be.

Tangy Shrimp Bisque

½ pound (8 ounces) raw
   shrimp
3 tablespoons bread crumbs
2½ cups Fish Broth, divided
   (see recipe on page 6)
4 tablespoons butter, divided
1 pinch of nutmeg

1 teaspoon lemon juice
½ cup cider
Pepper
1 egg yolk
½ cup cream

Serves 4–6

Looking to save your-
self some time? Rather
than discarding your
shrimp shells, freeze
them for making broth
another day.

1. Place the shrimp (still in their shells) in a saucepan and add enough water to cover. Bring to a boil, reduce to a simmer, and cook them for about 3 minutes, or until the shrimp turn pink. Remove from heat, drain, and allow shrimp to cool.

2. In a small bowl, mix the bread crumbs with 1 cup of the fish broth. Set it aside to soak for 10 minutes.

3. Meanwhile, peel the shrimp and remove their veins; discard the shells and veins. Melt half the butter in a soup pot. Add the shrimp, nutmeg, lemon juice, the bread crumb mixture, then the rest of the butter. Toss and simmer for 2 minutes.

4. Remove from heat and allow to cool slightly. In a blender or food processor, purée the shrimp mixture. Return it to the soup pot. Gradually add the cider and the rest of the fish broth. Reheat on very low heat.

5. Meanwhile, in a small bowl, whisk the egg yolk and cream together. Mix a little bit of the soup into it, stirring well to incorporate. Then add the egg mixture to the main soup pot. Stir until it thickens.

Smooth Moves: Blender vs. Food Processor

They seem interchangeable sometimes, but they're not. Blenders and food processors are different tools with different strengths. For ultrasmooth purées, a blender is the first choice. For rougher purées, or chopping jobs with drier ingredients, use a processor.

Bar Harbor Fish Chowder

¼ pound salt pork, diced
4 cups diced potatoes
3 medium onions, peeled and
    sliced
2 teaspoons salt, divided
3 pounds white-fleshed fish,
    such as flounder, haddock,
    or cod

2 cups milk
1 tablespoon butter
¼ teaspoon freshly ground
    black pepper

1. Fry the salt pork in a heavy kettle and then remove the pork with a slotted spoon; set aside. Add the potatoes, onions, and ½ teaspoon salt. Cover with hot water and cook over medium heat, covered, for 15 minutes, or until the potatoes are just tender.
2. Meanwhile, cut the fish into large chunks and put it in another saucepan. Add boiling water to cover and 1½ teaspoons salt. Simmer, covered, until the fish is fork tender, about 15 minutes.
3. While the fish is cooking, scald the milk by placing it in a small saucepan and bringing it to just below the boiling point over medium heat; do not allow the milk to boil.
4. When the fish is done cooking, remove it from the heat. Strain and reserve liquid. Remove any bones from the fish. Add the fish and strained liquid to the potato-onion mixture. Pour in milk and heat through, about 5 minutes. Mix in the butter and pepper. Serve immediately.

ℰ Frying vs. Sautéing

Frying means cooking at moderate temperature (ususally 340 to 360 degrees) in a large amount of oil, such as a pan filled two inches deep, or a pot filled with oil for deep-frying. Sautéing is a cooking method using small amounts of oil, usually measured in teaspoons or tablespoons, and very high heat—nearly at the oil's smoking point.

Oyster Halibut Soup

2 pounds halibut
½ pound (8 ounces) clams
½ pound (8 ounces) uncooked
    shrimp
½ pound (8 ounces) tomatoes

1 onion
2 cloves garlic
¼ cup olive oil
4 ounces white almonds
    (shelled and skins removed)

> **Serves 8**
>
> Leaving the bones in the fish while cooking will add flavor. Halibut bones are large and easy to remove after cooking.
>
> ∾

1. Using 3 pots, cook the halibut, clams, and shrimp separately, using all bones, shells, and so on, and enough water to cover in each case. For the halibut, bring the water to a simmer, reduce to low, and cook, covered, for about 12 to 14 minutes. Cover the pot containing the clams, bring to a boil, and remove from the heat immediately; let stand, covered, for 10 minutes, or until the shells open. Cook the shrimp, uncovered, over medium heat. As soon as the water begins to boil, lower the heat and simmer for about 2 or 3 minutes, or until the shrimp turn pink. Retain all cooking liquids.

2. Pour all of the cooking liquid into one pot. Peel and devein the shrimp. Shell the clams. Debone and skin the fish. Cut the halibut, clams, and shrimp into bite-sized pieces. Discard all bones, shells, and skins.

3. Chop the tomatoes coarsely, discarding the seeds. Dice the onion and garlic.

4. In a soup pot, heat the oil on medium heat. Place the vegetables in the oil and sauté for 3 minutes. Strain the vegetables, pressing the liquids into the pot. Discard the solids.

5. Add enough water to the retained cooking liquid to make a total of 10 cups of liquid; add to the soup pot. Bring to a boil. Mash the almonds almost to a paste. Add the almonds and the seafood pieces to the pot, turning off the heat. Let the soup sit for 5 minutes, covered, before serving.

Poultry Soups

Turkey Chili

Serves 4

If you like your chili spicy, do not remove the seeds from the jalapeño chilies.

1 pound uncooked turkey
½ of an onion
2 cloves garlic
2 tablespoons chopped jalapeño chilies
1 (15- to 16-ounce) can white beans
1 (15- to 16-ounce) can chickpeas (garbanzo beans)
2 tablespoons olive oil
4 teaspoons ground cumin

1 teaspoon summer savory
1 teaspoon marjoram
½ pound ground turkey
4 cups Basic Chicken Broth (see recipe on page 3)
¼ cup pearl barley
Hot sauce
Salt and pepper
Cheddar cheese, grated

1. Cut the turkey into ½-inch cubes. Mince the onion and garlic. Seed and chop the jalapeños. Drain and rinse the beans.
2. In a soup pot, heat the oil. Sauté the onion and garlic on medium heat for 3 minutes. Stir in the cumin, savory, and marjoram and cook for half a minute. Add both kinds of turkey, sautéing them until browned slightly. Pour in the broth and stir in the barley and the jalapeños. Bring to a boil, reduce to a simmer, and cook for 30 minutes.
3. Add the beans and a dash of hot sauce, and salt and pepper to taste; simmer for another 10 minutes. Top with the grated cheese and serve.

Saffroned Chicken Soup

9 cups Basic Chicken Broth
   (see recipe on page 3)
1 (3-pound) whole chicken
2 cups chopped onions
1 cup diced carrots
¾ cup diced celery
3 garlic cloves
2 tablespoons minced parsley
   (optional)

¼ teaspoon saffron
3 tablespoons butter
¼ teaspoon thyme
2 ounces dried noodles
1 cup corn kernels

Serves 8

Use wide egg noodles for this soup. They tend to hold up the best.

1. Pour the broth into a soup pot. Cut the chicken into pieces, reserving the neck, gizzard, and heart. Place all the chicken pieces and parts in the pot. Bring to a boil, reduce to a simmer, and cook for 1 hour.

2. With a slotted spoon, remove and discard the neck, gizzard, and heart. Also remove the chicken pieces, allowing them to cool slightly on a plate. Remove and discard the skin and the bones, then cube the chicken meat until you have 1 cup of it. (Save the rest for another recipe.)

3. Strain the broth and cool it to room temperature by placing the pot in a bath of ice water. Refrigerate it for 6 hours or overnight. Remove and discard the hardened fat layer that will have formed on top.

4. Chop the onions, dice the carrots and celery, and mince the garlic and parsley. Crumble the saffron.

5. Heat the butter in a soup pot. Sauté the onions, carrots, celery, garlic, and thyme for about 10 minutes on medium heat. Pour in the broth you made earlier and bring to a boil. Reduce to a simmer and cook for 15 minutes.

6. Add the saffron. Heat to just before the boiling point and add the noodles. Simmer for 10 minutes. Add the chicken cubes and corn, simmering for another 5 minutes. Garnish with the parsley.

Chicken Gumbo

Serves 8

Serve with warm and crusty rolls.

1 (3-pound) whole chicken
½ cup chopped celery
½ cup chopped onions
½ cup chopped green bell
   peppers
3 cloves garlic
2 teaspoons cayenne pepper
2 teaspoons black pepper
1 cup flour, divided in half

7 tablespoons olive oil, divided
8 cups Basic Chicken Broth
   (see recipe on page 3)
¾ pound (12 ounces) sausage
   (chorizo **or** andouille)
4 scallions
Salt and pepper
Hot sauce

1. Cut the chicken into serving pieces (breasts, thighs, etc.). Chop the celery, onions, green pepper, and garlic.
2. Combine the cayenne and black pepper and ½ cup flour in a bag. Place each chicken piece in the bag and shake until coated. In a large saucepan, heat 3 tablespoons of the oil. Brown the chicken pieces on all sides, turning a couple of times. Remove them with a slotted spoon and set aside. Add the other 4 tablespoons of oil to the skillet, scraping up the browned chicken bits with a wooden spoon. Whisk in the second ½ cup of flour. Cook over medium-low heat for 5 minutes. Take the pan off heat and add the celery, onion, green peppers, and garlic, stirring them in for 1 to 2 minutes.
3. Scoop this mixture into a soup pot and add the chicken broth. Bring to a boil, reduce to a simmer, and add the chicken. Cook for 40 minutes. Meanwhile, thinly slice the sausage and chop the scallions (white and green parts).
4. When the chicken is done cooking, remove from the pot, discarding the skin and bones. Coarsely chop the meat and set aside. Add the sausage to the soup pot and salt and pepper to taste; simmer for 10 minutes.
5. Stir the scallions into the pot along with the chicken pieces and a dash of hot sauce. Warm thoroughly and serve.

Corn and Chicken Soup

4 cups Basic Chicken Broth
    (see recipe on page 3)
12 ounces corn kernels
1 tablespoon sake
1 tablespoon curry powder
1 teaspoon salt
1 teaspoon sugar
1 egg white

½ pound (8 ounces) uncooked
    chicken meat
1 teaspoon cornstarch
1 egg
1 teaspoon sesame oil
2 cups water
Scallions, chopped (optional)

Serves 4

Instead of scallions,
try thinly shredded
lettuce or cabbage.

∽

1. In a soup pot, bring the broth to a boil. Reduce to a simmer and add the corn. Cook for 10 minutes.
2. Add the sake, curry powder, salt, and sugar, simmering for 5 minutes. Remove from heat.
3. Slice the chicken into thin shreds. Place the chicken in a bowl and stir in the egg white and cornstarch. Set aside.
4. In another bowl, whisk together the whole egg and the sesame oil.
5. In a small pan, bring 2 cups of water to a boil. Toss in the chicken mixture and cook for 20 seconds. Remove the chicken with a slotted spoon and drain the pan. Add the chicken to the broth-corn mixture. Gradually whisk in the sesame oil mixture. Take off heat and allow to sit briefly. Garnish with scallions and serve.

"Curry Powder" and "Garam Masala"

Curry powder is actually a blend of spices, invented by the British to resemble one of the famous masalas (spice blends) of India. In addition to ground coriander, cumin, mustard seed, turmeric, and other spices, good blends contain ground, dried curry (or kari) leaves, a typical spice of southwestern India. Garam masala (which means "hot spices") is also a mixture of spices used in Indian cooking, and is available premade in specialty stores and many supermarkets. It is usually a combination of spices such as cardamom, cinnamon, cloves, nutmeg, cumin, and peppercorns; but, like curry, there is no standard blend.

North African Chicken Soup with Fruit and Nuts

Serves 8

For a lean alternative in your next chicken recipe, substitute turkey. It has much less fat and much more protein than chicken, and it is often a better buy at the grocery store.

1 (4–pound) whole chicken
1 onion
3 cloves garlic (**or** 2 teaspoons roasted garlic)
1 cup diced dried apricots (unsulfured is best; they are dark brown)
4-inch piece ginger
4 tablespoons olive oil
1 teaspoon turmeric

1 teaspoon cinnamon
1 dash of ground cloves
5 cups Basic Chicken Broth (see recipe on page 3)
½ cup raisins (golden or brown)
1 teaspoon saffron
5 ounces uncooked couscous
½ cup sliced almonds
Harissa (optional)

1. Cut the chicken into serving pieces (such as breasts and thighs). Finely chop the onion and cloves. Peel the ginger (removing the thinnest layer possible) and finely chop or grate the root. Dice the dried apricots.
2. Heat the oil in a large saucepan. Brown the chicken parts for 10 to 12 minutes. Using a slotted spoon, remove them from the pan and reserve. Drain all but 2 tablespoons of fat from the pan.
3. Over medium heat, sauté the onion and garlic in the pan with the chicken fat for 3 minutes. Stir in the ginger, turmeric, cinnamon, and cloves, and cook for 1 minute.
4. Add the broth to the pan. Using a wooden spoon, scrape the bottom of the pan to loosen all the cooked-on bits. Add the apricots, raisins, saffron, and the reserved chicken. Bring to a medium simmer, cover, and cook for 45 to 60 minutes. Take off the heat.
5. Using a slotted spoon, remove the chicken pieces, discarding the skin and the bones. Remove all visible fat from the pan. Coarsely chop the chicken and set aside.
6. Add the couscous to the pan, replace the lid, and let stand for 5 minutes. Add the chicken and stir well. Replace the cover and let stand for 1 to 2 more minutes, off the heat.
7. Garnish with the almond slices and a very small dollop of the harissa, and serve.

Lime and Chicken Soup

3 limes
1 jalapeño chili
1 tablespoon minced cilantro,
*   plus 6 sprigs*
1 tomato
1 red onion
¼ pound (4 ounces) mild
*   yellow cheese*
2 corn tortillas
½ pound (8 ounces) uncooked
*   chicken breast*

5 cups Basic Chicken Broth
*   (see recipe on page 3)*
1 teaspoon oregano
1 teaspoon basil
1 bay leaf
Freshly ground black pepper
Salt

> **Serves 6**
>
> Chicken is perhaps the most dangerous raw meat. To prevent salmonella and other bacteria from being transmitted, thoroughly wash your hands and all utensils before and after handling it.
>
>

1. Juice 2 of the limes and cut the remaining lime into thin slices. Mince the jalapeño and the cilantro. Chop the tomato and the red onion. Cube the cheese. Cut the tortillas into strips.

2. Place the chicken in a large saucepan. Cover with water, bring to a boil, and cook for 5 minutes (blanching the chicken). Remove it to a plate and slice it into very, very thin strips, or shred it.

3. In a soup pot, combine the broth, lime juice, oregano, basil, jalapeño, bay leaf, and pepper. Bring to a boil, reduce to a simmer, and cook for 10 minutes.

4. Add the chicken, tomato, red onion, cilantro, and salt to taste. Bring to a boil, then reduce to a simmer and cook for 10 minutes. Remove the bayleaf.

5. Garnish with cheese cubes, slices of tortilla and lime, and cilantro sprigs.

Turkey Leftovers in Bread Bowls

Serves 6

Don't have time to make a bread bowl? Your local bakery should carry loaves to use instead.

2 teaspoons sugar
1⅓ cups warm water
1 envelope (or 2½ teaspoons) rapid-rise yeast
2 cups whole-wheat flour
1 cup bread flour (high gluten)
1½ cups white flour
2 eggs, separated
⅔ cup grated Monterey jack cheese

¼ cup cold water
4 cups chopped cooked turkey
4 cups Giblet Broth **or** Basic Chicken Broth (see recipes on pages 9 and 3)
Leftover vegetables, chopped (optional)
Salt and pepper

1. Using a small bowl, combine the sugar and the warm water. Shake in the yeast and let it sit at room temperature for 5 minutes.
2. In a large bowl, combine 1 cup of the wheat flour, all of the bread flour, and 1 cup of the white flour. Make a well in the center.
3. Whisk the egg yolks (reserving the whites); then add them to the yeast mixture. Add the cheese. Pour this mixture into the well of the flour mixture. Stir only enough to combine, adding more of the whole-wheat flour and white flour in equal measures until the dough is stiff. Punch it down.
4. Flour a wooden board. On it, knead the dough until it is smooth. Put it into a buttered or oiled bowl. Cover it with a towel and place it in a warm place to rise for 30 minutes. Punch down the dough and knead again for 5 minutes. Divide the dough into 6 portions. Refrigerate briefly (or up to 3 days).
5. Preheat the oven to 425 degrees. Roll out the dough into rough circles, about ¼-inch thick. Select 6 ovenproof soup bowls and butter the *outsides* of them. Put a bowl in the center of a round of dough. Pull the dough up around the bowl, completely covering the outside of it. Press the dough into place, but do not secure over the lip of the bowl (the bowls will be removed after baking). Repeat this process with each bowl and round of dough. Turn the bowls upside down on a cookie sheet.

(continued)

6. In a small bowl, whisk the egg whites and the cold water together. Brush half of this mixture lightly over all of the dough surfaces. Bake the bowls for 15 minutes.
7. Meanwhile, combine the meat, broth, and vegetables (if using) in a pot and bring to a simmer over medium heat. Add salt and pepper to taste.
8. Once the bread bowls are done cooking, slide the soup bowls out of the bread bowls. Return the bread bowls to the oven, empty side up, brushing the inside surface with the rest of the egg white mixture. Cook for 6 more minutes.
9. Fill the bread bowls with the turkey soup and serve immediately.

Chicken Chili

*4 cups cooked chicken (**or** turkey)*
1 large onion
1 tomato
2 tablespoons chopped cilantro
1 teaspoon chopped basil
2 cloves garlic
¼ cup olive oil

3 cups Basic Chicken Broth (see recipe on page 3)
2 teaspoons chili powder
1 pinch of ground cloves
2 (15- to 16-ounce) cans white beans, rinsed and drained
Tortilla chips

Serves 6

Garnish with the tomato and serve with tortilla chips on the side.

1. Cut the meat into ½-inch cubes. Chop the onion, tomato, and herbs. Finely dice the garlic.
2. Heat the oil in a soup pot on medium heat. Add the onion and garlic; cook on medium for about 3 minutes, lowering the heat as necessary to make sure the garlic doesn't burn.
3. Add all the other ingredients except for the tomato and the tortilla chips. Bring to a boil, reduce to a simmer, and cook on low for 1 hour (checking frequently to make sure the beans do not burn).

Turkey Chowder

1 onion
2 stalks celery
1 green bell pepper
3 carrots
3 russet potatoes
2 tablespoons butter
2 cups Giblet Broth **or** Basic
    Chicken Broth (see recipes
    on pages 9 and 3)
3 cups cooked turkey, cubed
1 cup corn kernels

3 cups milk
¾ teaspoon thyme
Salt and pepper
Fresh chopped parsley
    (optional)

1. Thinly slice the onion and celery, chop the bell pepper, slice the carrots, and dice the potatoes.
2. In a soup pot, heat the butter on medium heat. Add the onion and
   green pepper, sautéing for 4 minutes. Add the broth and the carrots,
   bring to a boil, reduce to a simmer, and cook for 5 more minutes.
3. Add the potatoes and celery, simmering the mixture for an additional
   10 minutes.
4. Stir in the turkey, corn kernels, milk, and thyme; salt and pepper to
   taste. Heat gently, but thoroughly. Garnish with parsley and serve.

Lemon Chicken and Okra Soup

1 broiler chicken, (2½ pounds)
Juice of 2 lemons
6 cups Basic Chicken Broth
    (see recipe on page 3)
1 large onion, peeled and chopped
3 medium tomatoes, peeled and
    chopped

1 (6-ounce) can tomato paste
2 cups sliced okra
⅓ cup uncooked long-grain rice
2 teaspoons salt
¼ teaspoon pepper
½ teaspoon ground red pepper
1 teaspoon ground turmeric

Serves 4

Out of chicken broth? Not to worry, the chicken in this soup will flavor the water.

1. Cut up the chicken into serving pieces (wings, legs, etc.). Rub lemon juice over the chicken pieces. Put the chicken in a large kettle with the broth. Bring to a boil, then simmer covered for 15 minutes.
2. Add all the remaining ingredients and simmer for 30 more minutes, until the chicken and rice are tender. Remove the chicken pieces with a slotted spoon; skin and debone them. Dice the meat and return to the kettle. Serve.

Curried Chicken Soup

1 tablespoon butter
1 teaspoon curry powder
¾ tablespoon flour
1½ cups Basic Chicken Broth
    (see recipe on page 3)
Paprika

1 egg yolk
¼ cup whole milk
¼ cup cooked chicken, cut into
    small pieces
Fresh chopped chives
    (optional)

Serves 2

If you transfer the egg back and forth between your cracked shells, the yolk with separate itself out.

1. Melt the butter in a saucepan. Add the curry and the flour and stir, cooking for 1 to 2 minutes. Pour in the broth and bring to a boil. Add paprika to taste. Turn the heat down to low.
2. In a small bowl, beat together the egg yolk and the milk. Gradually whisk this into the broth mixture. Stir in the chicken and heat on low for 5 minutes. Garnish with chives and serve.

Thanksgiving Turkey and Bacon Soup

8 slices bacon
6 cups Giblet Broth **or**
   Basic Chicken Broth
   (see recipes on pages 9
   and 3)
½ cup uncooked rice (any kind)
5 scallions, finely chopped
½ cup butter
¾ cup white flour
Salt

¼ teaspoon pepper
2 cups milk (any strength)
1½ cups cubed cooked turkey
3 tablespoons sherry

1. Cook the bacon; then lay it on paper towels to absorb the grease.
2. In a soup pot, combine the broth, rice, and scallions. Bring to a boil, reduce to a simmer, and cook 30 minutes.
3. In a large saucepan, heat the butter on medium-low heat. Whisk in the flour, salt to taste, and pepper, stirring for 1 minute.
4. Remove from heat, drizzle in the milk, and return to low heat. Stir until the mixture has thickened slightly.
5. Gradually stir the milk mixture into the rice mixture; stir in the sherry. Add the turkey. Crumble in the bacon; mix well and serve.

Chicken and Coconut Soup

3 pounds chicken
8 slices galangal (also called
   Thai ginger)
3 stalks lemongrass
8 chili peppers (red or green)
1 lemon
½ of an egg white
2 teaspoons cornstarch
4 cups Basic Chicken Broth
   (see recipe on page 3)

3 cups coconut milk
4 tablespoons fish sauce
   (Thai **or** Vietnamese)
½ teaspoon sugar
Salt
1 cup peanut oil
1 teaspoon black pepper
Coriander leaves

Serves 6–8

To add a flavorful
twist to this recipe,
substitute Thai broth
(see page 12) for a
basic chicken broth.

1. Cut the chicken into thin strips. Slice the galangal. Slice the bottom
   6–8 inches of the lemon grass, on the diagonal. Seed and coarsely
   chop the chilies. Juice the lemon.
2. In a bowl, mix together the chicken strips, egg white, and cornstarch.
   Refrigerate for 30 minutes.
3. Pour the chicken broth into a soup pot. Add the galangal, lemon
   grass, and chilies. Bring to a boil, cover, reduce to a simmer, and
   cook for 10 minutes. Remove the cover and stir in the coconut milk,
   fish sauce, sugar, and salt to taste, then simmer for 15 more minutes.
4. Meanwhile, using a skillet or wok, heat the peanut oil. Stir in the chicken
   pieces, separating them, and cooking just until they turn white. Drain.
5. Pour the broth mixture into individual bowls. Divide the chicken
   pieces among them. Sprinkle each bowl with lemon juice, pepper, and
   coriander leaves.

Low-Fat Chicken

*Nearly all of the fat in a chicken comes from its skin. You can
buy preskinned chicken breasts in the grocery store, but it's simple
to peel the skin off yourself before cooking. Choose white meat over
dark for the leanest meal.*

Hearty Winter Chicken and Noodle Soup

3 chicken quarters
(about 2 pounds total)
4 cups water
½ cup chopped celery,
plus 2 stalks, thinly sliced
2 tablespoons fresh chopped
parsley
1 teaspoon salt
1 teaspoon dried thyme,
crushed
¼ teaspoon pepper

1 bay leaf
4 medium carrots, sliced
3 medium onions, chopped
3 cups packaged dried wide
noodles
2 cups milk, divided
1 cup frozen peas
2 tablespoons all-purpose flour

1. Skin the chicken. Rinse the chicken and pat it dry with paper towels. Place the chicken, water, ½ cup chopped celery, parsley, salt, thyme, pepper, and bay leaf in a large Dutch oven. Bring to boiling; reduce heat. Simmer, covered, for 30 minutes.
2. Add the sliced celery, carrots, and onions; simmer, covered, for another 30 minutes, or until the chicken is tender and no longer pink. Remove from heat. Discard the bay leaf. Remove the chicken with a slotted spoon; let cool slightly. Debone the chicken; discard the bones. Chop chicken and set aside.
3. Heat the soup to boiling. Add the noodles; cook for 5 minutes. Stir in 1½ cups of the milk and the peas. Combine the remaining milk and the flour in a screw-top jar. Cover and shake until smooth; stir into the soup. Cook, stirring, until thickened and bubbly. Stir in chicken. Cook for 1 to 2 minutes more, or until heated through.

Quick Turkey Cassoulet

3 slices of bread (**or** 1 cup
   premade bread crumbs)
2 teaspoons olive oil
2 onions, chopped
1 carrot, chopped
2 cloves garlic, finely chopped
¼ pound turkey kielbasa
   sausage, thinly sliced
1½ cups diced cooked white
   turkey
1 (16-ounce) can Great
   Northern beans, drained
   and rinsed

1 (28-ounce) can whole tomatoes, drained and coarsely
   chopped
1 cup Basic Chicken Broth
   (see recipe on page 3)
½ cup dry white wine **or** dry
   red wine
1½ teaspoons chopped fresh
   thyme
½ teaspoon salt
½ teaspoon freshly ground
   black pepper

Serves 4

Save yourself some
time by substituting
1 cup of premade
bread crumbs for your
3 slices of bread.

1. Preheat oven to 350 degrees. Tear the bread into pieces and spread them on a baking sheet; bake for 6 to 8 minutes, stirring occasionally, until crisp and lightly colored. Set aside.
2. In a Dutch oven or flameproof casserole dish, heat the oil over medium heat. Add the onions, carrot, and garlic; cook, stirring, until the onions begin to soften, about 5 minutes. Add the kielbasa and cook, stirring, until it is lightly browned, about 5 minutes longer. Add the turkey, beans, tomatoes, chicken stock, wine, thyme, salt, and pepper. Bring the mixture to a simmer.
3. Sprinkle the cassoulet with the bread crumbs and bake for 20 to 30 minutes, or until browned and bubbling.

Chicken Ragout

Serves 4–6

This recipe can also be used as a sauce for your favorite homemade pizza or eaten with pasta.

2 tablespoons olive oil
1½ pounds boneless, skinless chicken thighs, cut in ½-inch pieces
¼–½ pound (4–8 ounces) Italian sausages, casings removed
½ of a medium-sized white onion, chopped
2 stalks celery, finely diced
2 carrots, peeled and finely diced
1 large clove garlic, minced

1 bay leaf
1 cup dry Marsala wine
½ pound fresh mushrooms, sliced
1 (14- to 16-ounce) can crushed tomatoes
1 cup Basic Chicken Broth (see recipe on page 3)
1 tablespoon tomato paste
3 generous pinches of ground cloves

1. Heat the oil in a large skillet over medium-high heat. Add the chicken thighs and Italian sausage. Stir, breaking up the sausage into small pieces; cook until the chicken is browned and the sausage is no longer pink. Add the onion, celery, carrots, garlic, and bay leaf, and continue to cook until the onion is softened. Stir in the Marsala. Bring to a boil, scraping up any brown bits that are stuck to the bottom of the skillet. Reduce the heat and simmer until half of the liquid has evaporated (about 15 minutes).
2. Transfer this mixture to a Dutch oven. Mix in the mushrooms, tomatoes, chicken stock, tomato paste, and cloves. Bring to a boil, then reduce heat and simmer, stirring occasionally, for 45 minutes. Remove bay leaf.

CHAPTER 4

Pork and Ham Soups

German Potato Soup with Ham

Serves 6

Potato skins contain many vitamins not found in the "meat" of the potato. Unless your recipe calls for a clean, "white" look, leave the skins on.

1 onion
3 leeks
2 pounds potatoes (any kind)
3 tablespoons butter
¼ teaspoon thyme
6 cups Basic Chicken Broth
  (see recipe on page 3)
  or water
1 meaty ham bone

½ pint cream
White pepper
Salt

1. Slice the onion, the white part of the leeks, and the potatoes.
2. In a soup pot, heat the butter on medium. Add the onions and cook for 3 minutes. Add the broth, leeks, potatoes, ham bone, and thyme. Bring to a boil, reduce to a simmer, and cook for 15 to 18 minutes.
3. Remove the soup pot from the heat and take out the ham bone. Cut the meat off the bone; discard the bone and shred the meat. Set aside.
4. Using a blender or food processor, purée the broth mixture. Return it to the pot, add the ham pieces, and reheat. Drizzle in the cream, season with pepper and salt, and serve.

 Common Vegetable Cuts
JULIENNE *are thin matchsticks,* ⅛" × ⅛" × 1½"
BATONS *are larger sticks,* ¼" × ¼" × 2"
DICE *are cubes of* ¼" × ¼" × ¼" *(small dice are called brunoise, and larger dice are usually just called cubes)*

Chinese Corn and Ham Soup

4 ears corn (white if possible)
½ cup minced ham
4 egg whites
3 tablespoons milk
5 cups Basic Chicken Broth
   (see recipe on page 3)
Salt

3 tablespoons cornstarch
3 tablespoons water
1 teaspoon sesame oil

> **Serves 6–8**
>
> Feel free to substitute canned or frozen corn in any recipe calling for fresh corn. It holds up well even over several hours of cooking.
>
>

1. Shuck the corn and remove the silk. Cut the kernels off the cobs with a sharp knife, discarding the cobs (or freeze them for use in making broth another day). Mince the ham.
2. In a bowl, beat the egg whites until they are frothy. Beat in the milk. Set aside.
3. Pour the broth into a soup pot and bring it to a boil. Sprinkle in some salt, add the corn kernels, and bring to a boil again. Simmer for 5 minutes, covered.
4. In a small bowl, whisk together the cornstarch, water, and sesame oil. Drizzle this mixture into the corn mixture and stir until the soup is both thick and clear.
5. Take off heat. Drizzle in the egg white mixture, stirring constantly. Stir in the ham and serve.

Common Vegetable Cuts

CHOPPED *items are cut roughly into small pieces, using a knife or food processor*
SLICES *are ⅛-inch thick unless otherwise specified*

Scandinavian Pork and Pea Soup

Serves 8

To keep onions from making your eyes tear, peel the onions in the sink with cold water running over them.

1 pound yellow split peas, rinsed

6 cups water

2 pounds lean bacon

3 medium carrots, peeled and diced

1 celery stalk, finely diced

4 medium leeks, peeled and chopped (white and light green parts only)

2 medium onions, peeled and halved

½ teaspoon dried thyme

1½ teaspoons salt

¼ teaspoon freshly ground black pepper

1 pound pork sausage links, cooked and drained

1. Soak the peas in cold water according to package directions. Put the peas in a large kettle with 6 cups of water. Cook slowly, covered, for about 1½ hours, until tender.

2. Meanwhile, put the bacon, carrots, celery, leeks, onions, thyme, salt, and pepper in another kettle. Cover with water. Cook slowly, covered, for 40 minutes, until the vegetables and bacon are tender. Remove the bacon; slice and keep warm. Using a slotted spoon, remove the vegetables and add them to the cooked split peas; add some of the broth in which the vegetables were cooked, if desired, to thin the soup.

3. Reheat, if necessary. Ladle the soup, including the vegetables, into wide soup plates and serve the sliced bacon and the cooked sausage links separately on a platter.

Portuguese Kale Soup

1 pound kale
1 pound small red potatoes
1 cup chopped onions
½ cup chopped carrots
3 pounds tomatoes
2 cloves garlic
1 pound chorizo sausage
1 tablespoon vegetable oil

2 tablespoons butter
8 cups Basic Chicken Broth
(see recipe on page 3)
Salt and pepper

Serves 6–8

For variety, feel free to substitute ½ pound of cabbage for half the kale, and 1 cup dry, red kidney beans (soaked overnight) for half the sausage.

1. Strip the kale leaves off their stems and cut diagonally into wide slices. Dice the potatoes. Chop the onions and carrots. Peel, seed, and chop the tomatoes. Mince the garlic. Prick the sausage and boil it in water for 5 to 10 minutes to release the fat; drain and cut it into ½-inch slices.
2. In a soup pot, heat the oil and butter together. Sauté the onions, carrots, and garlic for 3 to 5 minutes on medium heat. Add the broth and potatoes, bring to a boil, reduce to a simmer, and cook for 15 to 20 minutes.
3. With a masher or the back of a cooking spoon, mash most of the potatoes against the side of the pot.
4. Add the tomatoes and simmer for 10 to 15 minutes. Add both the kale and the sausage slices, cooking for another 5 to 10 minutes. Salt and pepper to taste.

Split Pea Soup

1 pound dried green split peas
2 tablespoons olive oil
1 medium onion, finely diced
2 carrots, peeled and diced
2 celery stalks, diced
2 cloves garlic, minced
½ teaspoon thyme
1 teaspoon black pepper
1 teaspoon Worcestershire sauce
½ teaspoon Tabasco sauce
2 bay leaves
2 whole cloves
2 pounds ham hocks
1 pound baking potatoes, peeled and diced
Salt and pepper

1. Rinse the split peas; soak them overnight in enough water to cover.
2. Heat the oil in a soup pot over medium heat. Add the onions, carrots, celery, garlic, thyme, pepper, Worcestershire, and Tabasco; sauté over medium heat for 5 minutes. Add the split peas along with their soaking liquid, the bay leaves, cloves, ham hocks, and potatoes to the soup pot and bring to a boil. Skim off any foam that appears on the surface. Reduce the heat and simmer gently for 2 hours.
3. Remove the ham hocks and allow them to cool. Cut the meat into small cubes and add to the pot. Add salt and pepper to taste. Remove bay leaves before serving.

Basque Bean Soup with Sausage

1 pound (16 ounces) white
   pea beans
1 onion
4 white turnips
6 potatoes
4 carrots
4 leeks
7 cloves garlic
1 small head white cabbage
½ pound (8 ounces) dried
   peas (green **or** yellow)

1 meaty ham bone
2 bay leaves
2 whole cloves
Basic Vegetable Broth
   (see recipe on page 4)
Salt
1 teaspoon thyme
12 small cooked sausages
Swiss cheese, grated (optional)

Serves 6

For a quicker soak,
put all the beans in
approximately 6 cups
of water, bring it to a
boil, and then set
aside for 1 hour.

〜

1. Soak the beans overnight in cold water, then drain.
2. Chop the onion. Cut the turnips and potatoes into small pieces. Slice the carrots and leeks (white and light green parts only), mince the garlic, and shred the cabbage.
3. Place the beans, peas, ham bone, bay leaves, cloves, and onion in a large soup pot. Add enough broth to cover all the ingredients by 3 inches. Bring to a boil, reduce to a simmer, and cook for 1 hour. Remove ham bone and allow it to cool slightly.
4. Add the turnips, potatoes, carrots, leeks, garlic, and thyme. Bring to a boil, reduce to a simmer, and cook for 15 minutes. Meanwhile, tear the meat off the ham bone, chop it, and set aside.
5. Add the cooked sausages, cabbage, and ham meat, simmering for 12 minutes. Discard bay leaves. Garnish with Swiss cheese and serve.

Pumpkin and Chili Soup

1 (4-pound) pumpkin
*¼ pound bacon (**or** ham)*
*2–3 Serrano chilies (**or** other medium-hot chilies)*
2 onions
1 tablespoon butter
2 teaspoons cumin

9 cups Basic Chicken Broth (see recipe on page 3)
*1½ cups grated Swiss, Havarti, **or** Muenster cheese*
3 tablespoons chopped parsley

1. Cut the pumpkin in half and scrape out the seeds and slimy threads. Quarter it and remove all peel and stalk. Cut the pumpkin flesh into very small pieces. Chop the bacon (or ham). Remove the seeds from the chilies and mince the flesh. Chop the onions.
2. In a soup pot, warm the butter and sauté the chopped bacon on medium until almost crisp. Add the onions and sauté for about 5 minutes. Add the pumpkin, chilies, cumin, and broth. Bring to a boil; reduce to a simmer and cook for 20 minutes.
3. As it cooks, grate the cheese and chop the parsley. Make sure the soup is warmed through but not boiling when you add them.

Corn and Bacon Soup

5–6 medium ears corn
   (to make about 3½ cups
   kernels)
4 strips bacon
2 medium leeks
¾ pound red **or** Yukon gold
   potatoes
2 tablespoons chopped parsley

1 tablespoon oil
1½ cups milk
2 tablespoons pimentos **or** thin
   strips of red bell pepper

Serves 4–6

For a quicker version, use 3½ cups of frozen corn kernels boiled for several minutes in 3 cups of water. Then move on to step 2.

1. Using a large saucepan, place the husked ears of corn and enough cold water to cover them. Bring to a boil; then reduce to a simmer and cook for 20 minutes. Reserve 3 cups of the cooking liquid (and freeze the rest if you like). After the corn cools slightly, use a sharp knife to slice off the kernels. (Freeze the cobs, if you like, for making vegetable stock another day.)
2. Slice the bacon strips into small pieces. Slice the leeks thinly. Peel the potatoes and dice them into ½-inch cubes. Chop the parsley.
3. In a soup pot, heat the oil. Sauté the bacon over medium heat for 3 minutes. Add the leek slices and cook, stirring occasionally, for about 1 to 2 minutes.
4. Add the reserved corn broth and potatoes. Bring to a boil, then reduce to a simmer, and cook for 15 minutes.
5. Heat the milk slightly; add it to the soup pot, along with the corn kernels and pimentos. Simmer very gently for about 10 more minutes. Add the parsley.

Spring Mixed Greens Soup

Serves 6–8

If you're looking to cut a few calories, substitute ½ cup of milk for the cream.

3 russet potatoes
8 cups mixed greens (wild ones such as chicory, burdock, dandelion, etc., and others such as beet tops, spinach, chard, etc.)
1 yellow onion
10 scallions
½ cup chopped dill
¼ cup chopped flat-leaf parsley
2 ham hocks
2 bay leaves
½ cup light cream

1. Peel and dice the potatoes. Tear the greens into pieces. Chop the onion and the scallions (white and green parts). Chop the dill and parsley.
2. Place the ham hocks in a soup pot and cover with cold water. Bring to a boil, reduce to a simmer, and cook for 1 hour.
3. Make sure that you have 12 cups of cooking liquid from the ham hocks; if not, add more water. Discard the ham hocks.
4. Add the potatoes, mixed greens, onion, scallions, bay leaves, dill, and parsley to the soup pot with the ham hock broth. Bring to a boil, reduce to a simmer, and cook for 30 minutes, stirring occasionally. Discard the bay leaves. Garnish with a drizzle of cream and serve.

Midwestern Swedish Yellow Pea Soup

*1 pound (16 ounces) dried
    whole Swedish yellow peas
    (split yellow peas can be
    substituted)
1 onion
4 medium russet potatoes
1½-pound pork loin (boneless)
12 cups Basic Chicken Broth
    (see recipe on page 3)*

*1 bay leaf
Salt and freshly ground black
    pepper*

(see recipe on page 3)

Serves 6–8

Split yellow peas can be substituted for the whole Swedish yellow peas.

1. Soak the dried peas overnight in cold water, then drain.
2. Chop the onion. Peel and quarter the potatoes.
3. Place the pork loin in a soup pot. Add the dried peas, onion, potatoes, chicken broth, and bay leaf. Bring to a boil, reduce to a simmer, and cook for 3½ to 4 hours. Skim off impurities as they form at the top.
4. Take the soup pot off the heat; remove the pork loin and potatoes using a slotted spoon. Once they have cooled slightly, shred the pork meat and chop the potatoes. Discard the bay leaf.
5. Add the meat and potatoes back to the soup pot and salt and pepper to taste. Reheat thoroughly, and serve.

White Bean and Ham Soup

Serves 6

Feel free to try this recipe with Beef or Vegetable Broth (pages 2 or 4).

¼ *pound (4 ounces) ham*
1 large carrot
1 onion
1 medium fennel bulb
6 cloves garlic
1 (14-ounce) can peeled tomatoes
2 tablespoons chopped sage
2 tablespoons olive oil

2 (16-ounce) cans cooked cannellini beans, drained and rinsed
4 cups Basic Chicken Broth (see recipe on page 3)
Pepper
Salt
Sage leaves (optional)

1. Slice the ham into thin strips, or dice it. Dice the carrot and onion. Chop the fennel and mince the garlic. Chop the canned tomato and the sage.
2. In a soup pot, heat the oil. Add the carrot, onion, fennel, and garlic, sautéing on medium for 5 minutes.
3. Stir in the beans, ham, chicken broth, tomato, sage, and pepper. Bring to a boil, reduce to a simmer, and cook for 20 minutes. Salt to taste and garnish with the extra sage leaves, if desired.

Puerto Rican White Bean and Sausage Soup

¾ *pound (12 ounces) dried*
   white beans
2 dry Spanish sausages
1 cup sliced banana squash
1 small yellow onion
3 scallions
2 tomatoes
2 teaspoons chopped oregano
½ of a red bell pepper
6 garlic cloves

10 cups water
⅛ teaspoon cayenne pepper
1 teaspoon white wine vinegar
Salt
1 teaspoon olive oil
⅓ cup Spanish sherry
5 cups Basic Chicken Broth,
   divided

Serves 4

Italian sweet sausage
without fennel can
be substituted for
Spanish sausages.

1. Soak the beans overnight in cold water, then drain.
2. Slice the sausage into ¼-inch-thick pieces. Peel the squash and cut it into ¼-inch-thick pieces. Chop the yellow onion, scallions, tomatoes, and oregano. Mince the red bell pepper and 4 of the garlic cloves. Peel the remaining 2 garlic cloves, leaving them whole.
3. In a soup pot, combine the water, beans, whole garlic cloves, onion, cayenne, vinegar, and salt. Bring to a boil, reduce to a simmer, and cook for 30 minutes.
4. Meanwhile, heat the olive oil in a saucepan. Add the minced garlic and the sausage; sauté on medium for 4 minutes. Add the tomatoes, oregano, sherry, squash, and scallions. Pour in 1 cup of the ham broth, scraping up the brown bits from the bottom of the pan. When the bean mixture is done cooking, add this mixture to the soup pot.
5. Add the remaining 4 cups of ham broth to the soup pot. Bring to a boil, reduce to a simmer, and cook for 30 minutes.

Spanish Bean Soup with Sausage

Serves 8

Precook sausage in the microwave to reduce the fat content. If you like crispy sausage in recipes, brown it beforehand and add it to the recipe during the last half-hour.

1 cup (8 ounces) dried chick-peas (garbanzo beans)
1 beef bone
1 ham bone
8 cups water
1 chorizo (Spanish sausage)
1 pound potatoes
1 onion

4 tablespoons olive oil
¼ pound (4 ounces) bacon
1 pinch of saffron threads
Salt

1. Soak the chickpeas overnight in cold water, then drain.
2. Place the two bones in a large soup pot; add the chickpeas and water. Bring to a boil, reduce to a simmer, and cook for 45 minutes.
3. Meanwhile, cut the chorizo into small pieces, and dice the potatoes and onion.
4. In a large saucepan or skillet, heat the oil. Sauté the bacon and onion on medium until the bacon is crisp. When the bone broth is done cooking, add the onion, bacon, potatoes, and saffron to the soup pot. Simmer for 15 minutes.
5. Remove the pot from the heat, stir in the sausage pieces, and salt to taste.

Texas Black-Eyed Pea Soup

2 cups dried black-eyed peas
1 pound ham
1 stalk celery
1 small onion
5 cloves garlic
2 serrano chilies
1 teaspoon minced thyme
2 tablespoons minced cilantro
¼ cup olive oil

12 cups Basic Chicken Broth
 (see recipe on page 3)
Salt and black pepper
Tabasco sauce
6 scallions (optional)

Serves 6

Black-eyed beans are actually legumes. You'll find them with the dried beans in your grocery store.

---

1. Soak the black-eyed peas overnight in cold water, then drain.
2. Dice the ham, celery, and onions. Chop the garlic, and seed the chilies, cutting them in half. Mince the thyme and cilantro.
3. Using a soup pot, heat the olive oil on medium. Add the ham, celery, onion, garlic, and chilies, sautéing for 4 minutes.
4. Pour in the chicken broth. Add the black-eyed peas and the thyme. Bring to a boil, reduce to a simmer, and cook for 1¼ hours.
5. Remove from the heat, add the cilantro, and cool slightly. Using a blender or food processor, purée until smooth. Add the salt, pepper, and Tabasco sauce to taste, and bring just to a simmer. Mince the scallions for garnish and serve.

Kielbasa and Bean Soup

1 pound (16 ounces) kielbasa
    sausage (low fat)
1 onion
1 stalk celery
2 (14½-ounce) cans whole
    tomatoes
2 teaspoons basil
1 teaspoon oregano
5 cloves garlic
½ chipotle pepper in adobo
    sauce

1 tablespoon olive oil
2 teaspoons thyme
5 cups Basic Chicken Broth
    (see recipe on page 3)
4 (15½-ounce) cans black
    beans, drained and rinsed
Salt and pepper

1. Thinly slice the sausage. Chop the onion and celery. Dice the canned tomatoes and mix with the basil and oregano. Mince the garlic. Drain and mince the chipotle.

2. Using a soup pot, heat the oil on medium. Add the onion, celery, and thyme, sautéing for 3 minutes. Add the garlic and cook for 1 additional minute.

3. Pour in the broth and scrape the bottom of the pan with a wooden spoon to loosen the cooked brown bits. Add the beans, tomatoes, kielbasa, and chipotle. Bring to a boil, reduce to a simmer, and cook for 20 minutes. Season with salt and pepper to taste, and serve.

Beef, Veal, and Lamb Soups

Lamb and Barley Soup

2½ pounds lean lamb meat
3 tablespoons butter
2 onions
3 stalks celery
6 cups water

3 tablespoons fresh chopped parsley
1 cup pearl barley
1 bay leaf
Salt and pepper to taste

1. Cube the lamb meat. Slice the onion and coarsely chop the celery and parsley.
2. In a soup pot, heat the butter. Cook the lamb on medium–high heat for 3 minutes, turning the pieces to brown on all sides. Remove the lamb from the pot and set aside. Drain and discard all but 3 tablespoons of the fat.
3. Reheat the fat and sauté the onion on medium for 3 minutes. Add all of the ingredients, including the cooked lamb; bring to a boil, reduce to a simmer, and cook for 2 hours. Discard bay leaf.

Scotch Lamb Soup

2 cups cubed lean lamb meat
2 onions
2 tablespoons oil
8 cups water
1 bay leaf
2 stalks celery

4 medium potatoes
2 cups chopped cabbage
3 carrots
⅓ cup pearl barley
⅓ cup chopped parsley

1. Cube the lamb meat and chop the onions.
2. In a soup pot, heat the oil. Brown the lamb pieces on medium-high heat, turning them to brown on all sides. Add the water, bay leaf, and onion; bring to a boil, then reduce the heat to low and cook for 1½ hours.
3. Dice the celery and potatoes. Chop the cabbage and grate the carrots coarsely. Add the celery, potatoes, and barley, cover, and bring to a boil. Reduce to a simmer and cook for 15 minutes. Add the cabbage and cook for 10 to 15 minutes longer. Remove the bay leaf.

Lamb and Fennel Soup

2 pounds lamb ribs
4 cups Basic Chicken Broth
    (see recipe on page 3)
4 cups water
2/3 cup finely chopped fennel
    fronds
1/2 cup chopped flat-leaf parsley
1/2 an onion

2 1/4 pounds tomatoes
1/8 teaspoon red pepper
6 slices crusty Italian bread

Serves 6

If possible, try to get wild fennel fronds for this recipe. You'll notice that it adds flavor to the soup.

∾

1. Trim off excess fat from the lamb ribs. Place the lamb in a soup pot and add the chicken broth and water; bring to a boil, then reduce to a simmer. For the first 30 minutes, regularly remove the impurities that rise to the top with a slotted spoon. Simmer for 1½ hours.
2. Finely chop the fennel fronds. Coarsely chop the parsley, finely slice the onion, and chop the tomatoes. Add these ingredients to the pot, along with the red pepper.
3. Return to a boil, reduce to a simmer, and cook for an additional 30 minutes.
4. Remove the lamb, discarding the skin and bones. Cut the meat into bite-sized pieces and return them to the pot to rewarm. While it reheats, place a slice of the bread in the bottom of each individual soup bowl. Pour the soup over the bread and serve.

Irish Stew

4–6 cups Basic Chicken Broth **or** Scotch Broth (see recipes on pages 3 and 7)
2½ pounds lamb meat
2 onions

2½ pounds potatoes
Salt and pepper
2 tablespoons chopped parsley (optional)

1. Preheat the oven to 375 degrees. Trim off excess fat and cut the lamb into pieces, through the bones. Thinly slice the onions and potatoes.
2. Place these 3 ingredients in layers in an oven-ready casserole dish, sprinkling each layer with salt and pepper. A layer of potatoes should be on top.
3. Pour in enough broth to fill the casserole halfway up. Cover. Bake for 2 hours. Uncover and bake for an additional 30 minutes. Sprinkle with parsley and serve.

Apounduquerque Ground Beef and Pork Meatball Soup

¾ pound ground beef
¾ pound ground pork
⅓ cup uncooked rice
1 egg
1 teaspoon oregano
1 teaspoon pepper
2 tablespoons olive oil

1 medium onion, finely diced
1 clove garlic, crushed
½ cup tomato paste
10 cups Basic Beef Broth (see recipe on page 2)
½ cup chopped cilantro

1. In a bowl, combine the beef, pork, rice, egg, oregano, and pepper. Mold the mixture into meatballs about the size of golf balls.
2. In a soup pot, warm the oil. Sauté the onion on medium for 3 minutes. Add the garlic and sauté for an additional 2 minutes. Stir in the tomato paste. Pour in the broth. Bring to a boil, add the meatballs, and reduce to medium-low. Cook, covered, for 30 minutes. Stir in the cilantro and serve.

Beef Soup with Black Olives

4 pounds beef
3 yellow onions
3 carrots
2 cloves garlic
3 anchovy fillets
4 tablespoons olive oil, divided
1 tablespoon tomato paste
1 teaspoon black pepper
1 cup flour
1 cup dry red wine

4 cups Basic Beef Broth
(see recipe on page 2)
1 tomato
8 black olives
2 tablespoons chopped parsley
1 teaspoon lemon juice

Serves 8

To serve, pour the soup into a bowl and then top each serving with a dollop of the olive mixture.

1. Cut the beef into 1½-inch cubes. Dice the onions and carrots. Mince the garlic and anchovies.

2. In a soup pot, warm 2 tablespoons of the oil on medium. Add the onions, carrots, and garlic, sautéing for 6 minutes. Add the anchovies, tomato paste, and pepper, cooking for 2 more minutes. Remove from heat.

3. Coat the beef with the flour. In a pan, heat the rest of the oil. On medium-high heat, brown the beef on all sides, turning several times. Drain the oil and discard.

4. Add the wine to the pan with the meat, stirring to loosen the cooked bits stuck to the bottom of the pan. Cook for 3 minutes. Add this and the beef broth to the soup pot with the vegetables. Simmer the mixture for 2 hours, checking to see if it needs more broth, wine, or water (or a combination of these) to keep the level of the liquid mostly covering the other ingredients.

5. Just before the soup is ready, coarsely chop the tomato, olives, and parsley; mix together, along with the lemon juice, and serve as a garnish.

New Mexican Beef Chili

3 pounds beef
2 onions
10 cloves garlic
7 fresh jalapeño peppers
¼ cup chili powder
2 tablespoons olive oil, divided
1 (28-ounce) can plum tomatoes
1 tablespoon red wine vinegar
  or red wine

6 cups water
4 cups cooked rice
Salt and pepper
Sour cream (optional)

1. Trim off the fat and cut the beef into ½-inch cubes; pat them dry with paper towels. Finely dice the onions and mince the garlic. Remove the stems and seeds, and mince the jalapeños.
2. In a dry saucepan, over medium heat, toast the chili powder for 1 minute or so, until the smell is heavenly. (Toast the entire ¼ cup of chili powder, or more, and reserve any that you don't use for guests to add as they like.)
3. In a large skillet, heat 1 tablespoon of the oil and brown the beef on all sides, turning several times. Drain off most of the fat and transfer the meat to a large stove-top ready casserole dish.
4. Warm the remaining tablespoon of oil in the skillet. Add the onions, garlic, and jalapeños. Cook them over medium heat for 3 minutes. Place them in the casserole dish with the meat. Stir in the chili powder and simmer everything for 2 minutes.
5. Pour in the plum tomatoes with their juice, the vinegar (or wine), and the water. Bring to a boil, reduce to a simmer, and cook, uncovered, for 1½ hours. About 15 minutes before the chili is done, add salt and pepper to taste.
6. Add some rice to each serving bowl and pour the chili over the top. Garnish with a dollop of sour cream if you like, and serve.

Beef and Onions in Red Wine Soup

1½ pounds beef
6 small yellow onions
2 tablespoons butter
2 teaspoons thyme
Pepper
2 tablespoons peanut oil
4 cups Red Wine Broth
    (see recipe on page 13)

10 cremini **or** button mushrooms
2 tablespoons fresh chopped
    chives

Serves 6

Don't be too impatient. The onions will take on a dark brown color when they're caramelized.

෴

---

1. Cube the beef. Thinly slice the onions.
2. Heat the butter in a sauté pan. Add the onions and thyme. Over medium heat, cook for 3 minutes, stirring often. Continue cooking, stirring constantly, until the onions are caramelized. Add the pepper, cover, and set aside.
3. Preheat the oven to 500 degrees. In an oven-ready pan, warm the peanut oil. Over high heat on the stove top, brown the meat on all sides. Put the pan directly into the oven and roast for 20 minutes. Remove the pan from oven, cover loosely to keep warm, and set it aside.
4. Pour the red wine broth into a soup pot. While it is coming to a boil, cut the mushrooms into quarters and chop the chives. Add the mushrooms and simmer for 3 minutes. Add the chives and cook for another minute.
5. Rewarm the onions in the oven, then place them in a mound in the middle of each serving bowl. Place the meat pieces around one side of each bowl, along with the mushrooms. Pour the broth over the top.

Beef and Beer Stew with Dried Fruit

Serves 6–8

Coarsely chop the remaining parsley, sprinkle it over the top to garnish, and serve.

3 pounds beef
Salt and pepper
2 yellow onions
½ cup dried pineapple
½ cup dried apples
18 pearl onions
2 tablespoons butter
3 tablespoons peanut oil

1 cup Basic Beef Broth
   (see recipe on page 2)
10 sprigs flat-leaf parsley
2 sprigs thyme
3 cloves
1 bay leaf
2 bottles dark beer

1. Cut the beef into 1½-inch cubes; pat the beef dry with paper towels and lightly coat them with salt and pepper. Thinly slice the onions. Chop the dried fruits coarsely. Preheat the oven to 325 degrees.
2. Place the pearl onions in a small saucepan and add enough water to cover them. Bring to a boil; boil them for 1 minute. Drain the pan and rinse the onions under cold running water. Remove their skins and set them aside.
3. Heat the butter in a sauté pan. Add the yellow onions, stirring them almost constantly over medium heat until they are dark brown. Remove the pan from the heat, cover, and set aside.
4. Using a large oven-proof casserole dish, heat the oil over medium heat on the stove top. Brown the meat pieces on all sides, for about 8 minutes. Remove the pieces with a slotted spoon, reserving the cooking liquid in the pan. Set aside the meat.
5. Turn the heat to high and add the beef broth. With a wooden spoon, loosen the bits of cooked meat stuck to the bottom of the pan, incorporating them into the broth. Cook over medium heat for 3 minutes. Remove the pan from the heat.
6. Layer the beef, onions, dried fruits, and pearl onions into the pan, using about a third of each ingredient in each of three layers.
7. Make a bouquet garni (see "Bag o' Spices" on page 8) with half of the parsley, the thyme, cloves, and bay leaf. Slightly bury the spice bag in the center of the mixture.
8. Pour the beer over the mixture. Bring to a boil, then cover the pan and place it in the oven. Cook for 1 hour.
9. Remove the bouquet garni and the bay leaf.

White Bean and Lamb Soup

1 pound dried white beans
1 cup chopped onion
1 clove garlic
1½ cups diced tomatoes
6 sprigs parsley
2 tablespoons butter
1 pound lamb shanks
10 cups water
1 bay leaf

1 tablespoon thyme
2 whole cloves
20 black peppercorns
Dill (optional)

> **Serves 4–6**
>
> If substituting canned beans for dry beans, decrease the water by three cups per cup of beans. Add canned beans later; cook for about half the time you would dried beans.
>
>

1. Rinse the beans and soak them overnight; drain.
2. Coarsely chop the onion, mince the garlic, dice the tomatoes, and tie the parsley sprigs into a bundle.
3. In a soup pot, melt the butter. Add the onions, garlic, and the lamb. Sauté on medium heat for 5 minutes until the lamb is browned. Add the beans, water, tomatoes, bay leaf, parsley, thyme, cloves, and peppercorns. Bring to a boil, reduce to a simmer, and cook for 2 hours.
4. Remove the lamb from the pot, discarding the skin and the bones. Cut the meat into bite-sized pieces and return it to the pot. Discard the bay leaf and parsley sprigs. Reheat, then garnish with a bit of dill, if desired.

Beef and Vegetable Soup

Serves 8

Refrigerating this soup after cooking allows the fat to rise to the top and form a hardened layer, which is easily removed.

1½ pounds beef short rib
1½ pounds stewing beef
¼ pound salt pork **or** uncut bacon
1 large yellow onion
1 large tomato
4 medium-sized sweet potatoes
3 scallions
1 large green pepper
½ pound fresh spinach
½ pound fresh kale
3 cloves garlic
2 tablespoons olive oil
12 cups water
½ teaspoon thyme
½ teaspoon pepper
1 (15½-ounce) can okra, drained

1. Cut the short rib into 3-inch pieces and the stewing beef into 2-inch cubes. Dice the onion and tomato, cube the sweet potatoes, and chop the scallions coarsely. Cut the green pepper into strips and trim the spinach and kale. Crush the garlic.
2. On medium-high heat, brown the pork and the short rib pieces on all sides. Add the stewing beef; brown it on all sides.
3. Add the water and bring it slowly to a boil. Add the thyme and pepper. Simmer it, covered, for 1 hour, frequently spooning off the impurities that rise to the top.
4. Meanwhile, heat the oil and sauté the onion, garlic, and scallions on medium for 3 to 5 minutes. Add the green pepper and cook for 1 additional minute. Set aside.
5. When the meat is ready, add the sautéed vegetables, along with the okra. Simmer for 30 minutes. Remove the short rib pieces and salt pork, and discard. Cool the soup to room temperature by placing the soup pot in a bath of ice water; then refrigerate for a few hours, or overnight. Remove the hardened fat layer that has formed on the top; reheat and serve.

Beef and Paprika Goulash

¾ pound sirloin
2 tablespoons peanut oil
2 cups finely chopped onion
2 cloves garlic, minced
1½ cups finely chopped red
   bell pepper

1 tablespoon paprika
   (any strength, to taste)
2 teaspoon caraway seeds
2 cups seeded and chopped
   tomatoes
Sour cream (optional)

1. Trim the meat to cut off excess fat, then cube it into ½ -inch pieces.
2. In a soup pot, heat the oil. Add the beef, stirring often over medium heat, until it just begins to brown. Add the onion, garlic, and bell peppers. Sauté for 5 minutes, stirring often. Stir in the paprika and caraway seeds. Add the tomatoes, bring to a boil, and reduce to a simmer. Cook for 1 hour, stirring occasionally.
3. Ladle the soup into bowls and garnish with dollops of sour cream.

> **Serves 4–6**
>
> You can substitute canned tomatoes for fresh ones. It can save you time, and won't affect the taste.
>
> ∾

Minestrone with Meatballs

24 cooked meatballs
1 (15-ounce) can navy **or** other
   white beans, drained
1 tablespoon dried minced onion
1 teaspoon basil
1 bay leaf
2 cups Basic Beef Broth
   (see recipe on page 2)
2 cups water

1 cup ditali, orzo, **or** other
   pasta
1 (16-ounce) can diced tomatoes (liquid retained)
1 (10-ounce) package frozen
   mixed vegetables, thawed
1 teaspoon sugar

> **Serves 6**
>
> Frozen vegetables retain more natural nutrients than fresh vegetables due to the loss of nutrient value at room temperature once a vegetable is picked.
>
> ∾

In a 4-quart saucepan, combine the meatballs, beans, onion, basil, bay leaf, broth, and water; bring to a boil. Add the pasta and cook for 15 minutes. Reduce to a simmer and add the tomatoes and their liquid, the vegetables, and sugar; heat through. Remove the bay leaf.

Moroccan Lamb and Garbanzo Bean Soup

¾ cup dried chickpeas (garbanzo beans)
4 (1-pound) lamb shanks (shoulder or neck can be substituted, as can 1¼ pounds lamb stew meat)
2 tablespoons ghee
2 onions, finely chopped
1 stalk celery, finely chopped
1 teaspoon turmeric
½ teaspoon (or to taste) cayenne pepper
1 teaspoon cinnamon
1 teaspoon finely chopped ginger root
1 pinch of saffron threads
8 cups any basic meat broth
¾ cup dried lentils, rinsed
6 tomatoes, seeded and coarsely chopped
2 tablespoons finely chopped parsley
½ cup finely chopped cilantro
1 cup plain yogurt
Salt and pepper

1. Soak the chickpeas overnight in cold water; drain.
2. In a soup pot, heat the ghee. On medium-high heat, lightly brown the lamb on all sides. Remove the lamb and set aside.
3. Add the onions and celery to the pot, sautéing for 3 minutes on medium heat. Add the turmeric, cayenne pepper, ginger, cinnamon, and saffron, stirring them in for another 3 minutes. Place the lamb back in the pot along with the chickpeas and the broth. Bring to a boil, reduce to a simmer, and cook for 1 hour. Regularly skim off and discard impurities that rise to the top.
4. Add the lentils and tomatoes and cook for another hour. Skim off any additional impurities as they form.
5. Using a slotted spoon, remove the bone if you are using one. Pull the meat off the bone, cube or shred it, and return it to the pot. Keep the soup pot on low heat. Stir in the parsley, cilantro, yogurt, and salt and black pepper to taste. Serve.

Italian Minestrone Cola Soup

2½-pound blade chuck roast

10 cups water

3 teaspoons salt, divided

1 small peeled onion, plus ¼ cup diced onion

½ cup celery leaves

1 bay leaf

2 slices bacon, diced

½ cup chopped fresh green beans

½ cup green peas

½ cup thinly sliced zucchini

½ cup diced celery

½ cup thinly sliced carrots

¼ cup chopped parsley

1 clove garlic, minced

1 (6-ounce) can tomato paste

1 cup cola

1 tablespoon olive oil

1 tablespoon Worcestershire sauce

1½ cups (12 ounces) cooked kidney beans

½ cup dry elbow macaroni

1 tablespoon Italian seasoning

¼ teaspoon black pepper

Parmesan cheese, grated (optional)

Serves 12

While the parmesan cheese isn't a necessity for this soup, it will give it an added flavor—and flair!

1. In a large pan, combine the meat, water, 2 teaspoons of the salt, the whole onion, celery leaves, and bay leaf. Cover and simmer about 2½ hours until the meat is tender.

2. Remove the meat and finely dice it, discarding any fat and bones (should yield about 2 cups of meat). Strain the broth (should measure 8 cups). Add ice cubes to the broth to harden the fat; remove and discard the fat.

3. In a 5- to 6-quart kettle or Dutch oven, combine the beef broth and the meat; warm on low heat.

4. Pan-fry the bacon until crisp. Add the bacon and the drippings and all the remaining ingredients, *except* the parmesan cheese, to the broth. Cover and simmer for about 30 minutes, until the vegetables and macaroni are tender. Serve sprinkled with parmesan cheese, if desired.

Pepper Pot Soup

Serves 8

For a different flavor, substitute chopped bacon for salt pork.

¼ pound salt pork
1½ pounds short rib of beef, cut into 3-inch pieces
1½ pounds stew beef, cut into 2-inch cubes
12 cups water
½ teaspoon dried thyme
1½ teaspoons salt
¼ teaspoon pepper
2 tablespoons olive oil
1 large onion, diced
2 cloves garlic, crushed
2 scallions, diced

1 large green pepper, cut into strips
1 (15½-ounce) can okra, drained
4 medium sweet potatoes, peeled and cubed
1 large tomato, peeled and cubed
½ pound fresh kale, washed and trimmed
½ pound fresh spinach, washed and trimmed

1. Place the salt pork and short rib pieces in a large kettle; brown the ribs on all sides. Add the stew beef and brown on all sides.
2. Add the water and slowly bring just to a boil. Using a spoon, skim off the fat that has risen to the top. Add the thyme, salt, and pepper; reduce to a simmer. Cook, covered, for 1 hour, occasionally skimming off any impurities.
3. While the meat is simmering, heat the oil in a skillet and sauté the onion, garlic, and scallions. Add the green pepper and sauté 1 minute more. Remove from heat and set aside.
4. After the meat is done cooking, add the sautéed vegetables and all the remaining ingredients, except the spinach, to the kettle. Continue to cook slowly, covered, for about 30 minutes, until the vegetables and meat are cooked. Remove from heat and cool slightly. Take out the short ribs and cut off and discard any fat. Cube the meat and return it to the kettle. Reheat the soup to serving temperature; then add the spinach and heat until the spinach has just wilted. Serve.

CHAPTER 6
Cheese, Cream, and Other Dairy Soups

Cream of Sorrel Soup

Serves 4

If you're looking for a nice change, replace the chicken broth with a vegetable broth in this soup.

2 cups sorrel leaves
2 tablespoons butter **or** vegetable oil
5 cups Basic Chicken Broth (see recipe on page 3)
½ cup whole milk **or** light cream

3 egg yolks
1 tablespoon of any fresh green herb, chopped

1. Tear the sorrel leaves away from the center rib and into a few larger pieces. Using an enamel or stainless steel soup pot, warm the oil, then add the sorrel, and stir until wilted down to about 3 tablespoons of leaves.

2. Add the stock and simmer for only about 2 minutes. Remove from heat and allow to cool very briefly. Using a wire whisk, lightly beat the egg yolks in a stainless steel bowl and mix in the cream. Temper this mixture by slowly adding about half of the hot broth to it, stirring constantly. Pour this mixture into the soup pot with the rest of the broth, making sure the mixture doesn't boil. Reheat on low. Garnish with a small amount of any green grass-style herb.

Cream of Broccoli Soup

1½ pounds broccoli
1 large stalk celery
1 medium onion
2 cups water
2 tablespoons butter
2 tablespoons flour
2½ cups Basic Chicken Broth
   (see recipe on page 3)

½ cup milk **or** cream
Salt and pepper

Serves 6–8

While cream will give you a richer, heartier texture, milk is a healthier option. Of course, half-and-half is always a good compromise!

1. Cut the broccoli into flowerets. Chop the broccoli stem, celery, and onion.
2. In a saucepan or steamer, boil the water and immediately add the broccoli stems, celery, and onion. Simmer for 10 minutes.
3. Meanwhile, steam the broccoli florets; then shock them in ice water. Drain and set aside, covered.
4. In another saucepan, melt the butter and whisk in the flour, stirring until it is smooth. Take the saucepan off the heat and allow to cool slightly. Whisk the chicken broth into the flour mixture. Bring to a boil, stirring it for 1 minute.
5. Add all the vegetables except the steamed broccoli and bring to a boil. Add the florets, then remove from heat. Stir in the milk (or cream). Salt and pepper to taste.

Cream of Mushroom Soup

Serves 6

Sauté the mushrooms and onions using ghee or nut oil to complement the flavor of this recipe.

½ pound fresh mushrooms (any kind, or a mix of types)
1 medium-sized yellow onion
3 tablespoons oil
3 tablespoons flour
*2 cups Basic Beef **or** Basic Chicken Broth (see recipes on pages 2 and 3)*

*2 cups total of milk, cream, plain yogurt, **and/or** sour cream*
*Celery seeds **or** caraway seeds (optional)*

1. Slice the mushrooms, including the stems, and dice the onion.
2. In a soup pot, heat the oil. Sauté the onion on medium heat for 3 minutes. Add the mushrooms and cook for 3 more minutes, stirring constantly. Remove from heat and allow the mixture to cool slightly.
3. Shake the flour over the mushroom mixture and whisk to blend. Stir in the broth and whisk in the dairy product(s). Heat thoroughly on a low to medium temperature. Garnish with seeds.

Cauliflower Cheese Soup

1 cup chopped onion
2 celery stalks
4 medium potatoes (russet or
*   Yukon gold)*
1 medium head cauliflower
2 cups shredded cheddar
*   cheese*
2 tablespoons butter
1 teaspoon curry powder
1 teaspoon mustard
1¼ cups skim milk

1½ cups peas
2 teaspoons dried dill
*   (more if fresh)*
¼ teaspoon dried rosemary
*   (more if fresh)*
Salt and pepper

Serves 8–10

If you can't find fresh peas, using frozen ones won't affect the taste in this recipe.

1. Chop the onion and dice the celery. Peel the potatoes and dice them into a ½-inch cubes. Finely chop the cauliflower. Grate the cheese.

2. In a soup pot, warm the butter on medium heat. Add the onion and celery, and sauté for 3 minutes. Add the potatoes and cauliflower. Pour enough water into the pot to cover all the ingredients. Add the curry and mustard. Bring the mixture to a boil, then reduce to a simmer and cook for 20 minutes.

3. Remove from heat and allow to cool slightly. Use a slotted spoon to remove the vegetables; working in batches, purée them. Add them back into the soup pot. With the pot still off the heat, stir in the milk gradually until the mixture is slightly thick.

4. Place the pot back onto low heat. Gradually sprinkle in the grated cheese, stirring until it just melts. Add the peas, dill, and rosemary, and cook for 5 to 10 minutes, until the peas are cooked.

5. Adjust the consistency with more milk, if necessary. Add salt and pepper to taste.

Cream of Asparagus Soup

1 pound asparagus
3 cups Basic Chicken Broth
  (see recipe on page 3)
2 cups water
3 tablespoons butter
3 tablespoons flour
*¼ cup sherry **or** ⅓ cup*
  white wine
1 small lemon

*1 cup milk **or** half-and-half*
Salt and pepper
Rye croutons (optional)

1. Trim off the woody ends of the asparagus. Chop the spears coarsely. (Discard the ends, or freeze them to use in making broth another day.)
2. In a soup pot, combine the broth, water, and asparagus. Bring to a boil, reduce to a simmer, and cook for 5 minutes. Keeping the liquids warm, carefully remove the asparagus using a slotted spoon. Once they have cooled, purée them in a blender or food processor. Return the puréed asparagus to the soup pot. Keep on very low heat.
3. In a saucepan, melt the butter. Sprinkle the flour over it, whisking the mixture constantly. Add the sherry (or wine), again whisking until it is smooth and bubbling slightly. Juice the lemon and mix it with about ½ cup of the asparagus liquid, then add this mixture to the saucepan. Slowly trickle the contents of the saucepan into the soup pot, stirring constantly. Simmer for 10 to 15 minutes.
4. Add the milk (or half-and-half) and salt and pepper to taste. Rewarm gently. Garnish with croutons and serve.

Cream of Onion Soup

2 cups milk
*1 tablespoon oil **or** butter*
5 cups minced yellow onion
2 teaspoons mustard (any kind)
*2 tablespoons white **or** rye flour*
3 cups water

1 teaspoon horseradish sauce
2 teaspoons total of pepper
* (any kind), Worcestershire*
* sauce, **or** soy sauce*
Salt to taste

1. In a saucepan, warm the milk very slowly, up to just before the boiling point. Take the pan off the heat, keeping it covered.
2. In a soup pot, heat the oil. Stir in the onions and mustard. Cook on low heat for 15 minutes.
3. Sprinkle the flour over the onion mixture, whisking constantly. Add the water, hot milk, and the seasonings, and warm to serving temperature.

> **Serves 6**
>
> A nut oil complements this soup recipe nicely. Or try a garnish of croutons and shredded cheese.
>
> ∾

Cream of Carrot Soup

1 pound carrots
1 large onion
½ cup chopped celery
2 cups peeled and diced potato
1 clove garlic, minced
1 tablespoon olive oil

1 teaspoon sugar
4 cloves
Pepper
4 cups Basic Chicken Broth
* (see recipe on page 3)*
Salt

1. Chop the carrots, onion, and celery. Peel and dice the potatoes.
2. In a soup pot, heat the oil. Add the carrots, onion, celery, potato, garlic, and sugar, and sauté on medium for 3 minutes. Reduce heat to low, cover the pot, and cook for 10 more minutes.
3. Uncover the pot and add the cloves, pepper, and chicken broth. Bring to a boil, reduce to a simmer, and cook 20 minutes.
4. Remove pot off the heat. Remove the cloves and allow the soup to cool slightly. Purée the soup in a food processor. Reheat and salt to taste.

> **Serves 6**
>
> If you don't have a food processor handy, throw it all in a blender to purée.
>
>

Roasted Corn and Chipotle Chowder

Serves 12

Prepare the red bell peppers in advance. Store them covered with olive oil in a glass jar in your refrigerator.

5 ears fresh corn, husked
2 red bell peppers
7–8 small red new potatoes
2 small cans chipotle chilies, drained
2 tomatoes
1 medium-sized yellow onion
3 cloves garlic
6 slices bacon
3 tablespoons butter
8 cups Basic Chicken Broth (see recipe on page 3)
Salt and pepper
1½ cups cream

1. Using a heavy cast iron pan, roast the corn on the grill for 5 minutes, turning often. Cut the kernels off the cobs, setting the kernels and 3 of the cobs aside. Roast the red bell peppers on the grill or under the broiler, turning them a few times, until the skin is blackened, about 8 minutes. Put the peppers in a sealed plastic bag.
2. Quarter all but 3 of the potatoes. Cover the quartered potatoes with water in a pan and simmer for 15 minutes. Meanwhile, seed and dice the chipotle peppers, tomatoes, and the remaining potatoes. Chop the onion and mince the garlic. Remove the burnt skin from the bell peppers and cut the flesh into small pieces, discarding the core. When the potatoes are done, coarsely mash them; set aside.
3. In a soup pot, fry the bacon on medium heat until almost crunchy. Remove the bacon and set aside. Drain off and discard the grease.
4. In the pot, melt the butter. Add the onion and sauté for 3 minutes. Add the garlic, sautéing for 2 more minutes. Dice the bacon slices and add them to the pot.
5. Pour in the broth, the 3 reserved corn cobs (*not* the kernels), the diced potatoes, the mashed potatoes, the chilies, and the tomatoes. Bring to a boil, add salt and pepper to taste, reduce to a simmer, and cook for 20 minutes.
6. Remove the cobs from the soup and discard. Add the corn kernels, red pepper pieces, and cream. Heat thoroughly, and serve.

Cucumber and Buttermilk Soup

3 cucumbers
2 tablespoons fresh chopped
  dill
1 lemon
2 tablespoons butter

2 tablespoons flour
4 cups buttermilk
White pepper

1. Peel the cucumbers and remove the heavily seeded core. Cut the flesh into slices. Chop the dill and juice the lemon.
2. In a soup pot, warm the butter and whisk in the flour, cooking for 3 minutes. Gradually whisk in the buttermilk. Bring almost to a boil. Add the cucumber slices and dill, simmering for 15 minutes.
3. Allow the soup to cool and then purée it in a food processor. Stir in the lemon juice and the white pepper. Reheat gently but thoroughly.

Serves 4

To quickly seed the cucumber, cut it in half, lengthwise. Use a teaspoon to scoop out the seeds.

Italian Cheese Soup

3 eggs
3 tablespoons grated parmesan
  cheese

6 cups Basic Chicken Broth
  (see recipe on page 3)

In a soup pot, bring the broth to a boil, then reduce it to a simmer. In a small bowl, beat the eggs until they are frothy; stir in the cheese. Very gradually, stir the egg mixture into the broth and continue to stir for a couple of minutes, until the eggs have cooked. Serve.

Serves 4

When you pour the egg mixture into the hot broth, you'll see small pieces of cooked egg. In Italy, the pieces are called "rags."

Northwest Cream of Cauliflower Soup with Hazelnuts

Serves 2–4

Raw cauliflower should be stored, in the refrigerator, in a plastic bag with tiny holes poked in it. Refrigerated, cooked cauliflower will last for about two days.

1 pound (16 ounces) cauliflower
1 carrot
1 stalk celery
¼ of a small onion
Hazelnuts, shelled (to yield
   1 tablespoon, chopped)
2 tablespoons butter

4 cups Basic Chicken Broth
   (see recipe on page 3)
1 cup milk
Salt and white pepper

1. Preheat oven to 275 degrees. Cut the cauliflower, carrots, and celery into 2-inch pieces. Chop the onion.
2. Roast the hazelnuts in the oven for 20 minutes. Rub them with a clean dishtowel to remove their skins. Chop them, along with the butter, in a food processor. Set aside.
3. In a soup pot, bring the chicken broth to a boil. Add the cauliflower, carrots, celery, and onion. Simmer for 12 minutes.
4. Remove from heat and allow to cool slightly. Transfer the vegetables and a small amount of the liquid to a blender or food processor; purée. Add the purée to the soup pot. Stir in the milk, salt, and white pepper, reheating gently but thoroughly.
5. Ladle the soup into bowls, garnish with some of the hazelnut butter, and serve.

French Cheddar Soup

1 small onion
1 green bell pepper
2 stalks celery
2 carrots
3 cups shredded cheddar
  cheese
4 tablespoons butter
4 tablespoons flour
3 tablespoons sherry

4 cups Basic Chicken Broth
  (see recipe on page 3)
2 cups milk
Salt and pepper
Fresh parsley (optional)

> **Serves 6**
>
> If you're looking to spice things up, this recipe also works well with Colby or Monterey Jack cheese.
>
>

1. Finely chop the onion, green pepper, celery and carrots. Grate the cheese.
2. Heat the butter in a soup pot. Sauté the vegetables on medium for 10 minutes, stirring frequently. Remove the pot from the heat and allow to cool slightly.
3. Shake the flour over the mixture. Pour in the sherry and chicken broth. Bring the mixture to a boil, stirring constantly. Add the cheese and stir until it melts. Drizzle in the milk, stirring all the time. Turn the heat to very low, cover, and heat the soup thoroughly for about 10 minutes; do not let it boil.
4. Chop the parsley. Salt and pepper the soup to taste. Ladle the soup into bowls, garnish with the parsley, and serve.

Potato Cheddar Soup

¼ pound (4 ounces) unsliced, rindless bacon

1 large onion

1½ pounds potatoes (any type **except** red)

½ teaspoon fresh minced sage

¾ cup shredded sharp white cheddar cheese

1 teaspoon mustard (any basic kind)

3 cups Basic Chicken Broth (page 3) **or** Potato Vegetable Broth (page 5)

1½ cups cream

1 dash of hot sauce (such as Tabasco)

Salt and pepper

Scallions (optional)

1. Cut the bacon, onion, and potatoes into a medium dice. Mince the sage. Grate the cheddar.
2. Heat an empty soup pot; then add the bacon. As it releases fat, turn the heat up to medium and cook until crisp. Drain off all but 1 tablespoon of the fat. Add the butter, onion, and sage to the soup pot with the bacon and grease; Simmer for 3 minutes, stirring constantly. Stir in the mustard and cook for 1 more minute.
3. Pour in the broth and add the potatoes. Bring to a boil, reduce to medium, and cook for 13 minutes. Mash some of the potatoes against the side of the pot, stirring briefly to thicken the mixture. Take off the heat.
4. Gradually stir in the cream, and then the cheese; stir constantly until it melts. Add the hot sauce, salt, and pepper to taste. Thinly slice the scallions for garnish.

Two Cheese Soup

½ cup finely chopped onion

½ cup finely chopped celery

½ cup finely chopped carrot

1 teaspoon fresh minced garlic

½ pound (8 ounces) Stilton
cheese

½ pound (8 ounces) Monterey
Jack cheese

2 tablespoons butter

1 bay leaf

⅓ cup flour

2 teaspoons cornstarch

3 cups Basic Chicken Broth
(see recipe on page 3)

1 pinch of baking soda

1 cup whole milk

½ cup finely chopped broccoli
florets

1 dash of cayenne pepper

¼ teaspoon black pepper

¼ cup chopped parsley
(optional)

Serves 8

Stilton cheese is England's richest blue cheese. You'll find it in cheese shops and some supermarkets.

∾

1. Finely chop the onion, celery, and carrot. Mince the garlic. Crumble both kinds of cheese.
2. Melt the butter on medium heat in a soup pot. Add the onion, celery, carrot, garlic, and the bay leaf. Sauté for 3 to 5 minutes.
3. Whisk in the flour and cornstarch, and cook for 2 minutes, stirring constantly. Pour in the broth. Add the cheese, baking soda, and milk. Stir well over low heat until the mixture thickens.
4. Add the broccoli and two types of pepper. Bring just to a boil, reduce to a simmer, and cook for 8 to 10 minutes. Chop the parsley for garnish. Remove the bay leaf and serve.

Tuscany Bread and Cheese Soup

Serves 4–6

Buy the sourdough baguette a few days before making this soup. It works best if it is slightly stale.

1 large sourdough baguette
4 cloves garlic
3 tablespoons olive oil, divided
Salt
1 large Spanish onion
2 stalks celery
2 leeks
1 (28-ounce) can whole tomatoes, drained
2 teaspoons thyme
½ teaspoon black pepper

1 pinch of cayenne pepper
6 cups Roasted Vegetable Broth (see recipe on page 8)
2 tablespoons basil
½ cup parmesan cheese
½ cup flat-leaf parsley (optional)

1. Preheat the oven to 300 degrees. Cut the baguette into ½-inch-thick slices. Crush 1 clove of the garlic and rub the bread slices with it, then cut the bread into 1-inch cubes. In a bowl, toss the bread cubes with 1 tablespoon of the oil and a dash of salt. Place them, in a single layer, on a baking sheet; bake for 40 minutes. When they are done, take them out of the oven and set them aside.
2. Meanwhile, coarsely chop the remaining garlic, the onion, celery, and leek. Dice the tomatoes.
3. In a soup pot, heat the rest of the oil. Add the onion, celery, leeks, and garlic. Cook on low for 4 minutes. Stir in the thyme, black pepper, and cayenne pepper. Add the broth, tomatoes, and basil; bring to a boil, then reduce to a simmer and cook for 20 minutes.
4. Remove from heat and stir in the bread cubes. Let it sit, covered, for 5 minutes. Grate (or shave) the parmesan and chop the parsley for garnish.

Cheddar Cheese and Ale Soup

4 strips bacon
2 tablespoons butter
½ of a small yellow onion,
  diced
¼ cup white flour

4 cups Basic Chicken Broth
  (see recipe on page 3)
1 bottle ale
6 ounces cheddar cheese
White pepper

1. In a saucepan, fry the bacon. Remove with a slotted spoon and allow to drain on paper towels. Discard half of the oil.
2. Add the butter and the onion to the pan, sautéing over medium heat for 5 minutes. Sprinkle in the flour and, stirring constantly, cook for 3 more minutes.
3. Add the broth, ale, cheese, and pepper, reheating gently but thoroughly. Ladle into bowls and garnish with the crumbled bacon.

> **Serves 4**
>
> This soup is best made (and served!) with a light to amber ale.
>
> ~

Cream of Greens Soup

1 (10-ounce) package frozen
  spinach
1 green bell pepper
1 zucchini
2 tablespoons olive oil

4 cups Basic Chicken Broth
  (see recipe on page 3)
Pepper
½ cup whole milk
Salt

1. Defrost the spinach, then squeeze out all excess moisture. Finely dice the green pepper and zucchini.
2. In a soup pot, heat the olive oil on medium. Add the bell pepper and sauté for 3 minutes. Add the spinach, chicken broth, and pepper. Bring to a boil, reduce to a simmer, and cook for 5 minutes. Drizzle in the milk, stirring constantly. Salt to taste and serve.

> **Serves 4**
>
> You can substitute 1 pound of fresh spinach or kale for this soup. To do so, simmer in the chicken broth for 10 minutes before starting to step 2 (in a separate pot).
>
> ~

Creamy Turkey Soup

Serves 8

Two cups of cubed white meat chicken (cooked) works well in this recipe.

1 onion, chopped
2 cups cubed cooked turkey
1 bouquet garni (see "Bag o' Spices" on page 8)
3 tablespoons butter
3 tablespoons flour

½ cup sherry
*4 cups Giblet Broth **or** Basic Chicken Broth (see recipes on pages 9 and 3)*
1 cup milk
Salt and pepper

1. In a soup pot, melt the butter on medium heat. Sauté the onion for 3 minutes. Whisk in the flour and cook, stirring often, for 1 minute. Stir in the sherry and broth, and add the bouquet garni. Simmer the mixture for 30 minutes.
2. Take off heat. Remove and discard the herb bag. Allow the soup to cool slightly. Stir in the milk and the turkey, return to heat, and bring *almost* to a boil. Simmer for 1 minute. Salt and pepper to taste, and serve.

Rich Tomato Bisque

Serves 8

Garnish with your favorite croutons.

4 tablespoons butter
2 onions, chopped
2 cloves garlic, minced
1 (28-ounce) can whole tomatoes, liquid retained
1 (46-ounce) can tomato juice

2 bay leaves
1 (8-ounce) package cream cheese
2 cups half-and-half
Salt and pepper to taste

1. Melt the butter in a soup pot. Add the onions and garlic and sauté over medium heat until the onions are soft. Add the tomatoes and their liquid, the tomato juice, and bay leaves; simmer for 20 minutes, stirring constantly, chopping the tomatoes with the side of a spoon.
2. Remove from heat and let cool slightly. Discard the bay leaves. Purée the solids with some of the liquid in a blender or food processor, along with the cream cheese. Return to the soup pot. Add the half-and-half and salt and pepper to taste. May be served hot or cold.

Basque Squash and Chestnut Soup

2 medium-sized yellow onions
2 medium-sized butternut
   squashes
1 russet potato
7 cloves garlic
1 bouquet garni (see "Bag o'
   Spices" on page 8)
8 whole unshelled chestnuts
1 cup grated sheep's milk
   cheese (semisoft)
⅓ cup olive oil

8 cups Basic Chicken Broth
   (see recipe on page 3)
2 cups whole milk
1 teaspoon salt
White pepper

Serves 4–6

Let the cheese soften while preparing this soup. When the soup is finished, garnish with the softened, grated cheese and serve.

1. Cut the onions into thick slices. Peel and seed the squashes; then cut them into 1-inch chunks. Coarsely chop the potato and crush the garlic cloves. Prepare the bouquet garni using a variety of your choice of fresh herbs. Roast and shell the chestnuts, then slice them very thinly. Grate the sheep's milk cheese.
2. In a soup pot, heat the olive oil. Add the onions and sauté on medium heat for 2 minutes. Add the garlic, squash, and potatoes; sauté for 3 minutes.
3. Pour in the broth and milk and add the bouquet garni, salt, and white pepper. Bring to a boil, then reduce to a simmer and cook for 1 hour. Remove the herb bag.
4. Remove from heat and allow to cool slightly. Using a blender or food processor, purée the soup. Return it to the soup pot and bring to a boil, then add the chestnuts and heat thoroughly.

Blue Cheese Soup

Serves 8

For an elegant flair, add ⅓ cup of dry white wine.

❧

2 tablespoons butter
½ cup finely chopped onion
½ cup finely chopped celery
½ cup finely chopped carrot
1 teaspoon minced garlic
⅓ cup flour
2 teaspoons cornstarch
3 cups Basic Chicken Broth
  (see recipe on page 3)
½ pound Stilton cheese,
  crumbled
½ pound cheddar cheese,
  crumbled

⅛ teaspoon baking soda
1 cup cream (heavy **or** light)
⅓ cup dry white wine
  (optional)
Salt
1 dash of cayenne pepper
¼ teaspoon freshly ground
  black pepper
1 bay leaf
¼ cup chopped fresh parsley
  (optional)

1. Melt the butter in a soup pot on medium heat, and add the onion, celery, carrot, and garlic. Cook until the vegetables are tender, about 8 minutes.
2. Whisk in the flour and cornstarch, stirring constantly; cook until it begins to bubble, about 2 minutes. Add the broth, the two cheeses, baking soda, cream, and wine (if using). Stir until smooth and thickened. Add the salt, cayenne, black pepper, and bay leaf. Bring to a slow boil and let simmer for 8 to 10 minutes.
3. Remove the bay leaf. Add milk or wine to thin if necessary. Garnish with the parsley and serve.

CHAPTER 7
Vegetable Soups

Oven-Roasted Butternut Squash Bisque

Serves 4

Toss the roasted squash seeds on top to garnish the soup. These seeds are edible.

3 pounds butternut squash
3 teaspoons sesame **or** olive oil
Black pepper
1 teaspoon cumin (curry
    powder can be substituted)
1 tablespoon orange zest
    (fresh is best)

4½ cups Basic Chicken **or**
    Vegetable Broth (see recipes
    on pages 3 and 4)
2 cloves garlic, sliced
½ teaspoon sugar
½ cup whole milk

1. Preheat the oven to 400 degrees. Cut the squash in half and scoop out the seeds and slimy threads. Rinse the seeds clean and dry them with a towel. Brush the exposed flesh of the squash halves with some of the oil and a bit of pepper. Put them on a foiled-lined baking sheet, cut side down; roast for 45 to 60 minutes, until tender.

2. While the squash roasts, coat the seeds with the rest of the oil and half of the cumin. Arrange the seeds on another foil-lined baking sheet in a single layer. Cover loosely with another piece of foil. Roast the seeds for about 10 minutes, turning them once.

3. Remove the squash from the oven and scoop the flesh into a soup pot. Add the chicken stock, orange zest, garlic, and the rest of the cumin. Bring to a boil, then reduce to a simmer and cook for 20 to 30 minutes.

4. Using a blender or food processor, blend the mixture. Return it to the pot and add the sugar and milk. Heat it thoroughly. Toss the squash seeds on top and serve.

Homemade Croutons

The weirder the bread, the better the crouton. Guests will "ooh" and "aah" when you announce that your squash bisque boasts a garnish of Irish soda bread croutons. Cornbread makes spectacular croutons, as do rye bread and pumpernickel. Toss with a few drops of oil, spread on a baking sheet, and bake at 325 degrees for 15 minutes, until crisp.

Cabbage and Tomato Soup

2 large onions
3 stalks celery
1 clove garlic
2 leeks (light green and white
   parts)
3 carrots
2 cups cubed new potatoes
1 cup shredded green cabbage
3 tablespoons olive oil
1 teaspoon rosemary

1 teaspoon parsley
1 teaspoon thyme
6 cups Basic Vegetable Broth
   (see recipe on page 4)
8 medium-sized whole tomatoes
   or 1 (16-ounce) can

Serves 6–8

Leeks tend to trap a
lot of sand and grit in
between their layers.
It's important to wash
leeks thoroughly
before using them.

1. Chop the onions and celery, and thickly slice the garlic and leeks. Slice the carrots and cube the potatoes (skin on). Shred the cabbage.
2. In a soup pot, heat the oil on medium and sauté the onions, celery, garlic, and leeks for 5 minutes. Add the carrots and potatoes, along with the herbs, to the pot. Pour in the vegetable broth. Bring to a boil, then reduce to a simmer, cover, and simmer for 1 hour.
3. Add the tomatoes, whole, to the top of the broth, if they are fresh. Cover and heat until you can slip off the skins. If using canned tomatoes, just stir them in with liquid included. Crush the tomatoes with the back of a large spoon. Rewarm the soup briefly.

Corn Chowder

Serves 4

For an extra thick and creamy chowder, substitute 2 cups of half-and-half for the milk.

5 medium ears of corn
½ cup chopped celery
½ cup chopped carrot
½ cup chopped onion
2 tablespoon butter
4 cups Basic Chicken Broth
    (see recipe on page 3)
½ cup dry white wine
½ teaspoon roasted garlic paste
½ cup polenta (from a prepared
    roll or leftover homemade)

2 cups milk **or** half-and-half
2 tablespoons fresh chopped
    thyme
¼ cup sherry
Salt and pepper
Red pepper flakes (optional)

1. In a 350-degree oven, roast the corn in their husks for about 45 minutes. Cool. Remove the husks and cut the kernels off the cobs.
2. Coarsely chop the celery, carrots, and onion. Sauté them on medium heat in the butter until tender. Add the broth, wine, roasted garlic, and the fresh corn kernels. Bring to a boil and simmer for 30 minutes.
3. Add the polenta and simmer for another 20 minutes. Purée the mixture in a blender or food processor; return it to the soup pot.
4. Add the milk, thyme, and sherry. Salt and pepper to taste. Reheat gently, and serve, garnished with a few red pepper flakes.

Using Vinegar Instead of Wine

If you don't have wine handy for your recipe, substitute one to two tablespoons of wine vinegar or cider vinegar mixed with one cup of water.

Mulligatawny Soup

2 tablespoons oil **or** butter
1 clove garlic, coarsely
   chopped
1 tablespoon curry powder
2 tablespoons white flour
4 cups Basic Chicken Broth
   (see recipe on page 3) **or**
   any vegetable broth

1 stalk celery, shredded
1 carrot, shredded
1 apple, peeled and finely diced
2 tablespoons uncooked white
   rice **or** potato starch
1–2 cups milk
1 tablespoon lemon juice

Serves 6

Stir the soup before adding the lemon juice at the end. Otherwise, it can curdle.

Heat the oil in soup pot and sauté the garlic on medium for 2 to 3 minutes. Whisk in the curry and flour, stirring for 1 minute. Add the broth, mixing everything together. Add the celery, carrot, apple, rice (or potato starch), milk, and lemon juice. Simmer for 15 minutes and serve.

Cabbage Soup

1 small head green cabbage
1 onion
1 leek
1 carrot
1 tomato
2 tablespoons butter

5 cups Basic Beef Broth
   (see recipe on page 2)
½ cup sauerkraut
Salt and black pepper
Sour cream (optional)
Fresh chopped dill (optional)

Serves 4–6

Garnish with sour cream and dill, if desired.

1. Coarsely shred the cabbage. Chop the onion, thinly slice the leek (white part only) and carrot, and cut the tomato into chunks.
2. Using a soup pot, heat the butter. Add the onion, leek, and carrot; sauté on medium for 5 minutes. Add the beef broth and bring to a boil. Reduce to a simmer, add the cabbage, sauerkraut, and tomato chunks, and simmer for 45 minutes. Salt and pepper to taste.

Mushroom Soup

Serves 4–5

Want a fast and easy way to slice mushrooms? Use an egg-slicer; it gets the job done in a snap.

¾ pound fresh mushrooms
    (any kind, or a mix of types)
3 cups Potato and Vegetable
    Broth (see recipe on page 5)
3 tablespoon flour
3 tablespoon butter **or** oil

1 cup whole milk
Salt and black pepper
2 tablespoons sherry

1. Using caps and stems, slice all but 4 or 5 of the mushrooms; set the uncut mushrooms aside.
2. Pour the broth into a soup pot and add the sliced mushrooms. Simmer on medium heat for *about* 30 minutes, making sure the mushrooms do not overcook and begin to disintegrate.
3. Using a slotted spoon, remove the mushrooms and set them aside, covered. Allow the broth to cool.
4. In a small pan, make a roux by melting the butter over medium heat and whisking in the flour until the mixture is smooth and begins to bubble. Add the roux to the broth in the soup pot, whisking constantly as the broth rewarms. Cook gently for 10 minutes, whisking often.
5. Whisk the milk, salt, and black pepper into the soup pot, making sure that it does not boil. Stir in the sherry.
6. Slice the remaining raw mushrooms. Place the cooked mushrooms in serving bowls and pour the broth over them. Garnish with the raw mushroom slices.

Mill Your Own Pepper

If possible, use freshly ground black peppercorns when pepper is called for in a recipe. These retain their flavor better than pre-ground pepper and you'll need less of it to get the same flavor. (As a general rule, use about half to start, then taste—you can always add more later!)

Tomato Soup with Cream and Cognac

16 medium tomatoes
1 large onion
⅓ cup walnut oil **or** butter
2 cups Basic Vegetable Broth
    (see recipe on page 4)
Crushed basil **or** oregano leaves
1 pint heavy **or** medium cream

1 teaspoon brown sugar
4–5 tablespoons cognac
Salt and pepper

Serves 6

For a different flavor, you can substitute 4–5 tablespoons of brandy for the cognac.

---

1. Peel the tomatoes by bringing a large pan of water to a rolling boil. Drop the tomatoes in the water for about 15 seconds (the tomato peels should just begin to split open), then drain. Rinse the tomatoes with cold water; peel the tomatoes and discard the skins. Cut the tomatoes into chunks and crush them in a bowl with the back of a large spoon. Finely chop the onion.
2. In a large soup pot, heat the oil on medium; add the onions and sauté them for about 1 minute. Add the tomatoes, 1 cup of broth, and a few crushed basil (or oregano) leaves. Simmer for 30 minutes.
3. Force the mixture through a sieve, removing only the seeds and any tough onion pieces. Put the sieved mixture back on low heat.
4. In a saucepan, warm the cream and the brown sugar until it is almost to the boiling point (do not let it boil); using a whisk, quickly pour it into the soup pot with the tomato mixture. Add the cognac, and salt and pepper to taste. Keeps for up to 1 week in the fridge.

Pumpkin and Apple Soup

Serves 6

If you like apple peels, leave them on while dicing. They will add a delicious flavor.

1 pound cooked pumpkin
1 large yellow onion
2 stalks celery
2 medium-sized tart apples
*1 ½ tablespoons butter **or** oil*
4 cups Basic Vegetable Broth
  (see recipe on page 4)
1 teaspoon ginger
1 teaspoon curry powder

½ teaspoon nutmeg
½ teaspoon cinnamon
2 cups milk
Chopped nuts (any kind,
  toasted or raw), optional

1. If using fresh pumpkin, preheat the oven to 350 degrees. Cut the pumpkin in half and remove seeds and slimy threads. Place each half cut-side down on foil-lined baking sheet; bake for 45 minutes.
2. Finely dice the onion. Dice the celery and apples.
3. In a soup pot, melt the butter. Sauté the onion on medium heat for about 2 minutes, until tender but not brown. Add all the vegetables, fruit, broth, and spices, including the flesh from the pumpkin (do not add the milk or nuts yet). Bring to a boil, then reduce to a simmer, and cook for 35 to 40 minutes.
4. Add the milk. Garnish with nuts, if desired.

Sunchoke Soup

8 cups Basic Chicken Broth (see recipe on page 3)
1 pound sunchokes
1½ pounds potatoes (russets are fine)
3 leeks (white and light green parts)
2 cloves garlic
¼ teaspoon thyme

¼ teaspoon diced (**or** ground) ginger
½ teaspoon marjoram
¼ cup half-and-half
Fresh chopped chives **or** green onion (optional)

Serves 6

A sunchoke, also known as a Jerusalem artichoke, is neither related to the artichoke nor is it from Jerusalem.

1. In a soup pot, boil the broth. While it's coming to a boil, peel the sunchokes, potatoes, and leeks, and cut them into ½-inch-thick pieces. Peel and coarsely chop the garlic and ginger.
2. Put all the vegetables in the pot with the broth, along with the thyme. Bring back to a boil, then reduce to a simmer and cook for about 25 minutes. Add the marjoram and cool the mixture for 10 to 20 minutes.
3. Using a blender or food processor, purée the mixture; add the half-and-half. Return it to the stove and reheat on low heat. Thin the soup with a bit more broth or water, if desired. Garnish with chives or green onion.

Yellow Bell Pepper Soup

Serves 4

This soup looks great garnished with bread cubes, grated parmesan cheese, and chopped parsley.

3 tablespoons olive oil (**or** any nut oil), divided

2 medium onions, diced

1 medium carrot, peeled and diced

1 stalk celery, diced

4 yellow bell peppers, seeded and cut into chunks

2 large russet potatoes, peeled and cubed

1 bay leaf

2 sprigs thyme

3 cups water

1 small loaf Italian bread, cut into ½-inch cubes

Salt and pepper

4 teaspoons grated parmesan cheese

1 teaspoon chopped flat-leafed parsley

1. In a soup pot, heat 2 tablespoons of the oil on medium. Add the onion, carrot, and celery and sauté for 10 minutes.
2. Add the peppers, potatoes, bay leaf, thyme, and water to the pot. Bring to a boil, then reduce to a simmer and cook for 25 minutes.
3. Meanwhile, heat the remaining oil in a skillet and sauté the bread cubes for a few minutes, until they are lightly browned.
4. When the soup is done cooking, take it off the heat and let it cool slightly. Remove and discard the bay leaf and thyme sprigs. Using a blender or food processor, purée the soup. Season with salt and pepper to taste. Garnish with the bread cubes, parmesan, and parsley.

Acorn Squash Soup with Cider

3 acorn squash
2 tablespoons butter
1½ cups diced onion
3 cups hard cider **or**
   nonalcoholic cider
4 cups Basic Chicken Broth
   (see recipe on page 3)
1 teaspoon ground cardamom
½ teaspoon cinnamon

1 dash of nutmeg
Salt and pepper to taste
1 tablespoon orange juice
Popcorn, popped (optional)

Serves 8

For a nice flavor variation, use ¼ cup of fruit brandy in place of ¼ cup of the cider.

1. Preheat the oven to 400 degrees. Cut the squash in half and scoop out the seeds and slimy threads. Place the squash halves cut-side down on foil-lined baking sheets; bake for about 35 to 45 minutes, until tender.

2. In a soup pot, melt the butter on medium heat and sauté the onions until soft. Scoop out the cooked squash flesh and add it to the pot along with the cider and chicken broth. Bring to a boil, reduce to a simmer, and cook for about 20 minutes.

3. Remove from heat and let cool slightly. Using a blender or food processor, purée the mixture. Return it to the pot, adding the spices and orange juice. Garnish with popcorn, if desired, and serve.

Big Fresh Tomato Soup

8–10 vine-ripened tomatoes, quartered

1 cup Basic Vegetable Broth (see recipe on page 4)

1 small onion, chopped

2 cloves garlic, chopped

*3 tablespoons olive oil **or** butter, divided*

2 tablespoons flour

*4 cups whole milk **or** half-and-half*

Salt and pepper

1 lemon

*Diced green onions **or** fresh chopped chives (optional)*

1. Put the tomatoes into a soup pot and crush them a bit with a wooden spoon. Add the broth and heat on medium.
2. In another pan, 1 tablespoon of the oil and sauté the onion for 2 minutes on medium heat. Add the garlic and sauté for 2 more minutes. Add this mixture to the soup pot; bring to a boil, reduce to a simmer, and cook until the volume is reduced by about a third.
3. In a medium-sized saucepan, heat the remaining oil on medium and whisk in the flour a bit at a time; cook, whisking constantly, until the mixture is smooth and light brown in color. Reduce the heat to low and gradually add the milk (or half-and-half) to the saucepan. Cook it until it thickens a little; do not let it boil. Add the dairy mixture to the soup pot and stir thoroughly; simmer for about 10 minutes.
4. Strain the soup through a sieve to remove the seeds. Allow it to cool slightly; then purée it in a food processor or blender.
5. Reheat on low. Season with salt and pepper to taste and a few squirts of lemon juice. Garnish with green onions or chives.

Escarole Soup

1 head escarole
1 large onion
1½ cups diced celery
3–4 cloves garlic
8 cups Basic Vegetable **or** Basic
   Chicken Broth (see recipes
   on pages 4 and 3)
2 bay leaves
2 tablespoons olive oil

1 teaspoon oregano
Salt and freshly ground black
   pepper
Parmesan cheese, grated
   (optional)

Serves 4

Grate the parmesan
and add it as garnish
along with an extra
sprinkling of freshly
ground black pepper.

1. Tear the escarole into small pieces. Dice the onion and celery. Mince the garlic.
2. In a soup pot, begin warming the broth, along with the bay leaves. In a large saucepan, heat the oil. Add the onion, garlic, celery, and oregano. Sauté for about 4 minutes on low heat. Add the escarole, stirring constantly, until it wilts. Transfer this mixture to the soup pot. Simmer gently for about 30 minutes. Remove the bay leaves.
3. Season with salt and pepper to taste.

Roasted Bell Pepper Soup

Serves 6

Bell peppers have different flavors depending on their color. Green is the most acidic and sour tasting. Red has the most peppery flavor. Yellow and orange have a gentle flavor.

6 large red bell peppers
1 large green bell pepper
1 large yellow bell pepper
3 large red onions
2 cloves garlic
⅓ cup fresh chopped green herbs (almost any combination)
3 tablespoons olive oil
4 cups water

¼ cup red wine **or** red wine vinegar
1 teaspoon chili powder
2 tablespoons lemon **or** lime juice
Salt and pepper

1. Grill or broil the peppers, whole, turning them with oven tongs until they are charred and blistered. Put them into paper or plastic bags to cool; seal the bags tightly.

2. Meanwhile, chop the red onions and mince the garlic and herbs. In a soup pot, heat the oil. Sauté the onions on medium for about 3 minutes. Add the garlic and sauté for another minute. Set aside to cool slightly.

3. Remove the skins, seeds, and stems from the peppers. Chop the red peppers. Slice the yellow and green peppers into narrow strips about 1 inch long. Using a blender or food processor, purée the onion and garlic mixture with 1 cup of the water and the *red* bell peppers.

4. Return the mixture to the soup pot and add the remaining 3 cups of water. Add the wine and chili powder. Bring to a boil, then reduce to a simmer and cook for 15 minutes.

5. Remove the mixture from the heat and stir in the lemon juice and herbs, and salt and pepper to taste. Just before serving, add the yellow and green pepper strips and heat thoroughly.

Spinach and Dill Soup

2 (10-ounce) packages frozen
   spinach (**or** 2 pounds fresh
   spinach)
1 pound russet potatoes
2 cups chopped onion
1 ½ teaspoon minced garlic
½ cup fresh minced dill
¼ cup fresh minced basil leaves

2 teaspoons salt **and/or** mustard
6 cups water
Plain yogurt **or** sour cream
   (optional)

Serves 6–8

Garnish with a dollop
of yogurt or sour
cream, if you like.

∽

1. Defrost the spinach (or, if using fresh, chop it). Cube the potatoes
   (peel on or off). Chop the onion. Mince the garlic, dill, and basil.
2. In a soup pot, combine the potatoes, onion, garlic, salt and/or mustard, and the water. Bring to a boil, reduce to a simmer, and cook for
   20 minutes.
3. Remove from heat and allow to cool slightly. Using a blender or food
   processor, purée the potato mixture along with the spinach, dill, and
   basil. Return to the pot and heat slowly and thoroughly.

Squash and Chili Pepper Soup

*1 squash (any fall-winter
  variety such as butternut)*
2 yellow onions
*1 chili pepper (any mild to
  medium-hot type, such as
  poblanos or serranos)*
*1 tablespoon cumin seeds
  (**or** ground cumin)*
2 tablespoons butter

*4 cups Basic Chicken Broth
  (see recipe on page 3)*
*1 cup cream, half-and-half,
  or milk*
*½ cup sliced almonds **or**
  pine nuts (optional)*

1. Preheat oven to 375 degrees. Cut the squash in half and remove the seeds and slimy threads. Place the two halves cut-side down in a baking pan and add ½ inch of water to the pan; bake for 35 to 50 minutes (depending upon the thickness of the squash), until tender.
2. Meanwhile, chop the onions. Seed and mince the chili. If using cumin seeds, heat a heavy frying pan (preferably cast iron) on medium. Add the cumin seeds to the pan and toast them, stirring periodically, until they darken and emit a roasted aroma. Remove the seeds from the pan and set aside. Using the same pan, add enough oil to just coat the bottom of the pan, and toast the nuts (if using).
3. When the squash is done, allow it to cool slightly; save the water from the pan. Peel the squash and cut the flesh into chunks. In a soup pot, warm the butter. Sauté the onions and chilies on medium for about 3 minutes. Add the squash, broth, and the water from the squash pan. Bring to a boil, then reduce to a simmer. Add the cumin seeds (or ground cumin) and simmer for 40 minutes.
4. Remove from heat and allow to cool slightly. Purée the soup in a blender or food processor and return it to the soup pot. Stir in the dairy product and reheat; do not allow the soup to boil once the dairy has been added. Garnish with nuts and serve.

Belgian Watercress Soup

*4 medium potatoes (Yukon
   gold **or** red)*
2 medium-sized yellow onions
2 bunches watercress
*3 tablespoons butter **or** oil*
1 cup milk

¾ cup plain yogurt
Croutons (optional)

Serves 6

If you're looking to
cut calories, use skim
milk in this soup.

ॲ

1. Place the potatoes, unpeeled, in a large saucepan with enough water
   to cover. Bring to a boil and cook for 20 to 30 minutes, depending
   upon their size. Reserve 2 cups of the water. Allow the potatoes to
   cool slightly.
2. Meanwhile, chop the onions. Cut off and discard the watercress
   stems and roughly tear the leaves. Dice the potatoes.
3. In a soup pot, melt the butter and sauté the onions on warm for
   2 minutes. Add the potatoes, the reserved potato water, and the
   watercress; simmer for 4 minutes.
4. Add the milk and yogurt. Heat thoroughly, but do not boil. Garnish
   with croutons, if you like, and serve.

Spinach and Cider Soup

Serves 6

Not a big fan of plain yogurt? Try substituting 1 cup of sour cream instead.

2 carrots
1 stalk celery
½ pound fresh spinach
1 clove garlic
1 tablespoon fresh chopped
   parsley
4 cups Basic Vegetable Broth
   (see recipe on page 4)
3 tablespoons olive **or** nut oil

2 tablespoons flour
1 teaspoon dill
½ cup apple cider
4 egg yolks
1 cup plain yogurt

1. Dice the carrots and celery. Remove the thickest stems from the spinach. Mince the garlic and chop the parsley.
2. In a soup pot, bring the broth to a boil. Add the carrots and celery, reduce to a simmer, and cook for 15 minutes. Remove from heat, cover, and set aside.
3. In a small saucepan, warm the oil. Sauté the onion on medium for 2 minutes. Add the garlic and cook for 1 minute more. Shake the flour over the mixture and whisk for about 2 minutes. Continuing to whisk constantly, add about ½ cup broth to the saucepan and cook for about 2 minutes.
4. Pour the onion mixture into the soup pot, stirring well. Add the spinach, parsley, dill, and cider to the pot. Bring to a boil, reduce to a simmer, and cook for 5 minutes.
5. Meanwhile, in a small bowl, beat together the egg yolks and yogurt until smooth. Pour this mixture into the soup pot, whisking it constantly. Heat thoroughly on low, making sure not to let the soup boil.

Multi-Mushroom Soup with Curry

1 ounce dried porcini and
    morel mushrooms (a combi-
    nation)
1½ cups chopped leeks (white
    part only)
2 cups fresh chopped
    Portobello mushrooms
1 tablespoon fresh chopped
    chervil (optional)
2 tablespoons oil **or** butter

2 tablespoons flour
1 tablespoons curry powder
4 cups milk
1 cube chicken bouillon
1 tablespoon sherry (optional)

Serves 4

Soak the dried mush-
rooms for a few hours
or overnight in room
temperature water.
Once soaked, they
are ready to use just
as you would fresh
mushrooms.

1. Boil about 2 cups of water, remove from heat, and soak the dried mushrooms in it for 15 to 30 minutes.
2. Meanwhile, chop the leeks, Portobellos, and fresh chervil. In a soup pot, heat the oil on medium. Sauté the leeks, stirring constantly, for 3 minutes; shake the flour and curry on them, and stir until everything is coated. Add the milk and the bouillon cube. Bring *almost* to a boil, reduce heat to low heat, and whisk the mixture. Add the fresh mushrooms and cook for 5 minutes.
3. Drain the soaked dried mushrooms and squeeze out any excess moisture. (Freeze the cooking liquid for later use, if you like.) Chop them roughly and add them to the soup, cooking for 1 more minute. Stir in the sherry, if using. Ladle into soup bowls and top with the chopped chervil.

Pumpkin Soup

Serves 6–8

For a tasty snack, place your washed pumpkin seeds on a baking sheet and sprinkle with some seasoned salt. Bake them for 10–15 minutes.

1 small pumpkin (2½–3 pounds)
1 onion (yellow **or** red)
2 tablespoons olive oil **or** butter
½ teaspoon cinnamon
½ teaspoon ground cumin
¼ teaspoon curry powder
5 cups Basic Vegetable **or** Basic Chicken Broth (see recipes on pages 4 and 3)

¼ cup orange juice (**or** a combination of fresh orange zest and freshly squeezed orange juice)
2 teaspoons grated fresh ginger (optional)

1. Cut the pumpkin in half and scrape out the seeds and slimy threads. (Wash and save the seeds for later use, if you like.) Cut the pumpkin into chunks (this makes it easier to peel) and remove the peel. Cut the flesh into small chunks. Chop the onion.
2. In a soup pot, warm the oil. Add the onion and sauté on medium for 3 minutes. Add the pumpkin, along with the spices; cook briefly, stirring, until well mixed. Pour in the broth and the orange juice. Bring to a boil, reduce to simmer, and cook for 30 to 40 minutes.
3. Remove from heat and let cool slightly. Using a blender or food processor, purée the mixture. Return it to soup pot to rewarm, adding a bit more orange juice or a little milk to achieve the desired thickness. Garnish with the fresh ginger, if using.

Storing Fresh Ginger

Peel and store fresh ginger in a freezer bag so that you always have some on hand. Slice the ginger into disks about the thickness of a quarter. You'll still be able to grate it if necessary, and it is the perfect size to drop in a cup of boiling water to steep for ginger tea.

Asparagus Soup

1 pound fresh asparagus
1 onion
5 cups Basic Chicken Broth
(see recipe on page 3)
¼ cup butter
¼ cup flour

White pepper
1 egg yolk
½ cup cream

Serves 6

Freeze the tough ends from the asparagus to use for making broth another day.

❧

---

1. Trim the tough ends from the asparagus and discard. Cut off the tips (do not discard) and slice the stalks. Chop the onion.
2. Put the asparagus tips in a saucepan with enough water to cover them. Bring to a boil, reduce to a simmer, and cook for 5 minutes. Drain and set the asparagus tips aside.
3. Pour 2 cups of the broth into a pot and add the asparagus stalks; bring to a boil, reduce to a simmer, and cook for 10 to 12 minutes. Remove from heat and allow to cool slightly. Force the stalks through a sieve, or purée them in a blender or food processor.
4. In a large soup pot, melt the butter. Sauté the onion on medium for 3 minutes. Whisk in the flour and cook for 1 more minute, stirring constantly. Drizzle in the rest of the broth, continuing to whisk until it thickens. Add the asparagus purée and white pepper. Reheat.
5. In a bowl, whisk together the egg yolk and the cream. Ladle some of the hot soup into this bowl, stirring well to incorporate. Add this mixture to the soup pot with the asparagus in it. Stir on low heat until it thickens. Add the asparagus tips, reheating thoroughly, but not allowing the soup to boil.

Green Peas for Color

The oldest trick in the book: Since asparagus, broad beans, and some other green veggies fade when cooked in a soup, chefs sometimes add a cup of frozen peas to the hot soup just before puréeing it. It revives the soup's color and adds a touch of sweetness.

Parsnip Soup with Pine Nuts

1 onion
1 pound parsnips
2 tablespoons butter
6 cups Basic Chicken **or**
  Vegetable Broth (see recipes
  on pages 3 and 4)

¼–½ teaspoon cayenne pepper
½ cup cream
3 tablespoons pine nuts

1. Chop the onion and slice the parsnips. Melt the butter on medium heat in a soup pot. Add the onion and parsnips; cook for 10 minutes, stirring often.
2. Pour in the broth and add the cayenne. Bring to a boil, reduce to a simmer, and cook for 20 minutes.
3. Meanwhile, toast the pine nuts in a single layer under the broiler for 1 to 2 minutes.
4. When it is done cooking, remove the soup from the heat and allow it to cool slightly. Using a blender or food processor, purée the mixture. Reheat without boiling. Stir in the cream. (Be sure not to allow the soup to boil once the cream has been added.) Garnish with nuts and serve.

Differences in Onions

Onions vary in sweetness. Vidalia tend to be the sweetest, followed by red, then yellow. White onions are the least sweet and are better in meat dishes than in soups.

Tomato Soup
with Curry and Red Pepper

3 pounds tomatoes
1 large onion
2 cloves garlic
1 dried hot red pepper
¼ cup butter
3 tablespoons curry powder

3½ cups Basic Chicken Broth
* (see recipe on page 3)*
1 bay leaf
½ cup sour cream

Serves 10

If you're looking for a cool, refreshing soup on a hot day, this soup can also be served chilled.

1. Chop the tomatoes into 2-inch chunks, removing the seeds. Dice the onions. Finely mince the garlic and red pepper.
2. In a soup pot, melt the butter. Sauté the onion and garlic on medium for 3 minutes, stirring constantly. Stir in the curry powder and cook for 5 more minutes.
3. Add the tomatoes, chicken broth, bay leaf, and red pepper. Bring to a boil, reduce to a simmer, and cook for 25 minutes.
4. Remove from heat and allow to cool slightly. Using a slotted spoon, remove and discard the bay leaf and the pepper pieces. In a blender or food processor, purée the mixture. Stir in the sour cream gradually. Heat gently but thoroughly; do not allow it to boil.

Which Tomatoes to Use

All tomatoes are not alike. Substitute plum tomatoes for a more robust flavor. Choose golden tomatoes for a more mellow taste. Reserve expensive varieties, such as hot-house, for recipes in which tomatoes are the main ingredient.

Mixed Vegetables and Herb Soup

2 tablespoons butter
3 cups mixed diced vegetables
1 tablespoons flour
5 cups Basic Beef Broth
    (see recipe on page 2)
2 cloves garlic, crushed
1 bay leaf
½ cup cream
White pepper

¼ cup grated cheese
    (such as pecorino Romano
    or Parmigiano Reggiano)
Salt
Nutmeg
3 tablespoons mixed chopped
    herbs (any combination)

1. In a soup pot, melt the butter on medium heat. Sauté the vegetables for 4 to 5 minutes. Whisk in the flour. Add the broth, stirring often as you bring it to a boil. Add the garlic and bay leaf. Reduce to a simmer and cook for 25 minutes.
2. When the mixture has cooked, discard the bay leaf and allow the soup to cool slightly. Drizzle in the cream and reheat the pot *almost* to a boil. Remove from heat and, again, allow to cool slightly.
3. Using a blender or food processor, purée the mixture along with the cheese. Return the mixture to the soup pot and reheat, but not boil. Add the pepper, salt, and nutmeg to taste. Garnish with the mixed herbs.

Texas Squash Blossom and Chili Soup

1 poblano chili
1 yellow summer squash
5 yellow cherry tomatoes
½ of a small onion
2 jalapeño **or** serrano chilies
2 cloves garlic
2 tablespoons olive oil
18 squash blossoms
6 cups Basic Chicken Broth
    (see recipe on page 3)

9 epazote leaves
1 teaspoon oregano
1 teaspoon basil
Salt and pepper
1 lime

Serves 6–8

If you can't find epazote leaves in your local store, look for Mexican tea. It's the same thing.

1. Place the whole poblano pepper on a baking sheet and broil it, turning it frequently, until the skin has blistered and darkened. Transfer the pepper to a plastic or paper bag and seal it tightly, setting it aside to steam (this makes it easier to peel).
2. Meanwhile, dice the squash and tomatoes. Finely chop the onion. Seed and dice the jalapeños (or serranos). Mince the garlic. Peel, seed, and dice the roasted poblano pepper.
3. In a soup pot, heat the oil. Add the squash, onion, garlic, and jalapeños; sauté for 4 minutes. Add the tomatoes, roasted poblano, and squash blossoms, and sauté for 1 minute.
4. Pour in the chicken broth and bring to a boil. Reduce to a simmer and add the epazote, oregano, and basil, and salt and pepper to taste. Garnish each serving with a thin curl of lime zest.

Tomato Bread Soup

Serves 2

Garnish each serving with a sprinkle of parmesan cheese.

1 tablespoon olive oil
1 leek, chopped (white part only)
4 cloves garlic, minced
2 cups peeled and chopped tomatoes
⅓ cup chopped fresh basil
½ teaspoon salt
1½ cups Basic Vegetable **or** Basic Chicken Broth, divided (see recipes on pages 4 and 3)

½ teaspoon pepper
2 cups cubed day-old Italian bread
2 tablespoons grated parmesan cheese (optional)

1. In a heavy saucepan, heat the oil on medium. Sauté the leeks and garlic, stirring occasionally, for about 3 minutes until softened. Stir in the tomatoes and basil. Bring to a boil. Boil gently for 5 to 10 minutes, or until slightly thickened.
2. Add 1 cup of the broth, the salt, and pepper. Bring to a boil, stirring. Remove from the heat. Stir in the bread. If necessary, add the remaining broth to reach the desired consistency.

Beef Broth and Tomatoes Soup

1 pound yellow onions

3 shallots

6 cloves garlic

1 (14-ounce) can whole plum
   tomatoes

½ teaspoon sugar

Salt to taste

½ teaspoon black pepper

6 cups Basic Beef Broth
   (see recipe on page 2)

6 slices French bread
   (optional)

1 cup grated Gruyère cheese
   (optional)

Serves 6

This recipe, similar to French onion soup, is also good served with swiss cheese.

1. Thinly slice the onions, shallots, and garlic. Drain the tomatoes and slightly mash them.
2. In a soup pot, warm the olive oil. Add the onions, shallots, and garlic; sauté for 3 to 5 minutes, stirring often. Add the sugar and seasonings, stirring almost constantly until the onions are dark brown (caramelized).
3. Stir in the tomatoes and beef broth. Bring to a boil, reduce to a simmer, and cook for 30 minutes.
4. Toast the bread and grate the cheese. Place a bread slice and some cheese in each serving bowl, then ladle soup on top.

Curried Zucchini Soup

Serves 8

Five cups of chopped zucchini equals about 6 "baby" zucchinis, 2–3 medium sized ones, or 1 "jumbo" backyard garden variety.

1 tablespoon olive oil
5 cups chopped zucchini
2 onions, chopped
1 stalk celery, diced
1 clove garlic, minced
2 teaspoons curry powder
¾ teaspoon salt
½ teaspoon cinnamon
¼ teaspoon pepper
1 teaspoon packed brown sugar

6 cups Basic **or** Roasted Vegetable Broth (see recipes on pages 4 and 8)

1. In a soup pot, heat the oil over medium heat; sauté the zucchini, onions, celery, garlic, curry powder, salt, cinnamon, and pepper, stirring occasionally, for about 10 minutes until softened.
2. Sprinkle with the brown sugar and pour in the broth. Bring to a boil, then reduce to a simmer; cook, covered, for 20 minutes, or until the vegetables are very tender.
3. In blender or food processor, puree the soup, in batches, until smooth. Pour into a clean soup pot. Reheat, but do not boil. Season with more salt and pepper to taste.

Bean and Legume Soups

Peas in the Pod Soup

1 pound fresh peas pods
2 tablespoons chopped onion
3 tablespoons chopped parsley
8 cups Basic Vegetable Broth
  (see recipe on page 4)
4 tablespoons butter

4 tablespoons flour
Salt and pepper
Diced cooked bacon (optional)

1. Cut off the small stem ends of the pea pods and pull off the thin strings along their back. Shell the peas, reserving both peas and pods. Chop the onion and parsley.
2. Bring the broth to a boil in a soup pot. Add the peas and the pods, reduce heat, and simmer for 7 minutes. Remove from heat. Strain, reserving the liquid. Force the peas and pods through a sieve, discarding the tough residue.
3. In another large container, heat the butter. Sauté the onion and parsley on medium for 3 minutes. Whisk in the flour and cook on low for 2 to 3 minutes. Add 1 cup of the reserved broth. Stir in the strained peas and pods.
4. Add the rest of the broth, stirring constantly over low heat. Cover and simmer for 5 minutes. Garnish with bacon, if desired.

The Interchangeable Bean

Substitute beans at will. Go to your local food co-op and try those different-looking beans in your next chili or bean soup. All beans taste fairly mild so you can't make a drastic mistake and you may find a new favorite.

Black Bean Soup with Curry

1 cup uncooked black beans
1 yellow onion
1 carrot
3 cloves garlic
1 tablespoon butter
1 tablespoon olive oil
2 tablespoons curry powder
1 ½ teaspoons ground coriander

10 cups Basic Chicken Broth
   (see recipe on page 3)
½ teaspoon salt
½ teaspoon black pepper
1 tablespoon chopped cilantro
   (optional)

> **Serves 4–6**
>
> Garnish each serving with chopped cilantro. It adds color and flavor.
>
> ∾

1. Soak the beans overnight in cold water, then drain. Cut the onion and carrot into a fine dice. Mince the garlic.
2. Using a soup pot or large saucepan, heat the butter and oil. Add the onion and carrot, sautéing for about 5 minutes on medium. Add the garlic and cook for 1 more minute. Add the curry and coriander and stir to combine for an additional 1 minute.
3. Pour in the chicken broth and beans, bringing the mixture to a boil. Reduce to a simmer and cook for 1½ hours.
4. Using a slotted spoon, remove about half of the beans and set aside. Cool the rest of the mixture slightly, then purée it in a blender or food processor. Combine with the whole beans back in the soup pot. Stir in the salt and pepper. Reheat if necessary. Chop the cilantro. Ladle the soup into bowls.

Thick Bean Broth

Any bean recipe gives you two options. Cook it longer and let the beans dissolve for a creamy texture. Serve it earlier in the cooking process, as soon as the beans are completely soft, for more distinct flavors in every bite.

Cuban Black Bean Soup

*1 pound (16 ounces) dried
  black beans*
4 cups cooked white rice
1 onion
1 red bell pepper
1 green bell pepper
1 tablespoon butter
*4 cups Basic Beef Broth
  (see recipe on page 2)*
2 bay leaves

½ teaspoon thyme
½ teaspoon oregano
½ cup rum (optional)

1. Soak the black beans overnight in cold water, then drain.
2. Cook the white rice if you do not have leftovers. Chop the onion and the red bell pepper coarsely. Dice the green bell pepper to a medium dice.
3. In a soup pot, heat the butter. Add the onion and sauté on medium for 3 minutes. Next add the beans, broth, bay leaves, thyme, oregano, and the red bell pepper (reserving the green one). Bring the mixture to a boil, reduce to a simmer, and cook for 1½ hours.
4. Remove about 1 cup of the beans with a slotted spoon and place them in a bowl. Mash them. Add them back into the soup pot, stirring a bit until the mixture thickens. Discard the bay leaves. Add the rum and green bell pepper dice. Cover and simmer for an additional 10 minutes.
5. Divide the rice among the serving bowls and pour the soup over the top.

Black Bean and Cumin Soup

1 cup dried black beans
1 onion
2 cloves garlic
1 stalk celery
1 carrot
7 cups broth
1 tablespoon oil
¾ teaspoon cumin
¾ teaspoon black pepper

Salt
Scallions (optional)
Plain yogurt (optional)

Serves 4–6

Any basic chicken, beef, or vegetable broth can be used for this soup.

1. Soak the beans overnight in cold water, then drain. Mince the onion and garlic. Finely dice the celery and carrot.
2. In a large saucepan or soup pot, bring the beans and the broth to a boil; reduce to a simmer and cook for 2 hours.
3. Using a smaller saucepan, heat the oil. Add the onion and garlic and cook for about 6 minutes over low heat. Add the celery and carrots and cook them for an additional 5 minutes.
4. Pour this vegetable mixture into the pan with the beans. Stir in the cumin and pepper. Simmer for 30 minutes. Remove from heat and let cool slightly. Purée the soup in a blender or food processor. Return the soup to the pot and reheat to serving temperature, adding salt to taste. Chop the scallions and use them as garnish for each individual serving, along with a dollop of plain yogurt.

Caribbean Black Bean Soup

Serves 4

Chop the cilantro and use as a garnish for each individual serving.

¾ pound (12 ounces) dried black beans
½ pound ham
1 yellow onion
2 tomatoes
4 scallions
1 teaspoon chopped oregano
6 cloves garlic
10 cups water
1 ham shank (ask the butcher to crack it)
1 bay leaf
¾ teaspoon black pepper
1 teaspoon red wine vinegar
Salt
1 tablespoon olive oil
⅓ cup Spanish sherry
Fresh cilantro (optional)

1. Soak the beans overnight in cold water, then drain. Cut the ham into ½-inch cubes. Quarter the onion. Chop the tomatoes, scallions, and oregano. Peel the garlic and mince 4 of the cloves, leaving the remaining 2 whole.

2. In a soup pot, combine the water, beans, ham shank, whole garlic cloves, bay leaf, onion, pepper, vinegar, and salt. Bring to a boil, reduce to a simmer, and cook for 45 minutes. Discard the ham bone and bay leaf.

3. Using a saucepan, heat the olive oil. Add the minced garlic, ham meat, tomatoes, oregano, sherry, and scallions. Sauté on medium for 6 minutes. Ladle out 1 cup of the cooked bean mixture and add it to the ham meat mixture. Stir, scraping up the brown bits from the bottom of the pan. Mix the contents of the saucepan into the soup pot with the bean mixture.

4. Bring to a boil, then reduce to a simmer and cook for 20 more minutes.

Lima Bean Soup

¼ cup cooked lima beans
⅓ cup cooked corn kernels
1 cup cooked peas
2 potatoes
4 carrots
2 stalks celery

1 onion
8 cups Basic Beef Broth
   (see recipe on page 2)
2 cups tomato juice **or** V-8
Salt and pepper

Serves 8–10

Lima beans from a can will work just fine in this recipe.

1. Cook the lima beans, corn, and peas separately, if you don't have left-overs. Dice the potatoes, slice the carrots, and chop the celery. Slice the onion and separate it into rings.
2. Using a soup pot, bring the broth to a boil. Add the potatoes, carrots, celery, and onion rings. Bring to a boil again, reduce to a simmer, and cook for 15 minutes.
3. Stir in the lima beans, corn, and peas. Pour in the tomato juice. Salt and pepper to taste. Simmer for 10 more minutes.

Lentil Soup

1 cup dried lentils
1 onion
1 clove garlic
2 tablespoons butter **or** oil
1 tablespoon tarragon

1 teaspoon paprika
1 bay leaf
4 cups Basic **or** Roasted
   Vegetable Broth (see recipes
   on pages 4 and 8)

Serves 6

Save yourself some time with this soup. Lentils only need to be rinsed, not soaked.

1. Rinse the lentils very thoroughly. Dice the onion and mince the garlic.
2. In a large saucepan or soup pot, melt the butter. Sauté the onion for 5 minutes over low heat. Stir in the tarragon, paprika, and bay leaf; then add the lentils next. Pour in the vegetable broth, bring to a boil, reduce to a simmer, and cook for 30 minutes.
3. Remove from heat and allow to cool slightly. Discard the bay leaf. Using a blender or food processor, purée the mixture. Reheat for 5 minutes.

Kidney Bean Chili

Serves 4

Garnish each individual serving with a few cooked corn kernels, some grated cheddar cheese, and a sprinkling of chopped cashews, if desired.

1 green bell pepper
1 stalk celery
½ an onion
1 carrot
1 zucchini
1 clove garlic
2 tablespoons vegetable **or** *nut oil*
1 (18-ounce) can chopped tomatoes
1 (15- to 16-ounce) can cooked kidney beans
1 cup tomato sauce
¼ cup water
2 teaspoons chili powder

¼ teaspoon hot pepper sauce
1 teaspoon basil
1 teaspoon oregano
¾ teaspoon black pepper
Cooked corn kernels, shredded cheddar cheese, **and/or** *chopped cashews for garnish (all optional)*

1. Chop the green bell pepper, celery, and onion. Shred the carrot and zucchini. Mince the garlic.

2. In a large saucepan or soup pot, heat the oil. Sauté all the fresh vegetables on medium for 3 minutes. Add all the remaining ingredients, except the garnishes. Bring to a boil, reduce to a simmer, and cook for 5 more minutes.

Red Lentil and Sweet Potato Soup

¾ cup dried red lentils

2 sweet potatoes

½ of an onion

2 tablespoons vegetable oil

3 cups water

2 cups orange juice

2 tablespoons brown sugar

1 tablespoon ginger

¼ teaspoon nutmeg

¼ teaspoon cinnamon

Salt and pepper to taste

1 dash of red pepper flakes

Serves 4–6

Tangerine or carrot juice can be substituted for the orange juice in this recipe.

1. Rinse the lentils thoroughly. Cut the sweet potatoes into 1-inch chunks and chop the onion.
2. In a large soup pot, heat the oil. Add the onion and sauté for 3 minutes on medium heat. Add the water, juice, sugar, and ground seasonings, bringing everything to a boil. Add the sweet potatoes and lentils. Bring to a boil, reduce to a medium heat, and cook the mixture, uncovered, for 20 minutes.
3. Reduce to a simmer, stirring the soup frequently, for another 10 minutes.

Lentil and Beer Soup

Serves 6

Lentils cook quicker than other beans, and never require soaking. They are also rich in iron and protein.

2 cups dried lentils
2 onions
2 stalks celery
3 carrots
4 cups beer (a dark German beer is best here)
4 cups Basic Chicken Broth (see recipe on page 3)

1 meaty ham bone (diced ham can be substituted)
2 tablespoons butter
Salt and pepper

1. Rinse the lentils, then drain. Finely dice the onions and cut the celery and carrots into very thin slices.
2. In a soup pot or large kettle, combine the beer, broth, and lentils. If using the ham bone (as opposed to diced ham) add it now. Bring to a boil, then reduce to a simmer; cook, covered, for 2 hours with the bone, or 1½ hours without it.
3. Uncover and remove the bone, breaking the meat into small pieces. Add the meat back to the pot and discard the bone. Or add the separate ham dice now. Leaving the cover off, reduce heat to a very low simmer.
4. Using a small saucepan or skillet, melt the butter. Add the onions, celery, and carrots, sautéing them for 10 minutes, without browning them. Add them to the soup pot, along with salt and pepper to taste. Rewarm the soup, and serve.

Lentil and Spinach Soup

1 cup dried lentils
2 (10-ounce) packages frozen
chopped spinach
½ of a yellow onion
3 tablespoons oil
1 teaspoon whole mustard
seed
4 cups Basic Chicken Broth
(see recipe on page 3)
4 teaspoons lemon juice

2 teaspoons black pepper
½ teaspoon coriander
Salt
Grated cheddar cheese
(optional)

Serves 4–6

This soup goes well
with thick slices of
fresh, warm Italian
bread.

1. Rinse the lentils thoroughly. Set the spinach out to thaw. Chop the onion.
2. Place the lentils in a large saucepan and add enough water to cover them by at least an inch. Bring to a boil, reduce to a simmer, and cook for 1½ hours.
3. In large soup pot, heat the oil on medium. Add the mustard seeds and cook 1–2 minutes, until they pop. Add the onion and cook for another 6 minutes.
4. Squeeze the spinach to remove excess moisture. Add the spinach to the soup pot containing the onions, along with the broth, lemon juice, pepper, and coriander. Stir in the lentils and salt to taste. Heat thoroughly. Garnish with grated cheddar cheese if desired.

Soybean Soup

Serves 2–4

You control the consistency with this soup. Drizzle in the flour mixture until it suits your taste.

1¼ cups uncooked soybeans
1 onion
1 small stalk celery
1 small carrot

2 cups seeded and diced
  tomatoes
3 cups water
2 tablespoons soy flour

1. Soak the soybeans overnight in cold water. Cover with fresh water in a saucepan, bring to a boil, reduce to a simmer, and cook for 1¼ hours. Drain and mash them.
2. Chop the onion and celery. Dice the carrot. Chop and seed the tomatoes.
3. In a soup pot, combine the water, onion, celery, and carrot. Bring to a boil, reduce to a simmer, and cook for 10 minutes.
4. Add the tomatoes and the mashed soybeans and simmer for 10 minutes. As soup is cooking, whisk the flour together with a bit of cold water. Drizzle in this thickener, stirring constantly, until you reach the desired consistency.

White Bean and Swiss Chard Soup

Serves 6

Cannellini beans can be substituted with any small white bean in this tasty recipe.

2 tablespoons olive oil
1 cup coarsely chopped onion
2 cups coarsely chopped Swiss
  chard (**or** bok choy)
1 tablespoon lemon juice

4 cups Basic Vegetable **or**
  Chicken Broth (see recipes
  on pages 4 and 3)
1 cup cooked cannellini beans

1. In a soup pot, warm the oil. Add the onion and sauté on medium for 2 minutes. Then add the Swiss chard and sauté for 3 minutes more.
2. Pour in the broth, the cooked beans, and the lemon juice. Bring to a boil, then reduce to a simmer. Cook for 10 minutes.

White Bean and Vegetable Soup

1 small zucchini

1 onion

2 tablespoons fresh chopped dill

3 tablespoon fresh chopped
    parsley

2 cloves garlic

1 lemon

4 tablespoons oil, divided

4 cups cooked Great Northern
    beans, divided

4 cups Potato and Vegetable
    Broth (see recipe on page 5)

2/3 cup dry white wine

1 teaspoon curry powder **or**
    garam masala

1 tablespoon water

Salt and pepper

Serves 6–8

For the differences
between curry
powder and Garam
Masala, see page 41.

---

1. Cut the zucchini into ¼-inch-thick slices. Chop the onion and herbs. Mince the garlic. Juice the lemon.
2. In a skillet, heat 2 tablespoons of the oil. Add the onion and sauté on medium for about 3 minutes. Add the garlic and sauté for 2 more minutes. Purée these ingredients in a blender or food processor, along with half of the beans.
3. Pour the purée into a soup pot and add the rest of the beans, the broth, wine, parsley, dill, and curry (or garam masala). Bring barely to a boil, reduce to a simmer, and cook for 20 minutes.
4. Using the skillet again, heat the remaining 2 tablespoons of oil. Add the zucchini pieces and the water. Sauté over medium heat, stirring frequently for about 7 minutes.
5. Add the zucchini to the soup pot, along with the lemon juice. Add water to thin the soup if necessary. Salt and pepper to taste, and simmer for 10 minutes. Serve.

White Bean and Parsley Soup

Serves 6

Compare the flavors of curly-leaf parsley and the Italian flat-leaf kind to find the one you prefer.

---

3 cups navy beans
2 onions
3 garlic cloves
1 teaspoon finely chopped
   rosemary
1 teaspoon finely chopped
   thyme
3 tablespoons olive oil, divided

12 cups Basic Chicken Broth
   (see recipe on page 3)
1 pound bacon slices
Italian flat-leaf parsley
   (optional)
Salt and pepper

1. Soak the beans in cold water overnight, then drain. Dice the onions, mince the garlic, and chop the rosemary and thyme.
2. In a large soup pot, heat 2 tablespoons of the oil. Add the garlic and onions and sauté for 3 minutes on medium heat. Pour in the broth and add the beans. Bring to a boil, reduce to a simmer, and cook for 1½ hours.
3. Meanwhile, heat the remaining tablespoon of oil in a skillet. Sauté the bacon on medium-high heat until crispy. Set the bacon aside on paper towels to cool.
4. When the soup is done cooking, use a slotted spoon to remove about 1½ cups of the cooked beans and allow them to cool slightly. Purée them in a blender or food processor with 2 cups of the liquid from the soup pot.
5. Stir the purée back into the soup pot. Add the rosemary and thyme, and salt and pepper to taste. Simmer for about 5 minutes to reheat. Chop the parsley and crumble the bacon; use as a garnish for each individual serving.

White Bean and Mushroom Soup

¾ *pound fresh cremini*
*(**or** button) mushrooms*
¼–½ *pound fresh shiitake*
mushrooms
1 large onion
2 medium potatoes
2 stalks celery
3 cloves garlic
4 tablespoons oil, divided
3 cups Mushroom Broth
(see recipe on page 9)
*3 cups Basic **or** Roasted*
Vegetable Broth (see recipes
on pages 4 and 8)

2 cups canned, cooked navy
*(**or** cannellini) beans,*
drained
½ *teaspoon dry mustard*
½ *teaspoon basil*
½ *teaspoon thyme*
¼ *cup dry white wine*
Salt and pepper
Fresh parsley (optional)

Serves 8

If you don't have any
fresh shiitake mush-
rooms, you can use
6–8 dried shiitakes,
soaked in water
overnight.

1. Slice the mushrooms. Chop the onion, dice the potatoes and celery, and mince the garlic.
2. In a soup pot, heat 2 tablespoons of the oil on medium. Add the garlic and onions, and sauté over medium heat for 3 minutes. Add the potatoes, celery, broths, and beans. Bring to a boil, then reduce to a simmer. Add the mustard, basil, thyme, and wine; cook, uncovered, for 15 minutes.
3. Add half of the cremini mushrooms to the soup pot and simmer for an additional 10 minutes. Remove the pot from the heat and let it stand for several minutes.
4. In a smaller saucepan, heat the remaining oil. Sauté the rest of the creminis and all the shiitakes. Cook, covered, for 10 minutes.
5. In a blender or food processor, purée the contents of the soup pot. Pour the purée back into the soup pot. Stir in the sautéed mush-rooms. Add salt and pepper to taste. Simmer, covered, for 10 minutes, adding water if necessary to adjust the consistency. Chop the parsley and use as a garnish for each individual serving.

White Bean Minestrone

Serves 8

You can also use
1/3 pound of fresh
spinach in place of
the Swiss chard.

¾ cup dried Great Northern
   beans (**or** white pea beans)
6 cups water
⅛ pound (2 ounces) salt pork
1 onion
3 stalks celery (leaves
   included)
2 tomatoes
1 carrot
1 potato
2 cups coarsely chopped white
   cabbage
2 small zucchini

4 leaves Swiss chard
5 sprigs parsley
3 tablespoons olive oil
1 teaspoon thyme
6 cups Basic Beef Broth
   (see recipe on page 2)
1 teaspoon basil
1 cup cooked small-size pasta
   (optional)
Grated parmesan cheese
   (optional)

1. Soak the beans overnight in cold water, then drain. Place in a large soup pot with the water. Bring to a boil, reduce to a simmer, and cook for 1 to 1½ hours. Drain and set aside.
2. Shred the salt pork, chop the onion, celery leaves, and celery. Seed and coarsely chop the tomatoes. Dice the carrots and potato. Coarsely chop the cabbage and the zucchini. Tear the Swiss chard (or spinach) into pieces and discard the stems. Chop the parsley.
3. In a soup pot, heat the salt pork. Add the onion, celery leaves, celery, tomatoes, carrot, potato, parsley, and thyme, stirring everything together. Sauté for 5 minutes.
4. Pour in the beef broth, and add the cabbage, zucchini, and cooked beans. Bring the pot to a boil, reduce to a simmer, and cook for 15 minutes.
5. Stir in the chard, basil, and the pasta (if using). Simmer for 2 to 4 minutes until the leaves wilt. Ladle into bowls, garnish with the parmesan, and serve.

Bean Soup with Mushrooms

½ pound (8 ounces) uncooked
  chickpeas (garbanzo beans)
1 ounce dried shiitake
  mushrooms
1 cup broad beans
1 Spanish onion
1 (28-ounce) can whole tomatoes
3 garlic cloves
1 bunch rosemary
½ cup grated parmesan cheese

2 tablespoons olive oil
2 bay leaves
Salt and pepper to taste
6 cups Basic Vegetable Broth
  (see recipe on page 4)
1 cup spelt (also called farro)

Serves 6

Broad beans are also known as fava beans. If you can't find either of these, lima beans can also be substituted.

1. Separately, soak the chickpeas in cold water and the dried mushrooms in room temperature water for several hours or overnight.
2. Drain the chickpeas. Strain the mushrooms to remove any unwanted debris, reserving the liquid. Chop the mushrooms coarsely. Shell and cook the broad beans. Chop the onion. Drain and dice the tomatoes. Mince the garlic and chop the rosemary leaves (reserving the stems). Grate the cheese.
3. In a soup pot, heat the oil. Add the onions and garlic and sauté for 4 minutes on medium heat. Tie the stems of the rosemary together and drop into the pot with the bay leaves, salt, and pepper; stir.
4. Add the chickpeas, the mushrooms and their liquid, the broth, tomatoes, and spelt. Bring to a boil, reduce to a simmer, and cook for 1 hour.
5. Stir in the cooked broad beans, grated cheese, and rosemary leaves. Simmer for 2 minutes. Discard the rosemary stems and bay leaves, and serve.

Tuscan Chickpea and Chard Soup

Serves 6

This recipe also works very well with Basic Vegetable Broth (page 4), which will make it vegan-friendly as well.

1 pound (16 ounces) butternut squash
*¾ pound (12 ounces) Swiss chard (**or** rainbow chard)*
1 onion
4 cloves garlic
1 tablespoon olive oil
2 teaspoons oregano
1 teaspoon rosemary

6 cups Basic Chicken Broth (see recipe on page 3)
2 (15½-ounce) cans cooked chickpeas
Salt and pepper

1. Peel, seed, and dice the squash. Coarsely chop the chard. Chop the onion and mince the garlic.
2. Heat the olive oil in a soup pot. Add the onion, oregano, and rosemary; sauté on low for 4 minutes. Add the garlic and cook for 1 additional minute.
3. Add the broth, chickpeas, and squash; bring to a boil, then reduce to a simmer and cook for 10 minutes. Add the chard and simmer for 10 minutes more. Sprinkle in the salt and pepper to taste, and serve.

Three Bean Soup

¾ cup dried Anasazi beans
⅔ cup dried lima beans
⅓ cup dried cowpeas
1 cup sliced leek
2 cups sliced carrots
2 parsnips
1 cup chopped celery
½ cup fresh chopped parsley
3 cloves garlic
3 tablespoons olive oil
8 cups water

1 bay leaf
2 teaspoons lemon juice
1 teaspoon onion salt
½ teaspoon hot pepper sauce
Freshly ground black pepper

Serves 8

Having trouble finding cowpeas in your local market? Try looking for black-eyed peas—a more recognized name.

1. In 3 separate bowls, soak the 3 kinds of beans overnight in cold water, then drain.
2. Slice the leek, using only the white and light green parts. Cut the carrots into thin slices. Trim the tough core from the parsnips. Chop the celery and parsley. Mince the garlic.
3. In a large soup pot, heat the oil on medium. Add the leek and stir for 3 minutes. Add the water, beans, carrots, whole parsnips, and bay leaf. Bring to a boil, reduce to a simmer, and cook for 1 hour with the lid on.
4. Using a slotted spoon, remove the parsnips and allow them to cool slightly. Remove and discard the bay leaf. Ladle out 2 cups of the liquid from the soup pot into a food processor or blender, add the parsnips, and purée until smooth.
5. Return the purée to the soup pot along with the parsley, garlic, lemon juice, onion salt, hot sauce, and black pepper to taste. Simmer for 10 minutes, then serve.

Lentil and Soybean Soup

1 cup soybeans
1 cup lentils
3 onions
3 carrots
3 stalks celery
5 cloves garlic
1 lemon
6 tablespoons olive oil
5 cups Roasted Vegetable Broth
   (see recipe on page 8)

Salt and pepper
Cinnamon
½ cup fresh chopped parsley

1. Soak the soybeans overnight in cold water, then drain. Rinse the lentils thoroughly.
2. Slice the onions and carrots. Coarsely chop the celery. Mince the garlic. Juice the lemon.
3. In a large saucepan or soup pot, combine the broth, soybeans, lentils, onions, garlic, and oil. Bring to a boil, reduce to a simmer, and cook for 45 minutes.
4. Add the celery, lemon juice, and salt, pepper, and cinnamon to taste. Bring back to a boil, adding extra cold water to cover all ingredients. Simmer for 45 minutes.
5. Chop the parsley and stir it into the soup pot; simmer for 2 more minutes and serve.

Brittany Bean Soup

1 pound (16 ounces) dried
   Great Northern beans
1 cup chopped tomatoes
2 cups sliced onions
2 leeks
3 cloves garlic
12 cups Potato and Vegetable
   Broth (see recipe on page 5)
1 bay leaf
2 sprigs thyme

Salt
½ cup cream
3 tablespoons butter
Freshly ground black pepper

Serves 6

When chopping the leeks, use only the white and light green parts.

1. Soak the beans overnight in cold water, then drain.
2. Chop the tomatoes. Thinly slice the onions and finely chop the leeks. Mince the garlic.
3. In a soup pot, combine the broth and beans. Add the tomatoes, onions, garlic, bay leaf, leeks, and thyme. Bring to a boil, reduce to a simmer, and cook for 1½ hours.
4. Remove from heat and allow to cool slightly. Discard the bay leaf and thyme stems. Using a blender or food processor, purée the entire contents of the soup pot. Return it to the soup pot and add salt to taste. Reheat it thoroughly on low.
5. Remove from heat. Stir in the cream and butter, mixing until the butter melts. Sprinkle with freshly ground black pepper and serve.

Black Lentil Soup

Serves 6–8

Out of vegetable broth? Water will work just as well for this recipe.

◯◡

1 pound (16 ounces) dried
   black lentils
1 Spanish onion
1 (28-ounce) can whole
   tomatoes, drained
2 tablespoons fresh chopped
   ginger root
3 cloves garlic
2 tablespoons peanut oil
  or ghee (see page 80)
2 tablespoons sugar
1½ teaspoons ground coriander

1 teaspoon garam masala
   (see page 41)
1 teaspoon salt
½ teaspoon cayenne
12 cups Basic Vegetable Broth
   (see recipe on page 4)
1 cup plain yogurt
½ cup chopped scallions

1. Rinse the lentils thoroughly. Chop the onion and dice the tomatoes. Peel and finely chop the ginger root. Mince 2 of the garlic cloves.
2. Using a large soup pot, heat the oil on medium. Add the onion, minced garlic, ginger, and sugar. Sauté for 10 minutes, stirring occasionally, until the mixture caramelizes. Add the seasonings, stir, and sauté for 5 minutes.
3. Add the tomatoes and simmer for 10 minutes. (The sauce will be quite thick.) Pour in the vegetable broth and add the lentils. Bring to a boil, reduce to a simmer, and cook for 1½ hours.
4. Remove from heat. Mince the remaining garlic clove and add it to the soup. Stir in the yogurt, adding a bit at a time and mixing well. Coarsely chop the scallions and add them as garnish to the individual soup bowls.

Tunisian Bean Soup

1 cup uncooked chickpeas
1 cup dried lentils
3 large onions
3 cloves garlic
1 cinnamon stick
3 tablespoons olive oil
1 teaspoon turmeric
1½ teaspoon cumin seeds
2 teaspoons ground cumin
2 bay leaves
6 cups Potato and Vegetable
   Broth (see recipe on page 5)

1 (28-ounce) can of crushed
   tomatoes
Salt and black pepper
¼–½ teaspoon cayenne pepper
2 tablespoons lemon juice
Fresh mint (optional)
Currants (optional)

Serves 6

Garnish each serving
with a few mint leaves
and currants, if desired.

૭

1. Soak the chickpeas overnight in cold water, then drain. Place the chickpeas in a large saucepan and add enough water to cover them by 3 inches. Bring to a boil, reduce to a simmer, and cook for 1 hour.
2. Meanwhile, rinse the lentils thoroughly. Finely dice the onion and mince the garlic.
3. When the chickpeas are ready, add the lentils and the cinnamon stick. Bring to a boil, reduce to a simmer, and cook for another 30 minutes.
4. While the chickpeas continue to cook, heat the oil in a soup pot. Add the onion, garlic, turmeric, cumin seeds, ground cumin, and bay leaves. Sauté on medium for 3 to 5 minutes. Add the broth and tomatoes to the soup pot. Bring to a boil, reduce to a simmer, and cook for another 15 minutes. Discard the bay leaves.
5. When the chickpeas and lentils are done, add them to the soup pot, discarding the cinnamon stick. Simmer for 5 minutes.
6. Season with salt, black pepper, and cayenne. Add the lemon juice.

Tuscan Bean Soup

Serves 6–8

Feel free to mix, match, and substitute at will with all of the dried beans called for in this recipe.

½ cup dried black turtle beans
½ cup dried Great Northern
   beans
½ cup cranberry beans
½ cup dried chickpeas
½ cup dried lentils
1 Spanish onion
2 stalks celery
3 cloves garlic
1 (28-ounce) can whole tomatoes, drained
3 tablespoons olive oil

1 bay leaf
1 teaspoon rosemary
½ teaspoon black pepper
8 cups Basic Vegetable Broth
   (see recipe on page 4)
½ cup uncooked white rice
1 cup cooked and shelled
   broad beans (also called
   fava beans) **or** lima beans
Salt
Scallions (optional)

1. Soak the black turtle beans, Great Northern beans, cranberry beans, and chickpeas in cold water, in 4 separate containers, overnight, then drain.
2. Rinse the lentils thoroughly. Chop the onion and celery, mince 2 of the garlic cloves, and dice the tomatoes.
3. In a large soup pot, heat the oil on medium. Add the onion, celery, and minced garlic; Sauté for 4 minutes. Add the rosemary, bay leaf, and black pepper, stirring them in. Add the broth, black turtle beans, Great Northerns, cranberry beans, chickpeas, lentils, and the tomatoes. Bring to a boil, reduce to a simmer, and cook for 1½ hours.
4. Add the rice and simmer for 20 minutes.
5. Add the broad beans and salt to taste ; simmer for an additional 2 minutes. Mince the remaining garlic clove and stir it into the soup. Remove and discard the bay leaf. Chop the scallions to add as garnish.

Italian Bean Soup

3 cups mixed dried beans
½ bunch spinach
1 small onion
1¼ cup tomatoes
1 large carrot
1 small stalk celery
2 cloves garlic
1 tablespoon olive oil
8 cups Basic Beef Broth
   (see recipe on page 2)

1 teaspoon oregano
½ cup cooked leftover pasta
   (small shells or similar)
Romano cheese (optional)

> **Serves 8**
>
> You can use any combination of dried beans for this recipe; it is a great way to clear your pantry of those partially used bags of beans.
>
>

1. Soak the beans overnight in cold water, then drain.
2. Tear the spinach leaves, discarding the stems. Chop the onion and crush the tomatoes. Julienne the carrot and celery, and mince the garlic.
3. In a large saucepan or soup pot, heat the oil to medium. Add the onion and garlic, and sauté for 3 minutes. Add the beans, broth, and oregano; bring to a boil, reduce to a simmer, and cook for 45 minutes.
4. Add the tomatoes, carrots, and celery. Simmer for 15 minutes. Stir in the spinach and the pasta and simmer for 5 minutes. Grate the Romano to use as a garnish for each individual serving.

Easy Slicing with the Mandolin

A slim metal or plastic board with a planelike blade, known as a mandolin, makes cutting delicate julienne strips and paper-thin slices into child's play. These once-rare tools have become widely available. Compact, inexpensive Japanese models, like the Benriner, are a great choice. They usually sell for about $25 and slip into a knife drawer easily.

Potato and Root Vegetable Soups

Garlic Soup

20 cloves garlic
2 cups diced onions
1 cup diced green pepper
3 cups chopped tomatoes, fresh or canned
3–4 slices dark bread
4 cups broth (beef is best)

Salt
Freshly ground black pepper
Grated cheese (your favorite), optional

1. Separate the garlic cloves and boil them in water in their skins for 30 second. Rinse in cold water, drain, and slip off the peels. Slice the cloves thinly. Dice the onions and the green pepper. Roughly chop the tomatoes. Cut the bread into small cubes.
2. Using a soup pot, heat the olive oil at medium to medium high, then add the onions and green peppers. Sauté for 4 to 8 minutes. Add the garlic and tomatoes. Simmer for 15 minutes.
3. Add the broth and bring the mixture to a boil. Reduce heat, salt to taste, and add enough of the bread cubes to reach the consistency desired. Garnish with black pepper and grated cheese.

Storing Potatoes and Other Root Vegetables

Tubers and roots contain lots of starch, which turns to sugar in the cold. Many people enjoy the resulting sweeter flavor, and keep these foods for long periods in unheated "root cellars," or refrigerator drawers. Whatever your taste preference, store root vegetables in a dark place, away from heat sources. They should not be stored in plastic bags, as they are living things and need to breathe.

Carrot and Apricot Soup

1 small white onion
1 clove garlic
²/₃ cup dried apricots
3 large carrots
1 bay leaf

2 cups orange **or** tangerine juice
¹/₃ cup whole milk **or**
    half-and-half
¹/₃ cup cottage cheese (small
    curd best) **or** plain yogurt

Serves 6

Unsulfured apricots work best with this recipe. They don't have any orange color added to them.

1. Slice the onion and the garlic clove, thinly. Chop the apricots and carrots. Put all of them into a soup pot with the bay leaf and citrus juice. Bring to a boil, then reduce to a simmer; cook for about 45 minutes, covered.
2. Remove from heat and allow to cool slightly. Using a blender or food processor, mix the two dairy products. Pour the contents of the soup pot into the blender with the dairy mixture and purée. Return the purée to the soup pot and heat thoroughly, but do not allow it to boil. Serve.

Slow-Cooker French Onion Soup

4 large yellow onions, thinly
    sliced
¹/₄ cup butter
3 cups Basic Beef Broth
    (see recipe on page 2)
1 cup dry white wine

¹/₄ cup medium dry sherry
1 teaspoon Worcestershire sauce
1 clove garlic, minced
6 slices French bread, buttered
¹/₄ cup Romano **or** parmesan
    cheese

Serves 6

To convert this to a stovetop method, simmer in a covered pot at a low temperature for 1 hour, adding water when necessary.

1. In a large frying pan, melt the butter on medium heat and sauté the onions until limp. Transfer to a slow cooker. Add the broth, wine, sherry, Worcestershire, and garlic. Cover. Cook on low for 6 to 8 hours.
2. Place buttered French bread on a baking sheet. Sprinkle with the cheese. Place under a preheated boiler until lightly toasted. To serve, ladle soup into bowl. Float a slice of toasted French bread on top.

Onion Soup

1½ pounds yellow onions
3 tablespoons butter
1 tablespoon olive oil
8 cups Basic Beef Broth
  (see recipe on page 2)
1 teaspoon salt
¼ teaspoon sugar
3 tablespoons white flour
½ cup dry white wine

Salt and pepper
3 tablespoons cognac
6–8 pieces of toast
1–2 cups grated Swiss cheese
  (optional)

1. Thinly slice the onions. In a soup pot, heat the butter and olive oil on low. Add the onions and sauté, covered, for 10 to 15 minutes.
2. Meanwhile, pour the broth into a saucepan and slowly bring it to a boil. Reduce the heat and leave the broth at a rolling boil.
3. Increase the heat to medium and stir in the sugar and salt. Cover and cook for about 10 minutes, stirring frequently, until the onions turn golden brown. Sprinkle the flour over the onions and stir for a few minutes. Add the wine and the broth that has been boiling. Simmer 30–40 minutes, adding salt and pepper to taste.
4. Grate the cheese. Trim the bread slices into rounds and place 1 in the bottom of each serving bowl. Sprinkle the toasted bread rounds with the cognac. Ladle the warm soup over the bread and garnish with cheese.

Celery Root and Mushroom Soup

3½ cups celery root (about 2
    medium ones)
2 russet potatoes
2 tablespoons olive oil, divided
5 Portobello mushrooms
Freshly ground black pepper

25 morel **or** shiitake mushrooms
4 cups Basic Chicken **or**
    Vegetable Broth (see recipes
    on pages 3 and 4)
3 teaspoons chopped celery
    leaves **or** flat-leaf parsley

Serves 4–6

If you'd like, the
mushroom stems can
be frozen to use for a
broth another day.

1. Preheat the oven to 375 degrees. Trim and peel the celery roots and peel the potatoes. Cut them into small cubes. Toss with 1 tablespoon of olive oil (you can add a bit of salt and pepper, too, if you like), spread out evenly on a baking sheet, and roast for 35 to 40 minutes.

2. Meanwhile, remove the stems from all the mushrooms. Thinly slice the mushroom caps.

3. Pour the broth into a saucepan and bring it to a simmer over medium heat. Chop the celery leaves (or parsley). When the vegetables are just about done roasting, warm the remaining olive oil in a large pot. Sauté the mushrooms on medium-high heat for 3 to 4 minutes.

4. Place a mound of mushrooms into each serving bowl. Add the roasted celery roots and potatoes on top. Ladle the broth over the vegetables. Sprinkle lightly with freshly ground black pepper. Garnish with the celery leaves and serve.

Using Different Mushrooms

Don't hesitate to substitute exotic dried mushrooms such as wood ear, enoki, and porcini in any recipe calling for fresh mushrooms. However, you might have to alter the amount used, depending on the type. Some mushrooms have very little flavor (such as buttons) and absorb the flavors of other ingredients. Others (such as shiitakes and dried morels) have a distinct taste and are best used in a recipe that does not have a lot of other intense, competing flavors.

Roots Soup

Serves 4

If you don't like sweet potatoes, a russet potato can be substituted in this soup.

1 small onion
2 medium carrots
1 medium parsnip
1 small celery root (**or** jicama)
1 medium-sized sweet potato
2 cloves garlic
4 cups Basic Vegetable **or**
    Mushroom Broth (see recipes
    on pages 4 and 9)
1½ teaspoons oil (**or** butter)

1½ teaspoons curry powder
3 tablespoons white flour
Salt and pepper
Cilantro sprigs (optional)

1. Peel all the vegetables. Chop the onion. Slice the carrots, parsnip, and celery root into ¼-inch-thick pieces. Cut the potato into ½-inch-thick slices and finely chop the garlic. In a saucepan, bring the broth to a boil.

2. In a soup pot, heat the oil. Add the onion and sauté on medium heat for 3 minutes. Add the garlic and curry powder, and sauté for 30 seconds. Sprinkle the flour over the top and whisk for 3 to 5 minutes. Add the boiling broth and the parsnip and carrots. In a small bowl, whisk the flour and water together until smooth; add this mixture to the soup pot. Bring to a boil, then reduce to a simmer, and cook for 15 minutes.

3. Add the potato and celery root, and salt and pepper to taste. Simmer for 10 to 20 minutes, until the vegetables are tender. Garnish each serving with a sprig of cilantro.

Borscht

4 large beets
⅓ cup barley flakes **or** rolled oats
1 teaspoon brown sugar
½ tablespoon lime **or** lemon juice

2 cups buttermilk **or** plain yogurt
Salt and pepper
2 scallions
Sour cream (optional)

Serves 2–4

To cut some calories, substitute plain yogurt for both the buttermilk and the sour cream in this recipe.

1. Remove the stems from the beets, but don't peel. Cover them with water in a large saucepan. Bring to a boil, then reduce to a simmer and cook for 30 to 40 minutes.
2. Remove from heat. Spoon out the beets and set them aside to cool. Transfer 1 cup of the beet cooking liquid to a smaller saucepan. (Reserve the remaining liquid.) Add the barley (or oats) and cook over medium heat for about 20 minutes, until all the liquid is absorbed. Remove from heat and let cool.
3. Peel the cooked beets and cut them into quarters. Using a blender or food processor, purée the beets with the barley, brown sugar, and lime (or lemon) juice. Add enough of the reserved beet liquid to thin slightly.
4. Pour the purée into a saucepan or soup pot. Add the buttermilk (or yogurt). Heat the soup thoroughly, but do not allow it to boil. Add salt and pepper to taste. Thinly slice the white parts of the scallions. Garnish each serving with a dollop of the sour cream (or yogurt) and a sprinkling of the scallions.

Peeling Cooked Beets with a Towel

To remove the skins of cooked beets or potatoes, wrap them in a clean, dry kitchen towel or paper towel, and rub off the thin outer skin. This is best done while they are warm from cooking. This is healthier and less wasteful than using a paring knife or vegetable peeler because most of the nutrients are in the skin and the layers directly beneath it. The beets will color your towel red, but most of the color will wash out.

Potato Pumpkin Soup

Serves 2–4

Your next Halloween pumpkin can become a delicious and economical soup.

1½ pounds raw pumpkin
2 potatoes
2 tablespoons butter
2½ cups Basic Chicken Broth
  (see recipe on page 3)
Salt and pepper

⅔ cup milk
Croutons (optional)
Fresh chopped parsley
  (optional)

1. Peel the pumpkin and cut the flesh into cubes. Peel the potatoes and cut them into 1-inch slices. Place both in a large bowl and add enough water to cover the vegetables by 2 inches. Let stand for 1 hour.
2. Drain and dry the vegetables with a clean dishtowel. In a soup pot, melt the butter and sauté the pumpkin and potatoes on medium-low for 12 minutes, stirring occasionally.
3. In a saucepan, bring the broth to a boil. Add it to the soup pot with the pumpkin and potatoes. Cover and simmer for 20 minutes.
4. Drain, reserving the cooking liquid. Allow the vegetables to cool slightly. In a blender or food processor, purée the vegetables. Return the reserved liquid and the vegetables to the pot. Simmer, uncovered, for 5 more minutes, adding salt and pepper to taste.
5. Thicken, if necessary, by boiling briefly with the cover off. Reduce heat to low and drizzle in the milk, stirring constantly. Garnish with croutons and parsley.

Turnip and Caraway Seed Soup

½ cup butter **or** oil (avocado
   oil is a good choice)
2 pounds small round turnips,
   peeled and sliced
2 onions, finely chopped
1 pinch of pepper
1 pinch of sugar
1 teaspoon caraway seeds
8 cups Basic Chicken Broth
   (see recipe on page 3)

¼ cup sour cream **or**
   plain yogurt
¾ cup cream
Goat cheese **or** blue cheese
   crumbles (optional)
1 tablespoon chopped dill
   (optional)

Serves 6–8

Thoroughly chilled in the refrigerator, goat cheese crumbles easily between the fingers, or by flaking it with the tines of a fork.

1. In a soup pot, melt the butter on low heat and sauté the onion for 5 to 6 minutes. Add the turnips, tossing them with the buttery onion. Sprinkle with the pepper, cover, and cook on medium until the vegetables are bathed in their own juices.

2. Uncover, add the sugar, and cook until the juices have mostly evaporated and the turnips are caramelized, tossing every few minutes. Add the caraway seeds and broth, and salt and pepper to taste. Bring to a boil, then reduce to a simmer and cook until the turnips begin to fall apart.

3. Remove from heat and allow to cool slightly. Using a food processor or a blender, purée the mixture. In a separate bowl, whisk the dairy products together. Pour the purée and the dairy mixture into the soup pot. Reheat slowly and thoroughly, but don't allow it to boil. Garnish each serving with the cheese crumbles and dill.

Autumn Roots Soup

Serves 4

Garnish with a dollop of yogurt (or sour cream) just before serving.

2 cups Basic Beef Broth
  (see recipe on page 2)
2 cups water
1 carrot
3 beets
1 parsnip
1 celery root
1 onion

2 potatoes (red, russet,
  or Yukon gold)
2 tablespoons butter **or** oil
  (avocado is a good choice)
2 tablespoons white flour
Plain yogurt **or** sour cream
  (optional)

1. In a saucepan, combine the broth and water and bring to a boil. Peel and grate all the vegetables.
2. In a soup pot, heat the oil. Sauté the onion on medium for 3 minutes. Sprinkle the flour over the onion and whisk for 3 to 5 minutes. Pour the boiling broth into the soup pot and mix well. Add the vegetables. Bring to a boil, then reduce to a simmer and cook for 20 minutes.

Salsify Soup

Serves 4

The salsify root has a faint oyster taste and looks a bit like an elongated turnip.

5 medium salsify roots
½ of a lemon
4 cups whole milk

Salt and white pepper
Fresh chives

1. Peel and thinly slice the salsify. Place it in a soup pot and cover with cold water. Squeeze the lemon and add the juice to the pot. Bring to a boil, reduce to a simmer, and cook for 10 minutes.
2. Remove from heat and allow to cool slightly. Purée the mixture in a blender or food processor. Transfer the purée to the soup pot and add the milk gradually, until the desired consistency is achieved. Bring almost to a boil, then stir in the salt and white pepper to taste. Reheat thoroughly, but gently. Chop the chives to use as a garnish for each individual serving.

Four Potato Soup

4 purple potatoes
3 Yukon gold potatoes
3 red bliss potatoes
1 Idaho **or** russet potato
1 Spanish onion
2 stalks celery
2 red bell peppers
½ of a habanero chili
4 cloves garlic

4 pounds chicken pieces
5 tablespoons peanut oil
8 cups water
2 teaspoon ground cumin
2 teaspoon paprika
¼ teaspoon cayenne
½ cup cream
Salt and pepper
4 tablespoons chopped cilantro

Serves 8

You can use virtually any variety or combination of potatoes in this recipe. Shoot for 3 to 4 pounds of total spud weight.

1. Peel all the potatoes and cut them into 1-inch cubes. Chop the onion and celery. Seed and chop the bell peppers and chili. Mince 3 of the garlic cloves.
2. Using a soup pot, heat 3 tablespoons of the oil. Add the chicken pieces and brown them on all sides. Pour in the water. Bring to a boil, reduce to a simmer, and cook for 10 minutes.
3. Using a slotted spoon, remove the chicken pieces, reserving the cooking liquid. Set the chicken aside to cool. Strain the cooking liquid, discarding the solids, and set aside.
4. Meanwhile, using a blender or food processor, purée the uncooked onion, celery, red peppers, the minced garlic, and the chili. Once the chicken has cooled, pull the meat off the bones, discarding the skin and bones. Chop the meat into chunks.
5. Using a soup pot, heat the remaining oil. Pour in the puréed vegetable mixture and simmer for 4 minutes. Add the cumin, paprika, and cayenne, stirring to coat well. Add 4 cups of the reserved cooking liquid from the chicken, the meat, and all the potatoes. Bring to a boil, reduce to a simmer, and cook for 20 minutes, adding more of the chicken cooking liquid if necessary.
6. Remove from heat and add salt and pepper to taste. Mince the remaining garlic clove and chop the cilantro. Stir in the cream, garlic, and cilantro, and serve.

Potato and Salmon Chowder

Serves 4–6

This chowder is also good with trout, tuna fillet, or any other oily fish.

1 pound salmon fillet
1 large onion
2 stalks celery
1 fennel bulb
6 red bliss potatoes
2 teaspoons thyme
1 teaspoon whole fennel seeds
2 bay leaves
4 cups Basic Vegetable Broth
   (see recipe on page 4)
1 cup tomato juice

2 tablespoons fresh chopped
   tarragon
4 tablespoons fresh chopped
   Italian flat-leaf parsley
   (optional)
1½ cups whole milk
Salt and pepper

1. Remove the skin from the salmon and cut the meat into 1-inch cubes. Chop the onion, celery, and fennel bulb. Cut the potatoes into 1-inch cubes.

2. Using a soup pot, melt the butter. Add the onion, celery, and fennel, cooking for 4 minutes on medium heat. Add the thyme, fennel seeds, and bay leaves, stirring to coat. Pour in the broth and tomato juice. Add the potatoes. Bring to a boil, reduce to a simmer, and cook for 20 minutes.

3. Add the salmon and simmer for another 5 minutes. Remove from heat and discard the bay leaves. Chop the tarragon and parsley. Stir the milk and the tarragon into the soup. Add salt and pepper to taste. Garnish with the parsley and serve.

Potato Soup with Roasted Garlic

1 large head garlic
1½ pounds russet potatoes
3 yellow onions
1 carrot
9 cloves garlic
*6 cups water **or** Potato and*
    Vegetable Broth (see recipe
    on page 5)

5 sprigs rosemary
1 (10-ounce) box tofu (silken
    kind)
Salt and white pepper

Serves 4–6

Use the leftover roasted garlic from this recipe as a spread on slices of warm sourdough or French bread.

---

1. Preheat oven to 350 degrees. Cut off and discard the very top of the whole garlic head. Place the garlic (top up) in a small baking dish with a lid, and drizzle some olive oil over the garlic. Cover and bake for 35 to 45 minutes, until tender. Set aside to cool.
2. Meanwhile, cut the potatoes into medium-sized chunks and chop the onion. Slice the carrot and peel the garlic cloves.
3. Using a soup pot, combine the potatoes, garlic, water (or broth), onion, carrot, and 4 of the rosemary sprigs. Bring to a boil, reduce to a simmer, and cook 25 minutes.
4. Take off heat and allow to cool slightly, discarding the rosemary sprigs. Break the tofu into pieces. Remove the pulp from the roasted garlic head by squeezing it from the bottom. (It will yield about 4 tablespoons of pulp.) Add the tofu and 2 tablespoons of the roasted garlic to the soup pot and mix well.
5. Purée the mixture in a blender or food processor. Return the pot to the heat and warm on low, adding salt and white pepper to taste. Garnish with the remaining rosemary sprig and serve.

Georgian Potato Soup

Serves 4–6

Mix the cream, cottage cheese, and flour first. The mixture needs to chill while preparing the rest of the soup.

6 cups diced potatoes
1 small onion
3 scallions
3 carrots
2 cloves garlic
1 tablespoon chopped parsley
2 small tart apples
$\frac{1}{3}$ cup chopped dried apricots
1$\frac{1}{4}$ cups cream
$\frac{1}{2}$ cup cottage cheese
2$\frac{1}{2}$ tablespoons flour

$\frac{1}{4}$ teaspoon cumin
2 teaspoon mustard
$\frac{1}{2}$ teaspoon white pepper
1 tablespoon hot pepper flakes
1 teaspoon dill
1 tablespoon oil
3 cups Basic Chicken **or** Vegetable Broth (see recipes on pages 3 and 4)
$\frac{1}{3}$ cup currants

1. Cut the potatoes into $\frac{1}{2}$-inch dice. Finely chop the onion and scallions. Julienne the carrots. Mince the garlic and chop the parsley. Peel the apples and cut them into $\frac{1}{2}$-inch dice. Chop the dried apricots.
2. In a mixing bowl, combine 1 cup of the cream, the cottage cheese, and the flour. Beat until smooth. Then whisk in the rest of the cream. Set aside in the refrigerator. In a small bowl, stir together all the spices and the parsley. Divide into 2 equal portions and set aside.
3. Using a soup pot, heat the oil. Add 4 cups of the potatoes, the onions, scallions, garlic, carrots, apples and half of the spice mixture. Stirring constantly, cook over medium heat for 4 minutes, scraping the bottom of the pan often. Pour in the broth and add the apple pieces and the other half of the spice mixture. Bring to a boil, reduce to a simmer and cook for 12 minutes, stirring often.
4. Remove from heat and allow to cool slightly. Using a blender or food processor, purée the mixture. Return it to the pot, add the remaining diced potatoes, and bring to a boil. Reduce to a simmer and cook for 15 minutes, adding a bit more broth or water as necessary.
5. Remove from heat. Stir in the refrigerated dairy mixture, the currants, and the apricots. Return to heat and simmer gently for 4 minutes, making sure not to let it boil. Serve.

Spicy Onion and Apple Soup

5 cups chopped tart apple
2 cups chopped onion
3–4 cloves garlic
2 tablespoons fresh minced
  ginger
2 tablespoons lemon juice
2 tablespoons oil
2 teaspoons dry mustard
1 teaspoon cumin
½ teaspoon cardamom
½ teaspoon allspice

¼ teaspoon cayenne pepper
Salt and pepper to taste
4 cups Basic Vegetable Broth
  (see recipe on page 4)
2 cinnamon sticks
Brown sugar (optional)
Raisins (optional)

Serves 4–6

Garnish with a sprinkling of brown sugar and raisins, and serve.

∾

1. Peel and chop the apples. Chop the onions and mince the garlic and ginger. Juice the lemon.
2. In a soup pot, heat the oil on medium. Add the onion, garlic, and ginger, sautéing for about 2 minutes. Add all the spices and sauté for another 3 to 4 minutes.
3. Add the apples, broth, cinnamon sticks, and lemon juice. Bring to a boil, reduce to a simmer, and cook for 10 minutes.
4. Remove from heat and allow to cool slightly. Take out the cinnamon sticks and purée the soup in a food processor or blender. Return to the pot and warm to serving temperature on medium heat.

Potato Purslane Soup

2 leeks
1 onion
2 large russet potatoes
1¼ cups purslane
1 cup watercress
1 tablespoon olive oil

3 cups water
1½ cups milk
Salt and pepper

1. Preheat the oven to 300 degrees. Cut the leeks into thin rings, using only the white and the light green parts. Dice the onion. Peel and cut the potatoes into a ½-inch dice. Remove the stems from the purslane and the heavy stems from the watercress. Place the leek pieces in a single layer on a foil-lined baking sheet. Bake for 35 minutes. Set aside.

2. While the leeks are cooking, heat the olive oil in a soup pot. Add the onion, sautéing for 8 minutes. Add the potatoes and the water, bringing the mixture to a boil. Reduce to a simmer and cook for 20 minutes.

3. Stir in 1 cup of the purslane and all the watercress, simmering for 2 minutes. Remove from heat and allow to cool slightly. Using a blender or food processor, purée the contents of the soup pot. Return it to the pot, stir in the milk and salt and pepper to taste, and reheat. Serve garnished with the remaining ¼ cup of purslane and the crisp leeks.

Potato and Vegetable Chowder

1 green bell pepper
1 red bell pepper
4 scallions
¾ pound baby potatoes
2–3 ears corn
2 tablespoon butter
1 teaspoon thyme

1 cup whole milk
Salt and pepper
3 cups Potato and Vegetable
  Broth (see recipe on page 5)

Serves 4–6

Substitute 1½ cups of frozen corn kernels if you're having trouble finding 2–3 fresh ears of corn.

1. Coarsely chop the green and red bell peppers. Cut the scallion into thick slices and cut the potatoes into chunks. Shuck the corn. Using a sharp knife, cut the kernels from the cobs, and discard the cobs (or defrost frozen corn).

2. Using a soup pot, heat the butter on medium. Add the bell peppers and scallions, sautéing for 3 minutes. Pour in the broth and add the potatoes and the thyme, bringing the mixture to a boil. Reduce to a simmer and cook for 15 minutes.

3. Add the corn and salt and pepper to taste, then drizzle in the milk, stirring constantly. Reheat gently and serve.

Potato Soup with Capers

1 pound baby potatoes
1 pound Yukon gold **or** russet
   potatoes
2 yellow onions
3 cloves garlic
1 tablespoon finely chopped
   ginger root
4 tomatoes
2 ears corn

4 tablespoons oil
4 pounds chicken pieces
2 teaspoons cumin seeds
6 cups Basic Chicken Broth
   (see recipe on page 3)
1 cup cream
2 tablespoons fresh chopped
   cilantro
3 tablespoons capers

1. Place the baby potatoes in a pot, cover with water, and bring to a boil; reduce to a simmer and cook for 12 to 18 minutes, until tender.
2. Meanwhile, peel the other potatoes and submerge them in a bowl filled with cold water. Finely chop the onions, garlic, and ginger root. Coarsely chop the tomatoes. Shuck (or defrost) the corn. Using a sharp knife, cut the kernels of the cobs, and discard the cobs.
3. Heat the oil in a large skillet. Place the chicken pieces, in a single layer, and brown for 7 minutes on each side. Using a slotted spoon, remove the pieces and set aside, reserving 1–2 tablespoons of the fat.
4. In a soup pot, combine the reserved fat, the onions, garlic, cumin seeds, and ginger, stirring for 10 minutes. Add the chicken broth. While it is coming to a boil, slice the big potatoes as thin as possible (as thin as potato chips if you can). Add them to the pan, along with the tomatoes and the chicken pieces. Reduce to a simmer and cook for 15 minutes, frequently skimming off any fat that rises to the top.
5. Remove from heat and allow to cool slightly. Take out the chicken pieces and set aside. Using a blender or food processor, purée the soup. Return the mixture to the soup pot and heat thoroughly on medium.

(continued)

6. Remove the skin and bones from the chicken pieces, cubing the meat and discarding the rest. Add the meat and the corn kernels to the pot. Cut the cooked baby potatoes into halves and add them to the soup pot.

7. Remove from heat. Chop the cilantro and add it to the pot, along with the capers. Drizzle in the cream, stirring constantly. Return the pot to the heat and bring the mixture to a gentle simmer; cook for 5 minutes, making sure not to let it boil.

Potato Soup with Watercress

2 leeks
3 medium russet potatoes
1 bunch watercress
3 tablespoons butter
6 cups Basic Chicken Broth
    (see recipe on page 3)

1 cup whole milk
Salt and white pepper
8 watercress leaves

Serves 4–6

If you'd like to spice up this recipe a bit, add 2 medium-sized onions for additional flavor.

1. Slice the leeks thinly, using only the white parts. Dice the potatoes and chop the watercress, reserving 8 whole leaves.

2. Using a soup pot, heat the butter. Add the leeks and sauté for 5 minutes on low heat. Pour in the broth and add the potatoes and watercress. Bring to a boil, reduce to a simmer, and cook for 5 minutes.

3. Remove from heat and allow to cool slightly. Using a blender or food processor, purée the mixture. Return it to the pot, adding the milk and salt and white pepper to taste. Reheat gently, but thoroughly. Garnish with the whole watercress leaves, and serve.

German Potato Soup with Marjoram

2 pounds russet potatoes
1 carrot
1 stalk celery
1 leek
1 onion
5 cups Basic Beef Broth
   (see recipe on page 2)
Salt to taste
¼ teaspoon white pepper
¼ teaspoon thyme

¼ teaspoon marjoram, plus
   extra for garnish
1 bay leaf
2 tablespoons butter
3 tablespoons flour

1. Cut the potatoes into ¼-inch-thick slices. Chop the carrot and celery. Thinly slice the leek (white part only) and the onion.
2. Using a soup pot, combine the potatoes and broth. Bring to a boil, then reduce to a simmer and add the carrot, leek, celery, onion, salt, pepper, thyme, marjoram, and bay leaf. Cook for 25 minutes.
3. Remove from heat. Pour the mixture through a strainer, reserving only the liquid and the potatoes. Discard all the other vegetables. Purée the potato mixture, return it to the soup pot, and set aside.
4. In a small sauce pan, melt the butter and whisk in the flour. Heat until it begins to bubble. Pour in 1 cup of the potato purée, whisking constantly to incorporate. Pour this butter-flour mixture into the soup pot with the rest of the potato mixture. Reheat gently but thoroughly. Garnish with marjoram and serve.

Potato-Leek Soup

4 large potatoes
3 leeks
1 stalk celery
1 yellow onion
1 cup water

1½ cups Basic Chicken **or** Beef
  Broth (see recipes on pages
  3 and 2)
1 cup whole milk
Fresh chives (optional)

1. Thinly slice the potatoes, leeks (white parts only), celery, and onion. Place them in a soup pot and cover with water. Bring to a boil, reduce to a simmer, and cook for 30 minutes.
2. Pour in the broth, and bring to a boil. Strain the soup, pressing all the liquids out of the vegetables and discarding the solids.
3. Chop the chives. Stir in the milk and reheat gently, but thoroughly. Garnish with the chives, and serve.

Serves 2–4

For this soup, make sure that you use only the white part of the leeks.

∽

Potato and Arugula Soup

1¼ pounds Yukon gold
5 cups arugula leaves
5 cloves garlic
3 slices multigrain bread

6 cups water
1 dash of red pepper flakes
Salt and pepper
Olive oil

1. Cut the potatoes into thick slices. Remove the stems from the arugula and tear the leaves. Thinly slice the garlic and cut the bread into cubes.
2. In a soup pot, combine the water and potatoes. Bring to a boil, reduce to a simmer, and cook for 15 minutes. Add the arugula and the garlic, and simmer for 5 more minutes.
3. Stir in the red pepper and bread pieces. Cover the pot, remove from the heat, and let stand for 10 minutes.
4. Reheat very gently. Ladle the soup into serving bowls and drizzle some olive oil over the top, then serve.

Serves 4–6

Yellow Finn potatoes can be substituted for Yukon gold potatoes in this recipe.

∽

Potato-Bean Soup

Serves 6

For added flavor, cook the beans in the vegetable broth. The best part is, you can use the leftover broth from the beans in the soup!

½ pound potatoes
1 cup sliced carrots
½ pound tomatoes
½ cup sliced leeks
½ pound zucchini
1 cup chopped green beans
4 cloves garlic
6½ cups Basic Vegetable Broth
    (see recipe on page 4)
½ cups uncooked macaroni

6 cups cooked white beans
Freshly ground black pepper
14 fresh basil leaves
½ cup parmesan cheese
⅓ cup olive oil
Salt

1. Dice the potatoes and slice the carrots into rounds. Chop the tomatoes and slice the leeks into thin rings. Dice the zucchini and coarsely chop the green beans. Peel the garlic.
2. In a soup pot, bring the broth to a boil. Add the potatoes, carrots, and green beans. Reduce heat and simmer for 20 minutes.
3. Add the leeks, zucchini, and macaroni, simmering for an additional 10 minutes. Add the white beans and the tomatoes, and simmer for 5 more minutes. Pour in a little water if the soup needs to be thinned. Reduce to a *very* low heat.
4. Grate the parmesan. Using a food processor, combine the garlic, black pepper, and basil leaves. Add some of the cheese and olive oil to the mixture, creating a paste. Gradually add the rest of the cheese and oil.
5. Ladle the soup into individual bowls and add a dollop of the oil and cheese paste.

CHAPTER 10

Grain and Nut Soups

Brussels Sprouts Soup with Nuts

Serves 6–8

It is not necessary to toast the nuts for this recipe, but is easy to do and definitely enhances the flavor.

½ cup whole almonds **or** walnuts, plus extra for garnish
1 large onion
1 large stalk of celery
1 large potato
1 large tomato
1 clove garlic
1½ pounds Brussels sprouts
1 tablespoon olive oil

⅓ cup dry white wine
1 bay leaf
2½ teaspoons mixed herbs and spices (such as dill and caraway)
1–2 tablespoon lemon juice
Salt and black pepper
Fresh parsley

1. Preheat oven to 275 degrees. Place the nuts in a single layer on a baking sheet. Bake for about 20 minutes, until you can smell the roasted aroma. Set them aside to cool.
2. Meanwhile, coarsely chop all the vegetables, making sure to trim off the bottoms of the Brussels sprouts and pull off the toughest leaves. When the nuts are cool, rub them with a dry dishtowel to remove the skins. In a food processor, grind the nuts until they are nearly the consistency of a nut butter.
3. In a soup pot, heat the oil. Sauté the onion over medium heat until golden. Add the celery, potato, tomato, garlic, about 1 pound of the Brussels sprouts, and the wine. Pour in enough water to cover all the vegetables. Bring to a boil, then reduce heat and add the ground nuts, the bay leaf, and the spice mix. Simmer for 35 to 40 minutes. Remove the bay leaf.
4. With a slotted spoon, remove the solid ingredients and allow them to cool slightly. Purée them in a blender or food processor (in batches, if necessary), and return them to the soup pot. Thin the soup with a bit of water if desired. Turn the heat to low and cover the pot.
5. In a saucepan or steamer, steam the rest of the Brussels sprouts in water for about 10 minutes, making sure they are still bright green. Add them to the soup pot, along with the lemon juice and salt and pepper to taste. Chop the reserved nuts and the parsley. Garnish each serving with a sprinkling of nuts and parsley.

Tomato and Hearty Grains Soup

2 medium onions
2 celery stalks
2 carrots
2 potatoes
2 tablespoons oil
1 (28-ounce) can crushed **or**
    puréed tomatoes
½ cup raw brown rice (**or**
    wild rice; don't use white)
¼ cup raw pearl barley
¼ cup raw millet (**or** quinoa)

2 bay leaves
2 teaspoons mixed herbs
    (whatever you like), plus
    extra for garnish (optional)
6 cups Roasted Vegetable Broth
    (see recipe on page 5)
Salt and pepper
Mustard (optional)
Chopped green onions
    (optional)

Serves 8

Garnish with green
onions or a bit more
of the mixed herbs.

1. Cut the onions into thin slices. Finely dice the celery, carrots, and potatoes (peels on or off potatoes).
2. In a soup pot, heat the oil and sauté the onions on medium for 2 to 3 minutes. Add all the rest of the ingredients. Bring to boil, reduce to a simmer, and cover. Cook for 1 hour, stirring every so often, since the grains tend to sink to the bottom of the pot. Discard the bay leaves.
3. Add salt and black pepper to taste, and a bit of mustard, if you like. If the soup is too chunky, add water to thin to the desired consistency. Simmer for another 15 minutes. Garnish with green onions or a bit more of the mixed herbs.

Tofu Soup with Rice

Serves 8

Bulgur is a crunchy, nutty wheat grain that can be substituted for rice or pasta.

6 cups Basic Chicken, Beef, or Vegetable Broth (see recipes on pages 3, 2, and 4)
6 cups mung bean sprouts
1 bunch scallions
1 bunch coriander
1 bunch mint
1 bunch basil
*1 tablespoon chili oil **or** hot pepper sauce*
2 lemons
4 cups cooked white rice
1 pound (16 ounces) firm tofu

1. Pour the broth into a large saucepan and heat on medium. Mince the sprouts, scallions, coriander, mint, and basil. In a bowl, toss them well with the chili oil and set aside to let the flavors mingle. Juice the lemons and cut the tofu into 1-inch cubes.
2. Stir the lemon into the hot broth. Place 1 cup of rice in the bottom of each serving bowl. Spoon the sprout and herb mixture on top of the rice and ladle the broth over the top.

Greek Rice and Lemon Soup

Serves 4

Garnish with black pepper and a bit of chopped parsley (or dill).

3 cups Basic Chicken Broth (see recipe on page 3)
½ cup uncooked long-grain rice
2 eggs
¼ cup lemon juice
Black pepper
*Parsley **or** dill*

1. In a medium saucepan, bring the broth to a boil. Add the rice, reduce to a simmer, and cook, covered, for about 20 minutes. Remove from heat and set aside, leaving the cover on.
2. In a medium bowl, whisk together the eggs and the lemon juice. Whisk in about 2 tablespoons of the hot rice broth. Drizzle this mixture into the rice mixture, stirring constantly, until it thickens.

Almond and Zucchini Soup

1 cup whole almonds
2 medium zucchini
4 cloves garlic
2 tablespoons butter
4 cups Basic Chicken **or**
    Vegetable Broth (see recipes
    on pages 3 and 4)
½ cup dry white wine

½ cup cream
Salt
Freshly ground black pepper
3–4 slices bacon (optional)

Serves 4

If you're looking to cut some calories, the bacon garnish is optional for this soup. It's tasty with or without.

1. Preheat oven to 275 degrees. Place the almonds in a single layer on a baking sheet. Bake them for about 20 minutes, until you can smell the roasted aroma. Set them aside to cool.
2. Meanwhile, cook the bacon and set it aside to drain on paper towels. Grate the zucchini and mince the garlic. Rub the almonds in a dry dishtowel to remove the skins; then grind the almonds in a food processor.
3. In a soup pot, melt the butter on medium. Stir in the zucchini and garlic and cook for 5 minutes, stirring almost constantly. Pour in the broth and the wine and simmer, uncovered, for 15 minutes. Stir in the almonds and remove from heat.
4. Allow the soup to cool slightly. In a blender or food processor, purée the mixture and then strain it back into the soup pot. Stir in the cream and add salt to taste. Reheat gently but thoroughly; do not allow it to boil. Crumble the bacon. Garnish each serving with a sprinkling of freshly ground black pepper and the crumbled bacon.

Storing Nuts
Squirrels freeze their nuts under the cold ground in winter. Maybe they're not so stupid after all. Nuts go rancid within a couple of months at room temperature. Store them in the freezer, in airtight containers.

Malaysian Peanut Soup

Serves 6

If you can't find Napa
cabbage at your local
store, try asking for
Chinese cabbage.
It's the same thing.

2 heads Napa cabbage
1 large onion
1 russet potato
2 sweet potatoes
1 (28-ounce) can whole tomatoes
1 tablespoon minced ginger
3 cloves garlic
5 tablespoons soy sauce (reduced
    sodium is best), divided
2 tablespoons lemon juice, divided
¼ teaspoon black pepper

1 pound dry roasted peanuts
    (no salt or additives)
2 tablespoons peanut oil
1 tablespoon sugar
2 teaspoons cumin
2 teaspoons coriander
1 teaspoon turmeric
¼–½ teaspoon cayenne
6 cups Basic Vegetable Broth
2 tablespoons Thai fish sauce
1 teaspoon hot pepper sauce

1. Trim and quarter the cabbages and chop the onion. Cut both kinds of
   potatoes into 1-inch cubes. Drain and dice the tomatoes. Mince the
   ginger and peel the garlic.
2. In a shallow dish, toss the cabbage with 2½ tablespoons of the soy
   sauce, 1 tablespoon of the lemon juice, and the pepper. Marinate in
   the refrigerator for 30 minutes.
3. Preheat the grill or broiler. Cook the marinated cabbage for about 6 minutes, turning them several times. Cut into 1-inch pieces and set aside.
4. Chop ½ cup of the peanuts. Set aside for the garnish. In a blender or
   food processor, purée the remaining peanuts into a thick paste. Set
   aside. Purée the garlic cloves and the ginger (together), and set aside.
5. In a large soup pot, heat the oil on medium. Add the garlic mixture,
   the onion, and the sugar; sauté for 3 minutes. Add the cumin,
   coriander, turmeric, and cayenne, stirring well. Add the tomatoes,
   increase the heat to medium-high, and cook until the mixture begins
   to bubble. Reduce to a simmer and cook for 5 minutes. Add the
   broth, both kinds of potatoes, the remaining soy sauce, and the fish
   sauce. Bring to a boil, reduce to a simmer, and cook for 20 minutes.
6. Add the cabbages, peanut paste, the remaining lemon juice, and the
   hot sauce. Simmer for 2 minutes. Garnish with the chopped peanuts.

Millet and Spinach Soup

1 (10-ounce) package frozen
   spinach
3 cups uncooked millet
1 large onion
3 cloves garlic
2 potatoes
1 carrot
1 teaspoon grated ginger
½ of a lemon
2 tablespoons nut oil
1 (14- to 16-ounce) can diced
   tomatoes

2 teaspoons curry **or** garam
   masala (see page 41)
8 cups Roasted Vegetable Broth
   (see recipe on page 8)
1 tablespoon chopped parsley
Salt and pepper
Plain nonfat yogurt (optional)

> ### Serves 8
>
> For added flavor, garnish each serving with a dollop of yogurt.
>
>

1. Defrost the spinach. Rinse the millet thoroughly. Chop the onion and mince the garlic. Dice the potatoes. Chop the carrot and grate the ginger. Squeeze the excess water from the spinach, and chop it coarsely. Juice the lemon.
2. In a large soup pot, combine the oil, millet, onion, garlic, potatoes, carrot, diced tomatoes in their juice, ginger, curry (if using garam masala instead, do *not* add it yet), and broth. Bring to a boil, reduce to a simmer, and cook for 1½ hours.
3. Chop the parsley and stir it into the soup, along with the spinach and lemon juice (if using garam masala, add it now). Add a bit more water if necessary to adjust the consistency. Simmer for another 10 to 15 minutes. Add salt and pepper to taste.

Yucatan Rice and Chicken Soup

Serves 6–8

If you're uncomfortable with throwing the tortilla chips in your soup, buy a package of small chips at your store and serve them on the side.

3 white onions
2 green bell peppers
1 dried chipotle chili
1 chipotle chili in adobo
    sauce, with 1 teaspoon of
    the sauce
3 cloves garlic
5 tablespoons peanut oil,
    divided
4 pounds chicken pieces
½ avocado leaf

10 cups water **or** Basic
    Chicken Broth (see recipe
    on page 3)
1 teaspoon epazote
½ cup uncooked white rice
3 scallions
½ cup chopped cilantro
¼ cup lime juice
2 cups yellow corn tortilla
    chips (optional)

1. Chop the onions and seed and chop the bell peppers. Mince both chipotle chilies and the garlic.
2. In a large saucepan, heat 3 tablespoons of the oil. Add the chicken pieces and brown them on both sides. Pour in the water (or broth); bring to a boil, reduce to a simmer, and cook for 15 minutes.
3. Using a slotted spoon, remove the chicken pieces, reserving the liquid. Strain the liquid and set aside 8 cups of it, discarding the rest. Tear the meat from the bones in chunks and set it aside, discarding the bones and skin.
4. Heat the remaining oil in a large soup pot. Add the onions, bell peppers, and garlic, and cook over medium heat for about 4 minutes. Add the avocado leaf, epazote, both chipotle chilies with their sauce; mix well. Add the chicken pieces and the 8 cups of reserved liquid. Bring to a boil, then reduce to a simmer; cook for 20 minutes, covered.
5. Add the rice and simmer for 20 more minutes.
6. Remove from heat, keeping it covered. Chop the scallions and cilantro, and stir them into the pot along with the lime juice. Cover the pot again and let the flavors mingle for 1 minute. Remove the avocado leaf. Garnish with the tortilla chips, and serve.

Barley and Wild Mushroom Soup

2½ pounds fresh mushrooms
    (a mix of any types)
1 large Spanish onion
1 stalk celery
2 carrots
5 tablespoons oil, divided
10 cups Mushroom Broth
    or Wild Mushroom Broth
    (see recipes on pages
    9 and 12)
½ dry white wine

2 teaspoons thyme
1 bay leaf
½ teaspoon black pepper
1 cup uncooked pearled barley
½ cup chopped Italian flat-leaf
    parsley
2 cloves garlic
1 tablespoon balsamic vinegar

> ### Serves 6–8
>
> For a heartier taste, you can use a dry red wine in place of a bottle of the white wine.
>
>

1. Slice the mushrooms, removing the stems and reserving them. Chop the onion, celery, and carrots.
2. In a large soup pot, heat 2 tablespoons of the oil. Add all the mushroom stems and a few of the sliced mushroom caps. Cover on low heat and cook for 5 minutes, until they begin to release juice. Add the broth and wine. Bring to a boil, reduce to a simmer, and cook for 20 minutes.
3. Strain the liquid from the soup pot into another container, reserving 8 cups and discarding the rest. Set aside. Heat the remaining oil in the soup pot on medium heat. Add the onions, celery, and carrots, and cook for 4 minutes. Stir in the thyme, bay leaf, and pepper, coating the vegetables. Add the remaining mushroom caps and sauté for 5 minutes. Pour in the reserved broth and add the barley. Bring to a boil, then reduce to a simmer; cook for 1 hour, covered.
4. Chop the parsley and mince the garlic. Remove the pot from the heat and stir in the balsamic vinegar, parsley, and garlic. Remove the bay leaf, and serve.

Wild Rice Soup

Serves 4

Watch the temperature on the stove once you've added the milk, almonds, and parsley. You want to reheat thoroughly, but don't bring it to a boil.

2 stalks celery
1 carrot
1 onion
½ green bell pepper
3 tablespoons fresh chopped
    parsley
1 tablespoon butter
3 tablespoons flour
¼ teaspoon black pepper
1½ cups cooked wild rice
1 cup water

1 cup whole milk
2 cups Basic Chicken Broth **or**
    Wild Mushroom Broth (see
    recipes on pages 3 and 12)
⅓ cup slivered almonds
Salt

1. Slice the celery, coarsely shred the carrot, and chop the onion, bell pepper, and parsley.
2. In a soup pot, heat the butter. Add the vegetables and sauté on medium for 4 minutes.
3. Shake on the flour and pepper. Stir in the cooked wild rice, water, and broth. Bring to a boil, reduce to a simmer, and cook for 15 minutes.
4. Remove from heat. Drizzle in the milk, stirring constantly. Add the almonds and parsley, and salt to taste. Reheat thoroughly, but do not boil.

Rice and Coriander Soup

¼ cup fresh minced ginger root
3 scallions
1¼ coriander leaves
5 cups Basic Vegetable Broth
   (see recipe on page 4)
1½ cups uncooked white rice
1 pound whole ginger root
   (in addition to the minced
   ginger above)
2 tablespoons salt, divided

1 tablespoon Chinese grain
   vinegar
½ cup sugar
½ teaspoon fresh chopped hot
   red pepper

Serves 6–8

You will have quite a bit of pickled ginger left over. Refrigerate whatever you don't use, and use it for other Chinese dishes.

1. Mince enough ginger root to make ¼ cup. Finely chop the scallions and the coriander leaves.
2. Pour the broth into a soup pot and add the rice; bring to a boil, reduce to a simmer, and cook for 1 hour.
3. Meanwhile, prepare the pickled ginger: Peel the whole ginger root and slice it very thinly. Boil water in a saucepan and add the ginger slices; boil for 20 seconds, then drain. Place the ginger slices in a bowl and sprinkle with 1 tablespoon of the salt. Let it sit at room temperature for 30 minutes. Drain and discard the liquid. Toss the ginger with the vinegar and the sugar, coating it well. Chop the hot red pepper and stir it in. Set aside.
4. When the rice mixture is done cooking, stir the remaining salt, the ¼ cup of minced ginger, the scallions, and 1 cup of the coriander leaves into the rice mixture. Remove from heat. Ladle the soup into serving bowls. Garnish each serving with the ¼ cup of coriander leaves and some of the pickled ginger.

Mushroom and Barley Soup

Serves 8

The blend of diced onions, carrots, and celery commonly used as a flavor base for soups is called a mirepoix.

6 cup water, divided
1 ounce dried shiitake mushrooms
2 cups sliced fresh mushrooms
  (any kind)
2 onions
2 carrots
2 stalks celery
2 tablespoons oil
3 tablespoons pearl barley
1 bay leaf

$^1/_8$ teaspoon thyme
$^1/_8$ teaspoon pepper
Salt
2 cups Basic Vegetable **or** Beef
  Broth (see recipes on pages
  4 and 2)

1. Boil 1 cup of the water, remove from heat, and soak the dried shiitakes in it for 15 to 30 minutes. Meanwhile, slice the fresh mushrooms and chop the onions, carrots, and celery; then chop the
   soaked mushrooms, reserving the soaking liquid.
2. In a soup pot, heat the oil. Add the fresh mushrooms and the onion,
   sautéing on medium for 8 minutes.
3. Add the broth, the remaining water, carrots, celery, soaked mushrooms, and their soaking liquid. Bring to a boil, reduce to a simmer,
   and cook for 45 minutes.
4. Add the barley, bay leaf, thyme, and pepper, simmering for another
   40 minutes. Discard the bay leaf, salt to taste, and serve.

Rice and Egg Soup

6 cups Potato Vegetable Broth
    (see recipe on page 5)
1 cup Basic Vegetable Broth
    (see recipe on page 4)
3 eggs
1 lemon

1½ cups cooked long-grain rice
Black bread cubes **or** croutons
    (optional)

Serves 6

Garnish with a few bread cubes (or croutons), and serve.

Place the broths in a soup pot on medium-high heat. Juice the lemon and whisk it into the eggs in a small bowl. Whisk in a few table-spoons of the hot broth, stirring constantly to incorporate. Drizzle this mixture into the soup pot, stirring and heating to combine. Stir in the cooked rice and heat for a few minutes.

Tortilla Soup

Serves 6

Make sure you have extra tortilla chips and cheese. If you serve them on the side, your guests can add more to their liking.

4 whole green chilies
2 medium-sized tomatoes
1 onion
2 cloves garlic
3 corn tortillas
¼ cup shredded cheddar
  cheese
2 tablespoons olive oil
1½ cups Basic Beef Broth
  (see recipe on page 2)
1½ cups water

1½ cups Basic Chicken Broth
  (see recipe on page 3)
1½ cups tomato juice
1 teaspoon ground cumin
1 teaspoon chili powder
Freshly ground black pepper
4 teaspoons Worcestershire
  sauce

1. Roast the chilies on the grill or under the broiler, turning them a few times, until the skin is blackened. Transfer the peppers to a paper or plastic bag, seal it tightly, and set aside to steam (this makes them easier to peel).

2. Meanwhile, drop the tomatoes into a pan of boiling water for about 15 seconds, until the peels just begin to split open; drain and rinse the tomatoes under cold water. Peel, seed, and dice the tomatoes. Chop the onion and mince the garlic. Cut the tortillas into ½-inch-wide strips and shred the cheese. Peel, seed, and dice the roasted chilies.

3. Using a soup pot, heat the oil. Add the onion, chilies, and garlic, sautéing on medium heat for 5 minutes. Add the tomatoes, both kinds of broth, water, tomato juice, cumin, chili powder, pepper, and Worcestershire sauce. Bring to a boil, reduce to a simmer, and cook for 45 minutes.

4. Add the tortillas and cheese; mix well and simmer for 10 minutes.

CHAPTER 11
Pasta Soups

Spaghetti Soup

Serves 6–8

If you want to add a twist to this spaghetti soup, substitute grated parmesan cheese for the cheddar cheese.

1 pound (16 ounces) dried red kidney beans
1 Spanish onion
3 cloves garlic
3 tablespoons peanut oil
1 pound hamburger meat
2 tablespoons chili powder
1 tablespoon oregano
1½ teaspoon ground coriander
1 dash of cinnamon
1 dash of allspice

1 dash of ground cloves
1 dash of cayenne pepper
2 bay leaves
1 (28-ounce) can diced tomatoes
8 cups water
3 cups cooked spaghetti
1 cup grated cheddar

1. Soak the beans overnight in cold water to cover, then drain. Chop the onion and mince the garlic.
2. Place the beans in a large saucepan with enough water to cover them. Bring to a boil, reduce to a simmer, and cook for 1½ hours. Drain, reserving 1 cup of the cooking liquid, and set aside both.
3. Using a soup pot, heat the oil. Add the ground beef and brown it, breaking it up with a wooden spoon as it cooks. With a slotted spoon, remove the meat and set it aside to drain on paper towels, reserving the oil in the pan.
4. Add the onion and garlic to the soup pot, and sauté them for 3 minutes. Add the chili powder, oregano, coriander, cinnamon, allspice, cloves, cayenne, and bay leaves. Stir for 5 minutes.
5. Add the tomatoes and their liquid and simmer for 2 minutes. Place the beef back in the pot, add the water, and bring to a boil. Reduce to a simmer and cook, uncovered, for 10 minutes. Stir in the beans and some of the reserved cooking liquid. Simmer for 2 minutes.
6. Remove the bay leaves. Grate the cheese. Put some of the cooked spaghetti in each bowl, ladle the chili mixture over the spaghetti. Garnish with the grated cheese.

Macaroni and Cheese Soup

1 small carrot
1 small stalk celery
1 small onion
¼–½ pound (4–8 ounces)
  cheddar cheese
1 cup uncooked elbow macaroni
¼ cup butter
4 cups Basic Chicken Broth
  (see recipe on page 3)

½ teaspoon white pepper
2 tablespoons cornstarch
2 tablespoons water
1 (8-ounce) can corn kernels,
  drained
½ cup peas (optional)

Serves 6

Out of corn starch? Potato starch can be substituted for corn starch in this soup.

1. Finely chop the carrot, celery, and onion. Cube the cheese.
2. In a pot, cook the macaroni in unsalted water, according to the directions on the package. Rinse it in cold water, and set aside.
3. In a large skillet, melt the butter. Add the carrots, celery, and onion, sautéing for 3 minutes on medium heat. Remove the pan from the heat and set aside.
4. In a soup pot, combine the milk and cheese. Stirring constantly, cook on medium-low heat until the cheese melts. Add the chicken broth and pepper; mix well.
5. In a small glass, whisk the cornstarch into the water until smooth; add it to the soup pot. Simmer, stirring constantly, for 1 minute. Add the macaroni, the sautéed vegetables, the corn, and peas (if using). Reheat on low.

Chicken Tortellini Soup

Serves 6

Save your leftovers for a day before making this soup. Any kind of leftover cooked vegetables can be used in this recipe.

1 onion
2 cloves garlic
2 cups cubed cooked chicken
1 tablespoon oil
6 cups Basic Chicken Broth
   (see recipe on page 3)

1 teaspoon dill
9 ounces tortellini (fresh **or**
   dried)
2 cups leftover cooked vegetables
¼ teaspoon pepper
Romano cheese (optional)

1. Chop the onion, mince the garlic, and cube the chicken.
2. In a soup pot, heat the oil. Sauté the onion and garlic for 3 minutes on medium heat. Add the chicken broth, tortellini, vegetable mix, chicken cubes, dill, and pepper. Bring to a boil, reduce to a simmer and cook for 7 minutes for fresh tortellini and 15 minutes for dried tortellini.
3. Grate the cheese as a garnish, and serve.

Armenian Noodle Soup

Serves 6–8

If you'd like to add a personal touch to your cooking, try growing fresh mint in a small pot on your windowsill.

1 onion
6 tablespoons butter
8 cups Scotch Broth
   (see recipe on page 7)
½ cup tomato sauce

2 cups uncooked egg noodles
   (¼-inch wide)
1 tablespoon fresh chopped
   mint (optional)

1. Finely chop the onion. In a saucepan, heat the butter. Sauté the onion for 3 minutes on medium heat.
2. In a soup pot, combine the broth and tomato sauce, and bring to a boil. Stir in the noodles. Simmer for 4 minutes.
3. Add the onions to the soup pot. Chop the mint. Ladle the soup into the individual bowls, garnish with the mint, and serve.

Minestrone with Penne

2 large Spanish onions
6 cloves garlic
3 carrots
3 stalks celery
1 medium head green cabbage
10 large kale leaves
1 (28-ounce) can plum tomatoes
1 (16-ounce) can chickpeas
   (also called garbanzo beans)
½ cup olive oil

½ teaspoon thyme
2 bay leaves
12 cups water
1 cup (8 ounces) penne pasta
Salt and pepper

Serves 10

Experiment with vegetable pastas such as tomato or spinach. They frequently have a more substantial consistency and more nutrients than regular pasta.

1. Chop the onions, garlic, carrots, celery, cabbage, and kale. Cut the plum tomatoes in pieces, reserving their liquid. Drain and rinse the chickpeas.
2. Using a soup pot, heat the oil. Add the onions, garlic, carrots, and celery, and cook for 6 minutes. Add the cabbage, kale, thyme, and bay leaves, stirring well for 1 minute. Add the water, tomatoes, and chickpeas, bringing to a boil. Reduce to a simmer and cook for 45 minutes. Discard the bay leaves.
3. Add the penne and simmer for 15 minutes. Add salt and pepper to taste, and serve.

Pasta e Fagioli

Serves 4

Borlotti beans are traditionally used in this Northern Italian dish, but there are many versions of this recipe. Feel free to substitute your favorite bean.

1 tablespoon olive oil
1 medium onion, chopped
1 cloves garlic, finely chopped
1 large carrot, sliced in ¼-inch rounds
1 small zucchini, chopped
1 tablespoon fresh basil, chopped
2 tablespoons (tightly packed) fresh chopped parsley leaves
½ cup (tightly packed) fresh spinach, stems removed
*1–2 cups coarsely chopped fresh **or** canned tomatoes*
*1 cup canned kidney beans (**or** your favorite bean), including the liquid*

*4 cups Basic Chicken Broth (see recipe on page 3) **or** water*
2 tablespoons lemon juice
½ tablespoon white wine vinegar
1 teaspoon dried oregano
Salt and freshly ground black pepper to taste
1 cup (8 ounces) cooked short pasta (such as spirals, bowties, elbows)
*Grated Swiss **or** parmesan cheese (optional)*

1. Heat the olive oil in a heavy saucepan or Dutch oven. Add the onion, garlic, and carrot, and cook until the onions begin to turn brown and caramelize. Add the zucchini, basil, parsley, and spinach. Cook until the basil and spinach are wilted. Add all the remaining ingredients except the pasta and cheese, and stir to combine. Bring the mixture to a boil, then simmer gently for 20 to 30 minutes.
2. Divide the pasta among the serving bowls, ladle the soup over the top, and sprinkle with grated cheese.

Artichoke and Orzo Soup

8 baby artichokes
2 cups water
2 tablespoons lemon juice
1 yellow onion
2 tablespoons olive oil
6 cups Basic Chicken Broth
   (see recipe on page 3)
2 large eggs

¼ pound (4 ounces) uncooked
   orzo pasta
¼ cup grated Parmigiano
   Reggiano cheese

1. Trim the artichokes to remove the outer leaves. Mix the water and lemon juice, and dip the artichokes into it. Cut the top inch off the artichokes and trim the stem, then dip them again. Discard the dipping liquid and dry off the artichokes. Cut them in half, lengthwise. Cut each in half again, into ⅛-inch pieces. Very finely dice the onion.

2. In a large saucepan, heat the oil and add the onion. Sauté on medium for 3 minutes, stirring often. Stir in the artichoke slices and cook for an additional 5 minutes. Remove from heat, cover, and set aside.

3. In a soup pot, bring the chicken broth to a simmer. Add the orzo and simmer for 6 minutes. Place the serving bowls (or tureen) in the oven to warm. Add the artichoke mixture to the broth mixture and stir well. Reduce heat to lowest setting.

4. Grate the cheese. In a medium bowl, whisk the eggs slightly, then whisk in the cheese. Ladle the soup into the warmed serving bowls, drizzle with the egg and cheese mixture, and serve.

Pasta and Tofu Soup with Roasted Garlic

Serves 6–8

You can store the left-over roasted garlic in the refrigerator to use another day.

1 whole head garlic, plus 8
   cloves
8 cups garlic broth
¼ pound (4 ounces) firm tofu
1 tablespoon peanut oil
2 teaspoons low-sodium soy
   sauce
2 tablespoons sesame oil
3 tablespoons balsamic vinegar

Salt and black pepper
2 cups cooked pasta shells
2 large eggs
Scallions

1. Roast the whole garlic head: Preheat oven to 350 degrees. Cut off and discard the very top of the whole garlic head. Place the garlic (top up) in a small baking dish with a lid, and drizzle some olive oil over the garlic. Cover and bake for 35 to 45 minutes, until tender. Allow to cool. Squeeze out the roasted garlic pulp and discard the rest.
2. In a blender or food processor, purée 1 cup of the broth with 2½ tablespoons of the roasted garlic. Set aside. Mince the 8 fresh garlic cloves and cut the tofu into small cubes.
3. Using a soup pot, heat the oil. Add the minced garlic and sauté on low heat for 6 minutes. Add the roasted garlic purée and the remaining broth. Bring to a boil, reduce to a simmer, and cook for 5 minutes.
4. Add the soy sauce, sesame oil, balsamic vinegar, tofu, and salt and pepper to taste, stirring on low heat until thoroughly warmed. Cover and leave on low heat while you whisk the eggs in a small bowl. Uncover and drizzle the eggs on top of the soup. Simmer for 5 minutes.
5. Chop the scallions. Divide the cooked pasta among the serving bowls. Ladle the soup over the top, and garnish with the scallions, and serve.

Pork and Escarole Soup with Ditalini

2 tablespoons olive oil

2 cloves garlic, minced

1½ cups sliced pork (½-inch pieces)

3 cups (tightly packed) thinly sliced escarole

6 cups Basic Chicken Broth (see recipe on page 3)

½ cup ditalini pasta

1 tablespoon chopped fresh oregano

½ teaspoon dried thyme

3 tablespoons grated parmesan cheese, plus extra for garnish

Salt and freshly ground black pepper

Serves 4

1½ teaspoons of dried oregano can be substituted for the 1 tablespoon of fresh oregano called for in this soup.

---

1. In a soup pot, heat the olive oil on medium-low. Add the garlic and sauté until soft. Add the pork, increase heat to medium-high, and brown quickly. Reduce heat back to medium-low. Add the escarole and cook until it just begins to wilt. Add the broth, increase heat to high, and bring to a boil. Reduce to a simmer and add the oregano, thyme, and parmesan; simmer for 5 minutes. Add salt and pepper to taste.

2. Cook the pasta until al dente, according to package directions. Drain and stir it into the soup. Ladle into warm soup bowls and sprinkle with parmesan.

Using Pork Elsewhere

Although pork is not really "the other white meat," today's pigs are not fat. In fact, pork tends to be leaner than beef. Substitute pork for beef in any recipe, but remember to remove the fat from around the edges.

Quadretti and Chickpea Soup

Serves 4 to 6

Fresh is always better! If you can find it, substitute 2 teaspoons of fresh rosemary for 1 teaspoon of dried rosemary.

4 plum tomatoes
3 cloves garlic
3 tablespoons olive oil
1 teaspoon dried rosemary
  (**or** 2 teaspoons fresh)
2 cups canned chickpeas
  (garbanzo beans), drained
  and rinsed
Salt and freshly ground pepper

4 cups Basic Beef Broth
  (see recipe on page 2)
½ cup quadretti pasta
¼ cup grated parmesan cheese

1. Drop the tomatoes into a pot of boiling water for about 15 seconds (until the peels just begin to split); drain and rinse under cold water. Peel, seed, and roughly chop the tomatoes. Mince the garlic cloves.
2. In a large soup pot, heat the oil on medium. Add the garlic and sauté for 3 minutes. Stir in the tomatoes and rosemary. Reduce heat to medium-low and cook until the tomatoes have reduced, about 15 minutes.
3. Add the chickpeas and salt and pepper to taste; cook for about 5 minutes. Pour in the broth, cover, and cook another 15 minutes.
4. Using a slotted spoon, remove about ½ cup of the chickpeas. Mash them with a fork or purée them in a blender; return the purée to the soup and heat thoroughly.
5. Cook the pasta until al dente, according to package directions. Drain, stir into soup, and heat through. Remove from heat, stir in the parmesan, and serve.

Curry-Style Tomato Noodle Soup

1 tablespoon peanut oil **or** ghee (see page 80)
1 onion, finely chopped
2 cloves garlic, finely minced
1 tablespoon curry powder
2 (28-ounce) cans chopped plum tomatoes, including liquid

4 cups Basic Chicken Broth, divided (see recipe on page 3)
¼ teaspoon cinnamon
Salt and pepper
4 cups cooked egg noodles

Serves 8

After cooking the egg noodles, sprinkle a few drops of olive oil on the drained pasta to keep it from sticking together.

∼

1. In a large saucepan or soup pot, warm the oil on medium-low heat. Add the onion and sauté for 5 minutes. Add the garlic and curry powder, and sauté for a 3–4 minutes, stirring constantly. Add the tomatoes, along with their liquid, to the pot. Add 2 cups of the broth, the cinnamon, and a sprinkling of salt and pepper. Simmer over medium-low heat, partially covered, for 25 minutes.

2. Remove from heat and allow to cool slightly. Purée the soup in a blender, in small batches, and return it to the pot. Add the remaining broth and salt and pepper to taste; heat to serving temperature. Divide the cooked noodles among the serving bowls and ladle the soup over the top.

Linguine with Beef and Black Bean Chili

2 tablespoons vegetable oil
1 pound ground beef
¾ cup finely diced onion
1 jalapeño chili pepper, seeded and thinly sliced
2 tablespoons chili powder
1 tablespoon ground cumin
2 cloves garlic, finely chopped
1 (15-ounce) can black beans, rinsed well and drained

1 (16-ounce) can crushed tomatoes
2 tablespoons chopped fresh cilantro
1 cup water
1 cup Basic Beef Broth (see recipe on page 2)
Salt and freshly ground pepper
1 pound (16 ounces) linguine

1. In a soup pot, heat the oil on medium and brown the meat, stirring with a wooden spoon to break it up. Add the onion, jalapeño, chili powder, cumin, and garlic, and cook until the onion is golden brown. Add the beans, tomatoes, cilantro, water, and broth. Bring to a boil, reduce to a simmer, and cover; simmer for 15 minutes.
2. Cook the linguine until al dente, according to package directions; drain.
3. Skim off any fat that has accumulated on the top of the soup. Add the cooked linguine and salt and pepper to taste. Stir over medium heat until the pasta is well coated with sauce and the mixture begins to simmer. Serve.

Orzo and Egg Soup

8 cups Basic Chicken Broth
   (see recipe on page 3)
½ cup uncooked orzo pasta

3 eggs
½ cup lemon juice

Serves 6–8

Orzo is actually rice shaped pasta. In fact, you can substitute ½ cup of rice if you'd like. (See page 180 for Greek Rice and Lemon Soup.)

1. In a soup pot, bring the broth to a boil. Stir in the orzo, reduce to a simmer, and cover; cook for 10 minutes. Remove from heat, keeping covered to allow the pasta to cook further.
2. In a medium bowl, beat the eggs until they are frothy. Drizzle in the lemon juice, beating until it thickens. Place the soup pot with the orzo on low heat. Drizzle about 2 cups of the hot pasta broth into the egg mixture, beating constantly; then stir all the egg mixture into the soup pot. Serve immediately.

CHAPTER 12
Stews

Gone-All-Day Stew

Serves 6

Cut up the veggies the night before to give yourself a head start on this one-dish meal.

1 (10¾-ounce) can condensed tomato soup
1 cup water
¼ cup flour
2 pounds beef chuck, cut into 1-inch cubes
3 medium carrots, cut diagonally into 1-inch pieces
½ cup diced celery

6 medium-sized yellow onions, quartered
4 medium potatoes, peeled and cut into 1½-inch cubes
2 beef bouillon cubes
1 tablespoon Italian herb seasoning
1 bay leaf
Salt and pepper

Preheat the oven to 275 degrees. In a bowl, mix together the soup, water, and flour until smooth. In a roasting pan with a cover, combine this mixture with all the remaining ingredients; bake for 4 to 5 hours. Remove from the oven and discard the bay leaf. Add salt and pepper to taste, and serve.

Sloppy Joe Stew

Serves 4

For a healthier touch, this stew is also delicious with ground turkey.

1 tablespoon olive oil
1 pound ground beef
½ cup chopped onions
½ teaspoon salt
1 dash of pepper

1 (14-ounce) can diced tomatoes
2 large potatoes, peeled and sliced
1 cup sliced carrots
½ cup chopped celery

Warm the oil in a large, heavy skillet over low heat and brown the hamburger, stirring it with a wooden spoon to break it up. Drain off the fat. Stir in the onions, salt, and pepper. Add all the remaining ingredients, mixing well. Bring to a boil, reduce to a simmer, and cook until the potatoes are tender, about 20 minutes.

Carolyn's Southwestern Chicken Stew

3 pounds chicken pieces
(breasts, thighs, legs), skin
and fat removed
¼ cup flour, plus 1 tablespoon
¼ cup olive oil
2 tablespoons minced garlic
5 cups Basic Chicken Broth
(see recipe on page 3)
1 (14-ounce) can whole tomatoes, roughly chopped
1 (6-ounce) can tomato paste
16 pearl onions
1½ teaspoons seasoned salt
1½ teaspoons ground cumin
4 sprigs oregano
4 sprigs thyme

1 bay leaf
¼ teaspoon crushed red
pepper flakes
½ pound (8 ounces) kielbasa
2 cups cubed new potatoes
2 cups coarsely chopped
zucchini
2 cups coarsely chopped
carrots
2 cups coarsely chopped
yellow squash
1 (8-ounce) can whole kernel
corn
Fresh chopped cilantro
(optional)

Serves 6

To cut down on the fat, you can substitute smoked turkey sausage for the kielbasa.

1. In a bag, coat the chicken pieces with the ¼ cup of flour. Heat the oil in a soup pot or Dutch oven and brown the chicken. Using a slotted spoon, remove the chicken and set aside. Drain off all but 1 teaspoon of the drippings.
2. Whisk the remaining flour and the garlic into the drippings, mixing for 30 seconds. Stir in next 10 ingredients starting with chicken broth and ending with red pepper flakes. Bring to a boil; reduce to a simmer and cook, uncovered, for 20 minutes.
3. Add the chicken pieces and the kielbasa; cover and simmer 20 minutes longer.
4. Skim off any fat that has accumulated on the top. Add all the vegetables. Simmer, covered, for 30 minutes. Discard the bay leaf. Garnish with the cilantro, and serve.

Brunswick Stew

2 (2½-pound) whole chickens
8 cups (2 quarts) water
1 tablespoon salt
1½ cups ketchup, divided
2 tablespoons light brown sugar
1½ teaspoons dry mustard
1½ teaspoons fresh grated
  ginger
½ of a lemon, sliced
1 clove garlic, minced
1 tablespoon butter
¼ cup white vinegar
3 tablespoons vegetable oil

1 tablespoon Worcestershire
  sauce
¾ teaspoon hot sauce
½ teaspoon pepper
2 (28-ounce) cans diced tomatoes
2 (15-ounce) cans whole kernel
  corn, including liquid
2 (15-ounce) cans creamed-style
  corn
1 large onion, chopped
¼ cup (firmly packed) light
  brown sugar
Salt and pepper to taste

1. Place the chickens in large soup pot or Dutch oven. Add the water and salt, and bring to a boil; cover, reduce heat, and simmer for 45 minutes, or until the chicken is tender. Drain off all but 4 cups of the cooking liquid.
2. Remove and discard the skin and bone from the chickens. Shred the meat and add it to the pot with the reserved cooking liquid.
3. In a small saucepan, combine ½ cup of the ketchup, the sugar, mustard, ginger, lemon, garlic, butter, vinegar, oil, Worcestershire, hot sauce, and pepper; cook on medium heat, stirring occasionally, for 10 minutes.
4. Stir the ketchup mixture into the soup pot with the chicken and broth. Add the remaining 1 cup ketchup and all other remaining ingredients; simmer, stirring often, for 4 hours or until thickened.

Montana Stew

2 tablespoons all-purpose flour
1 tablespoon paprika
4 teaspoons chili powder,
    divided
2 teaspoons salt
2½ pounds beef, cubed
3 tablespoons oil
2 medium onions, sliced
1 clove garlic, minced
1 (28-ounce) can diced tomatoes

1 tablespoon cinnamon
1 teaspoon ground cloves
½ teaspoon crushed red pepper
2 large potatoes, cubed
2 cups roughly chopped carrots
Salt and pepper

Serves 8

Hearty stews are just right for family reunions and tailgate picnics.

∾

---

1. In a small bowl, mix together the flour, paprika, 1 teaspoon chili powder, and salt; coat the beef in this mixture. Heat the oil in a large soup pot or Dutch oven and brown the beef.
2. Add the onion and garlic, and cook until soft; then add the tomatoes, the remaining chili powder, cinnamon, cloves, and peppers. Cover and simmer for 2 hours.
3. Add the potatoes and carrots. Simmer for about 45 minutes, until the vegetables are tender. Add salt and pepper to taste, and serve.

A Bowl You Don't Have to Wash!

Use squash as a soup bowl. Many small squashes make excellent complements to soups and stews. Cut them in half, remove the seeds and prebake in the microwave or oven. Ladle your soup or stew into the squash for a festive look.

Tomato-Seafood Stew

½ pound shrimp, shelled and
  deveined
1 tablespoon olive oil
1 cup chopped onion
2 garlic cloves, minced
1 (16-ounce) can diced tomatoes, including liquid
1 (8-ounce) can tomato sauce
1 potato, peeled and chopped
1 medium green pepper,
  chopped
1 celery stalk, chopped

1 medium carrot, shredded
1 teaspoon dried thyme,
  crushed
¼ teaspoon black pepper
4 dashes hot sauce
1 (20-ounce) can whole baby
  clams, drained
2 tablespoons fresh chopped
  parsley

1. Cut the shrimp in half lengthwise. Heat the oil on medium in a soup
   pot and sauté the onion and garlic for about 3 minutes, until the
   onion softens. Stir in the tomatoes and their liquid, the tomato sauce,
   potato, green pepper, celery, carrot, thyme, black pepper, and hot
   pepper sauce. Bring to a boil, then reduce to a simmer. Cover and
   simmer for about 20 minutes, until the vegetables are tender.
2. Add the shrimp, clams, and parsley. Bring to boiling, reduce to a
   simmer, and cover; cook about 2 or 3 minutes, until the shrimp
   turns pink.

Scandinavian Beef and Vegetable Stew

3 pounds stewing beef
3 pounds beef marrow bones
12 cups (3 quarts) water
2 bay leaves
3 whole cloves
1 teaspoon rosemary
2 teaspoons salt
½ teaspoon freshly ground
　black pepper
6 carrots, peeled and sliced

1 medium-sized cabbage,
　cut into eighths
1 onion, chopped
¼ cup cider vinegar
1 tablespoon brown sugar
1 tablespoon flour
3 tablespoons cold water

Serves 8

This hearty stew will
soon become a
winter favorite!

1. Cut the stewing beef into bite-size pieces, trimming off any excess fat. In a soup pot, boil the beef bones in the water for 1½ hours. Remove and discard the bones, reserving the marrow. Strain the broth through a sieve or cheesecloth to remove any impurities. Return the broth to the soup pot.
2. Add the stewing beef, bay leaves, cloves, rosemary, salt, and pepper to the broth. Simmer, covered, for 2 hours, or until the beef is tender. Periodically skim off any fat as it rises to the top.
3. Add the reserved marrow to the soup pot. Bring the mixture to a boil, reduce to a simmer, and add the carrots and cabbage; cook, covered, for 20 minutes, or until the vegetables are just tender. Remove the bay leaves.
4. Using a slotted spoon, remove the meat and vegetables from the broth. Arrange in a serving dish and cover to keep warm. Simmer the onion in the broth for 5 minutes. Add the vinegar and sugar. Whisk together the flour and water; add it to the broth, stirring constantly until the mixture is thickened and smooth. Add salt and pepper to taste. Pour the sauce over the meat and vegetables, and serve.

French Chicken and Pork Stew

1 (⅓-pound) boneless pork
   shoulder chop
1 (3- to 4-pound) whole chicken
8–10 small white onions, peeled
½ pound small mushrooms
4 cups Basic Beef Broth
   (see recipe on page 2)

¼ cup dry white wine
2 tablespoons Dijon mustard
2 tablespoons fresh chopped
   parsley
1 teaspoon cornstarch
1 teaspoon water

1. Cut the pork into ¾-inch cubes. Cut the chicken into serving pieces (breasts, thighs, wings, etc.).
2. In a large, deep skillet, cook the pork in its own fat on medium heat until browned. Remove the pork with a slotted spoon and set aside.
3. Add the chicken and onions to the pan with the pork drippings. Cook on medium heat for about 20 minutes, turning the chicken pieces occasionally, until the chicken and onions are well browned. Using a slotted spoon, remove the meat and vegetables from pan and set aside.
4. Add the mushrooms to the pan and sauté them in the drippings until soft; remove from pan and set aside.
5. Add the broth to the pan and bring to a boil, scraping the bottom of the pan with a wooden spoon to loosen any cooked bits; continue to boil until the liquid has reduced by about half. Return the chicken, onions, and mushrooms to pan. Add the wine and mustard; bring to a boil. Cover, reduce heat, and simmer for about 30 minutes, until the chicken is cooked through. Stir in the reserved pork and the parsley; bring to simmer again.
6. With a slotted spoon, remove all the meat and vegetables from the pan and transfer to a warm serving platter. Whisk together the cornstarch and water until smooth; add this mixture to the pan juices and quickly bring to a boil, whisking constantly until it thickens. Pour the broth over the chicken and vegetables, and serve.

Hearty Quick (or Slow) Tomato Stew

4 cups (1 quart) tomato juice

1 (14½-ounce) can Italian
   stewed tomatoes

2 cups water

2 medium potatoes, unpeeled,
   chopped

1 (15-ounce) can chickpeas
   (garbanzo beans), drained
   and rinsed

1 (15-ounce) can kidney beans,
   drained

1 cup uncooked lentils, rinsed

1 large onion, chopped

1 cup diced red pepper, seeded

1 cup diced green pepper,
   seeded

1 (10-ounce) package chopped
   frozen spinach

2 carrots, julienned

2 tablespoons dried parsley

2 tablespoons chili powder

2 teaspoons dried basil

2 teaspoons garlic powder

1 teaspoon ground cumin

Topping:

½ cup sour cream

½ cup yogurt

¼ cup fresh chopped chives

Serves 6

Garnish each serving
with a dollop of the
sour cream, yogurt
and chives mixture.

1. Quick method: Combine all the ingredients except the toppings
   in a large Dutch oven. Bring to a boil, reduce heat, and simmer for
   30 minutes, or until lentils are tender.
2. Slow method: Combine all the ingredients except the toppings in a
   slow cooker. Set on low and cook for about 6 hours.
3. Mix the topping ingredients together in a small bowl.

African Pork and Peanut Stew

Serves 4

The lemon juice called for in this recipe is a nice addition. It refreshes the flavor right before serving.

2 tablespoons peanut oil, divided
2 pounds boneless pork butt, cut into 1-inch cubes
1 onion, chopped
2 cloves garlic, minced
½ teaspoon curry powder
½ teaspoon ground coriander
½ teaspoon ground cumin
½–1 teaspoon crushed red pepper flakes
½ teaspoon ground ginger
¼ teaspoon cinnamon
1 bay leaf

1 teaspoon salt
2 cups Basic Chicken Broth (see recipe on page 3)
1 tablespoon tomato paste
½ cup chunky peanut butter
2 plum tomatoes, seeded and chopped
1 green bell pepper, seeded and cut into 1-inch pieces
½ teaspoon lemon juice
¼ cup chopped cilantro
½ cup chopped unsalted peanuts

1. In a large heavy pot, heat 1 tablespoon of the oil on high. When hot, add the pork cubes and brown on all sides. Add the onion and cook until soft. Stir in the garlic, curry powder, coriander, cumin, and crushed red pepper. Cook 1 minute. Add the ginger, cinnamon, bay leaf, salt, chicken broth, and tomato paste. Bring to a boil, then cover and simmer on low for 45 minutes.
2. Add the peanut butter and stir well to blend. Cook the stew another 3 minutes, uncovered, for the flavors to blend. Stir in the chopped tomato and bell pepper. Simmer for 2 or 3 more minutes, until the vegetables just begin to soften.
3. Add the lemon juice. Garnish with the chopped cilantro and peanuts, and serve.

Polish Stew

1 pound Polish sausage, cut in
  ½-inch pieces
3 tablespoons oil
1½ pounds beef, cubed
2 onions, sliced
2 cups sliced mushrooms
1 (1-pound) can sauerkraut
1 cup dry white wine

1 (8-ounce) can tomato sauce
2 teaspoons soy sauce
1 teaspoon caraway seeds
¼ teaspoon vegetable sea-
  soning

Serves 8

Start your preparation
for this stew early in
the day. It requires a
baking time of 2–2½
hours.

1. In a heavy ovenproof skillet, sauté the sausage over medium heat for
   15 minutes. Using a slotted spoon, remove the sausage and set aside.
   Add the oil to sausage drippings and brown the beef for 15 minutes.
   Remove the beef with a slotted spoon and set aside. Preheat the oven
   to 375 degrees.
2. Add the onion to the skillet with the drippings and sauté for about
   3 minutes, until the onion softens; using a slotted spoon, remove and
   set aside.
3. Add the mushrooms to the skillet with the drippings and sauté,
   along with the sauerkraut and wine, for about 3 minutes. Add all
   the remaining ingredients, along with the sausage, beef, and onion,
   mixing well. Cover and bake for 2 to 2½ hours; stir the mixture
   every 30 minutes.

New Hampshire Goulash

Serves 6

For a nice variation to this recipe, try substituting cooked rice for the noodles.

3 tablespoons oil
3 pounds beef stew meat, cut
   in 1-inch cubes
3 cups chopped onions
1 cup chopped green peppers
1 clove garlic, minced
1 (16-ounce) can tomato sauce
1 tablespoon chili powder

½ teaspoon soy sauce
2 (5-ounce) cans mushrooms
1 tablespoon paprika
3 tablespoons brown sugar
¼ teaspoon pepper
1½ cups sour cream (optional)
Cooked egg noodles, buttered

1. Heat the oil in a large, heavy skillet on medium heat, and brown the meat well on all sides. Add all the remaining ingredients except the sour cream and noodles; mix well. Cover and cook at a low simmer for about 2½ to 3 hours, until beef cubes are tender.
2. Stir in the sour cream just before serving (if using). Serve over hot buttered noodles.

Hearty Smoked Sausage Stew

Serves 8

Prepare this stew the night before. You can leave it to cook in your slow cooker during the day and come home to a finished meal.

1 pound dried red kidney beans
6 cups Basic Chicken Broth
   (see recipe on page 3)
2 cups water
1 pound smoked sausage, sliced
1 cup barley
2 bay leaves

½ teaspoon garlic powder
1 teaspoon thyme
Salt and pepper

1. Rinse the beans and soak them overnight in a bowl with enough cold water to cover. Drain and rinse again.
2. Mix together all the ingredients, except the salt and pepper, in a large slow cooker; cover and cook on low for 8 hours. Discard the bay leaves. Add salt and pepper to taste, and serve.

Grandma's Beef Stew

⅓ cup flour
1 teaspoon salt
¼ teaspoon freshly ground
   black pepper
2 pounds stewing beef, cut
   into cubes
¼ cup shortening
4 cups water
1 tablespoon lemon juice
1 tablespoon Worcestershire
   sauce

1 teaspoon sugar
1 large onion, sliced
2 bay leaves
¼ teaspoon allspice
12 small carrots, trimmed and
   scraped
12 small white onions, trimmed
8 small new potatoes, peeled

Serves 8

This recipe may bring back memories of your grandmother's warm and cozy kitchen.

---

1. Mix together the flour, salt, and pepper. Toss the beef cubes in the mixture; shake off excess.
2. In a soup pot, melt the shortening on high heat. When the fat is very hot, add as many of the beef cubes to the pan as you can without crowding them, and brown on all sides; remove with a slotted spoon and set aside; repeat this process until all the beef is browned.
3. In a saucepan, bring the water to a boil. Return all the meat to the pot and add the boiling water. Stir in the lemon juice, Worcestershire sauce, sugar, onion, bay leaves, and allspice. Reduce the heat, cover, and simmer for about 1½ to 2 hours, until the meat is tender.
4. Add the carrots, onions, and potatoes; cover and cook for about 20 to 25 minutes, until the vegetables can be pierced easily with a fork. Discard the bay leaves before serving.

Oniony Beef Stew

1 (2½-pound) boneless beef
   chuck roast
1 tablespoon vegetable oil
3 cups chopped onion
1 clove garlic, crushed
1 (8-ounce) can tomato sauce
1½ teaspoons caraway seeds
1½ teaspoons salt
1 teaspoon dill seeds
¼ teaspoon pepper
1½ teaspoons Worcestershire
   sauce

2 tablespoons brown sugar
   (optional)
1 cup sour cream
1 pound (16 ounces) cooked
   noodles

1. Trim off the excess fat from the roast and cut the meat into 1-inch cubes. In a soup pot or Dutch oven, heat the oil on medium heat and sauté the beef cubes, onion, and garlic until the beef is browned.
2. Add all the remaining ingredients except the sour cream and noodles. Simmer, stirring occasionally, for about 1½ hours, until the meat is tender.
3. Stir in the sour cream and cook, stirring often, until heated thoroughly, but do not let the mixture boil. Serve over hot cooked noodles.

Coastal Oyster Stew

1 pound (16 ounces) shucked
  oysters, with their liquid
2 cups water
½ cup diced onions
½ cup diced celery
6 tablespoons sweet butter
1½ cups heavy cream
2 tablespoons fresh chopped
  parsley

1 tablespoon fresh chopped
  chervil
Salt and freshly ground black
  pepper

Serves 4

For an authentic flair, serve oyster crackers with this stew. You'll definitely impress your guests.

1. Pick through the oysters, removing any bits of shell. Place them in a small saucepan with their liquid and the water. Heat slowly until the oysters begin to curl, about 5 minutes. Remove the oysters and set aside. Strain the liquid and set aside.
2. In a soup pot, melt the butter on medium-low heat and sauté the onion and celery about 6 minutes, until tender. Add the reserved oyster liquid and the heavy cream. Heat *almost* to the boiling point, reduce heat, and simmer for 10 minutes. Add the oysters, parsley, chervil, and salt and pepper to taste; simmer for 1 minute. Serve with crackers.

Cuban Chicken Stew

Serves 4

To collect the lime juice, cut the lime into quarters over a bowl. Squeeze the juice out one quarter at a time.

2 tablespoons butter
3 pounds boneless, skinless
   chicken, cut into bite-size
   pieces
1 cup finely diced onions
1 clove garlic, minced
1 teaspoon cayenne pepper
2 teaspoons paprika
1 cup Basic Chicken Broth
   (see recipe on page 3)

3 cups milk
2 large yuccas, peeled and
   diced into 1-inch-thick cubes
4 ears yellow corn, shucked,
   cut into 1-inch-thick slices
Juice of 1 lime

1. Melt the butter in a soup pot over medium heat and cook the chicken pieces until no longer pink. Remove the chicken with a slotted spoon and set aside.
2. Add the onion, garlic, cayenne, and paprika to the chicken drippings in the soup pot and cook, stirring constantly, until the onion is translucent. Add the stock, milk, yucca, corn, and chicken to the pot. Bring *almost* to a boil, reduce heat to a simmer, and cover. Cook, stirring occasionally, for about 1 hour, until the yucca is tender.
3. Remove from heat, stir in lime juice, and serve.

Potato and Garbanzo Stew

1 tablespoon olive oil
1 Spanish onion, chopped
2 cloves garlic, minced
3 fresh tomatoes, coarsely
   chopped, divided
1 teaspoon paprika
⅓ cup chopped fresh basil
1 teaspoon oregano
2 large russet potatoes, diced
1 cup Basic Chicken Broth
   (see recipe on page 3)
   ***or** water*

1 (15-ounce) can garbanzo
   beans (chickpeas), drained
¼ cup basil, chopped
Salt and pepper
½ cup fresh chopped parsley
   (optional)

Serves 4

For added color, garnish each individual serving with fresh chopped parsley before serving.

1. In a soup pot, heat the oil on medium. Add the onion, garlic, 2 of the tomatoes, the paprika, and oregano. Sauté, stirring occasionally, for 5 minutes. Add the potatoes and broth. Cover and bring to a boil; boil for 5 minutes, stirring occasionally.
2. Add the chickpeas. Reduce heat to a simmer and cook for about 5 minutes, until the potatoes are done. Add the remaining tomato, basil, and salt and pepper to taste; heat for 3 minutes.

Chicken Fennel Stew

Serves 6

Fennel looks somewhat like celery, but it has a mild licorice flavor. It can be eaten raw or cooked.

1 cup dried white beans
8 cups water
1 large yellow onion, chopped
2 large cloves garlic, minced
2 celery ribs, chopped
1 small fennel bulb, diced
2 cups Basic Chicken Broth
   (see recipe on page 3)
2 (2-ounce) turkey sausages,
   casings removed
1 teaspoon salt

1 large boneless, skinless
   chicken breast, cut into
   ½-inch pieces
4–5 small new red potatoes,
   scrubbed and diced
½ teaspoon dried thyme
1 cup green beans, trimmed
   and cut into ½-inch pieces

1. Rinse the beans and soak them overnight in enough cold water to cover. Drain and rinse them again.
2. Put the beans in a soup pot with the water. Bring to a boil and add the onion, garlic, celery, fennel, and broth. Reduce to a simmer and cook for 1½ hours.
3. Brown the sausage in a skillet on medium heat, using a wooden spoon to break them up. Add the chicken to the skillet and cook until brown around the edges, about 5 minutes. Add the sausage and chicken to the soup pot with the bean mixture. Add the potatoes, salt, thyme, and green beans. Return to a simmer and cook, covered, for 45 minutes.

Chicken Stew with Garlic

1 whole head garlic

2 tablespoons olive oil, plus 1
   teaspoon

1 (3-pound) whole chicken, cut
   into serving pieces (breasts,
   thighs)

1/8 teaspoon garlic salt

1/8 teaspoon oregano

1/2 teaspoon freshly ground
   black pepper, divided

1 red bell pepper, coarsely
   chopped

1 yellow bell pepper, coarsely
   chopped

1 orange bell pepper, coarsely
   chopped

2 fresh tomatoes, chopped

1 cups Basic Chicken Broth
   (see recipe on page 3)

24 pearl onions, peeled

3 medium white potatoes, peeled
   and cut into 1-inch cubes

2 ears of corn, cut into 2-inch
   chunks

1 small yellow squash, sliced

1 tablespoon fresh chopped sage

1/4 teaspoon salt

> ### Serves 4 to 5
>
> Look in your pantry.
> One (14-ounce) can
> of whole tomatoes
> with the juice can be
> substituted for the
> 2 fresh tomatoes.
>
>

1. Preheat the oven to 400 degrees. Slice off and discard the very top of
   the garlic head. Place the garlic on a piece of foil large enough to wrap
   it in. Drizzle the garlic with the 1 teaspoon of olive oil, wrap it in the
   foil, and bake for 40 minutes, until soft. Remove and set aside to cool.

2. Season the chicken parts with garlic salt, oregano, and 1/4 teaspoon of
   the pepper. In a large soup pot heat the remaining olive oil on medium-
   high heat. Add the chicken and sauté until browned, about 5 minutes
   per side. Using a slotted spoon, remove the chicken and set aside.

3. Pour off all but 1 tablespoon of the drippings in the pot. Add the bell
   peppers and sauté on medium heat for 2 minutes. Squeeze the
   roasted garlic pulp out of its skin and add it to the pot. Stir in the
   tomatoes with their juice, the broth, and the chicken. Bring to simmer
   over high heat. Reduce to low and simmer for 15 minutes.

4. Stir the onions, potatoes, corn, squash, and sage into the stew.
   Simmer for 15 more minutes. Season with salt and the remaining
   1/4 teaspoon pepper. Serve immediately in shallow bowls.

CHAPTER 13

Healthy Choices

Chilled Cucumber-Mint Soup

Serves 4

This is a refreshing summertime soup—and there's no cooking!

1 cucumber, halved, peeled, and seeded
¼ cup chopped scallions
¼ cup chopped fresh mint

2 cups low-fat milk
1 cup plain low-fat yogurt
Salt and pepper to taste

Purée the cucumber, scallions, and mint in a food processor or blender. Add the milk and yogurt and process until smooth. Transfer to a large bowl and stir in the yogurt. Season with salt and pepper. Cover and chill for 1 to 2 hours before serving.

Light and Lean Chowder

Serves 2–4

If you don't have fresh broccoli handy, substitute green beans. They hold up well while slow cooking and offer similar nutritional value as broccoli.

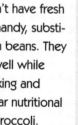

1 (14½-ounce) can reduced-sodium, fat-free chicken broth
1 cup small broccoli florets
1 cup sliced mushrooms
½ cup chopped onion
1 tablespoon margarine
2 tablespoons flour

¼ teaspoon salt
⅛ teaspoon pepper
1 (13½-ounce) can evaporated skim milk
1 (8-ounce) can corn kernels, drained
1 tablespoon chopped pimiento

1. In a small saucepan, combine the broth and broccoli and bring to a boil. Reduce the heat to low, cover, and simmer for 5 minutes. Set aside.
2. In a large saucepan on medium heat, sauté the mushrooms and onions in the margarine until tender. Stir in the flour, salt, and pepper. Add the milk all at once and heat, stirring continuously, until it begins to bubble; continue to stir, letting the mixture bubble, for 1 minute more. Stir in the broccoli and broth mixture, the corn, and pimiento. Heat thoroughly and serve.

Broccoli-Leek Soup

2 tablespoons olive oil
2 medium leeks, finely chopped
  (white parts only)
1 pound red potatoes, peeled
  and finely chopped
1½ pounds broccoli florets and
  stalks, cut into 1-inch pieces
5 cups reduced-sodium, fat-free
  chicken broth

Salt and white pepper
2 tablespoons fresh chopped
  chives (optional)

Parmesan Topping:

½ cup plain nonfat yogurt
¼ cup grated parmesan cheese
1 pinch of white pepper

Serves 8

For added color and flavor, garnish each individual serving with chives before serving.

∾

1. In a large soup pot, heat the olive oil on medium. Add the leeks and sauté for 3 to 5 minutes, until softened. Add the potatoes and broccoli, and sauté for 2 minutes, stirring frequently. Add the broth and bring to a simmer. Cover partially and simmer for 15 to 20 minutes, until the vegetables are tender when pierced with a knife.
2. Remove from heat and allow to cool slightly. In a blender or food processor, purée the soup. Add salt and pepper to taste. Reheat to serving temperature.
3. Make the parmesan topping: Combine the yogurt, cheese, and pepper in a small bowl and whisk until combined.
4. Ladle the soup into bowls and spoon the parmesan topping on top.

Any Squash Soup with Apples and Potato

Serves 6-8

Butternut, Hubbard, Delicata, buttercup squash, or a combination all work well with this soup.

*3 pounds of squash (butternut, Hubbard, Delicata, or buttercup—**or** a combination)*
1 tablespoon olive oil
3 carrots
2 medium-sized yellow onions
1½ pounds apples (any variety)
*1 pound potatoes (white **or** red)*

5 cloves garlic
2 thyme sprigs
*8 cups of reduced-sodium, fat-free broth (chicken **or** vegetable)*

1. Preheat the oven to 400 degrees. Cut squash(es) in half, scoop out and discard all the seeds and slimy threads. Brush the exposed flesh with half of the olive oil. Peel and chop the carrots and onions into large chunks; toss them with the rest of the olive oil.

2. Place the squash, carrots, and onions on a foil-lined baking sheet along with the squash, cut-side down. Roast the carrots and onions for 45 minutes and remove. Roast the squash for 15 more minutes after that.

3. Cut the apples into large chunks. Peel and cut the potatoes into medium-sized chunks. Cut the garlic into small pieces. Place all of them in the soup pot, along with the broth and thyme. Add the scooped-out flesh of the squash and the carrots and onion. Bring to a boil, then reduce to a simmer and cook for 30 minutes.

4. Remove from heat and allow to cool slightly. Remove the thyme stems. Using a blender or food processor, purée the soup. Return it to the pot and reheat gently. Serve.

Chili Bean Soup

1 pound dried pink beans
6–8 cups water
1 teaspoon garlic salt
1 teaspoon onion salt
¼ teaspoon dried thyme
¼ teaspoon dried marjoram
1¼ cups reduced-sodium, fat-
free beef **or** *chicken broth*

1 (16-ounce) can chopped
tomatoes
1 packet chili seasoning mix
1 cup hot water

Serves 6

This soup requires some advanced planning. The dried pink beans must be soaked overnight in cold water.

1. Rinse the beans and soak them overnight in cold water to cover. Drain.
2. Place the beans in a large pot and add the water, garlic salt, onion salt, thyme, and marjoram. Bring to a boil, reduce the heat to low, and cover; simmer for 2½ to 3 hours until tender. Add hot water if necessary to keep the beans from boiling dry.
3. Spoon out 1 cup of the beans and about ½ cup of liquid from the pot; using a potato masher, mash them thoroughly. Return them to the pot, along with the broth, tomatoes, chili mix, and the 1 cup hot water. Stir well and heat for at least 10 minutes to blend the flavors. Ladle into soup bowls and serve.

Pumpkin Cheese Soup

Serves 6–8

The pumpkin is used as an ingredient in the soup and as a soup tureen. It makes a great centerpiece for your table.

1 (5–6 pound) whole pumpkin
2 teaspoons reduced-fat margarine, melted
2 tablespoons water
1 large onion, chopped
2 large carrots, shredded
2 celery stalks, chopped
4½ cups reduced-sodium, fat-free vegetable broth
1 clove garlic, minced
½ teaspoon salt
½ teaspoon pepper
½ teaspoon nutmeg
¾ cup plus 2 tablespoons 1 percent milk
1 cup low-fat cheddar cheese, grated
6 tablespoons dry white wine
⅓ cup minced fresh parsley

1. Preheat the oven to 350 degrees. Cut off the top of the pumpkin (reserving it) and scoop out and discard the seeds. Brush the inside with the melted margarine. Replace the top and place the pumpkin on a foil-lined baking sheet. Bake for about 45 minutes, until tender when pierced with a fork. (The pumpkin should be a bit droopy but still hold its shape well.)

2. Meanwhile, heat 2 tablespoons of water in a soup pot. Add the onion, carrots, and celery and cook for about 10 minutes, until soft. Add the broth, garlic, salt, pepper, and nutmeg. Cover and simmer for 20 minutes.

3. Remove from the heat and let cool slightly. Working in 2 or 3 batches, purée the vegetable mixture in a blender or food processor. Pour back into the soup pot and stir in all the milk. Reheat gently. Add the cheese and wine, and heat until the cheese melts, stirring frequently to avoid scorching.

4. Place the hot pumpkin on a serving platter and ladle in the soup. Sprinkle with the parsley. To serve, ladle out soup at the table, scooping a little bit of pumpkin into each serving.

Autumn Soup

4 cups fat-free chicken broth
1 cup chopped onion
2 slices bread, cut into cubes
2 tart apples, cored and
    coarsely chopped
1 (1-pound) butternut squash,
    halved lengthwise and
    seeded

1 teaspoon salt
1 teaspoon diced marjoram
1 teaspoon diced rosemary
1 teaspoon pepper
2 eggs
½ cup buttermilk

Serves 6

Use powdered buttermilk for cooking, and reconstitute only what you need for this recipe.

1. Combine the broth, onion, bread cubes, apples, squash, salt, marjoram, rosemary, and pepper in a large, heavy saucepan. Bring to a boil, reduce the heat to low, and simmer, covered, for 45 minutes.

2. Remove from heat. Take out the squash halves and let cool slightly. Scoop out the squash flesh from the skins and return the flesh to the saucepan; discard the skin. Working in batches, purée the soup in a blender or food processor. Return the purée to the pan.

3. In a small bowl, beat together the eggs and buttermilk. Stir a little of the hot soup into the egg mixture, and then add it to the soup. Reheat gently for 5 minutes to blend the flavors; do not boil. Ladle into bowls and serve.

Sweet Potato–Ginger Soup

Serves 6

Whole root ginger can be stored in the freezer in a sealed, plastic bag for up to six months.

1 tablespoon olive oil
1 onion, chopped
2 tablespoons fresh minced ginger
1 (1½-pound) butternut squash, peeled, seeded, and diced
4 large sweet potatoes, (about 1½ pounds total), peeled and diced

1 large russet potato, peeled and diced
8 cups (2 quarts) reduced-sodium, fat-free chicken broth
½ cup plain low-fat yogurt

1. Heat the oil over medium heat in a soup pot for 30 seconds. Add the onion and sauté until translucent, about 5 minutes. Add the ginger and cook for about 1 minute. Add the squash, sweet potatoes, russet potato, and broth. Bring to a boil, reduce the heat to low, cover, and cook until the vegetables are tender, about 30 minutes.

2. Remove from heat and allow to cool slightly. Working in 1-cup batches, purée in a food processor or blender until smooth. Pour into a clean saucepan, stir in the yogurt, and reheat gently. Ladle into bowls and serve.

When Are Onions "Translucent," and When Are They "Caramelized?"

After a few minutes of sizzling gently in oil or butter, onions wilt as their cell walls collapse, giving up their juices. This gives the once-opaque raw onion a watery, "translucent" appearance. The edges, once rough and sharp, are then "soft." As the water evaporates from the juices, the onions' natural sugars concentrate on the exterior of the pieces, and brown in the heat. The first stages of this transformation give onions a golden appearance. Since browned sugar is known as caramel, the browning of onions is often referred to as "caramelizing."

Artichoke Hearts Soup

*4 large artichokes (**or** 6
   smaller ones), cleaned*
*Juice of 2 small lemons,
   divided*
16 cups (1 gallon) water
1 tablespoon salt
3 medium-large taro roots

1 medium leek
3 stems of celery leaves
1 tablespoon garlic powder
1 teaspoon marjoram
3 tablespoons yogurt

> **Serves 8**
>
> Use a knife to cut off the leaves and trim around the solid core attached to the stem of the artichoke. Remove the fibrous, inedible material to expose the "heart."
>
>

1. Trim the *uncooked* artichokes to hearts (see the sidebar on this page for instructions). Cut each heart into a few small, bite-sized pieces. Place them in a bowl of water with the juice of 1 of the lemons to prevent the artichokes from becoming black.
2. Bring the 1 gallon of water in a soup pot to a boil. Add the salt and the artichoke pieces, after rinsing them off. Simmer for 20 minutes or until all the artichoke hearts are well cooked.
3. While the artichokes are cooking, peel, clean, and cut the taro roots into ½-inch cubes. Soak in fresh water and set aside. Chop up the leek and the celery leaves. When the artichokes are cooked, remove them from the cooking water and set aside.
4. Add the taro root, celery, and leeks to the water in the soup pot. Bring to a boil, reduce to a simmer, and cook for another 15 to 20 minutes until the taro roots are soft. With a hand-held blender, blend the root vegetables with the cooking water until puréed. Adjust the flavor; add water if the soup is too salty, or add salt if needed.
5. Return the artichoke hearts to the pot. Add the garlic powder, marjoram, and the juice of the remaining lemon. Bring to a light boil, then reduce to a simmer and cook for 3 minutes. Add the yogurt to the soup just before turning off the heat. Mix well and serve.

Low-Salt Pepper Soup

Serves 4

Using green peppers will give this soup a strong "peppery" taste. Red or yellow bell peppers will result in a mild, sweet taste.

4 bell peppers, cut in half and seeded

½ tablespoon olive oil, plus 1 teaspoon

2 cloves garlic, minced

1 medium-sized yellow onion, chopped

1 medium potato, peeled and cut into 1-inch pieces

1 cup low-sodium, fat-free chicken broth

½ cup low-fat milk

1. Preheat the oven to 350 degrees. Place the peppers open-side down on a baking sheet and brush with the teaspoon of olive oil. Bake until tender (about 30 minutes).
2. Meanwhile, sauté the garlic and onion in the ½ tablespoon of olive oil for a few minutes. Add the potato and chicken broth. Bring to a boil, then cover and reduce the heat. Simmer for 15 minutes, or until the potato is tender. Add a little water if it starts to dry out.
3. When both the peppers and the potato mixture have cooked, place them in a food processor or blender and purée until smooth. Return the mixture to the saucepan, stir in the milk, and warm over low heat to serving temperature.

Navy Bean Soup

3 tablespoons olive oil, divided
1 leek, chopped (about ½ cup)
1 cup tomato sauce or purée
2 (12-ounce) cans navy beans, drained
2 cloves garlic, minced
5 cups reduced-sodium, fat-free chicken broth
1 teaspoon chili powder
Juice of ½ of a lemon
2 tablespoons fresh chopped sage
6 small slices white or wheat bread, toasted

Serves 6

Two tablespoons of fresh rosemary can be substituted for the 2 tablespoons of fresh sage called for.

1. Heat 2 tablespoons of oil in a large soup pot or Dutch oven; add the leek and cook until golden brown. Add the tomato sauce, beans, and garlic, stirring to combine. Add the chicken broth, chili powder, and lemon juice, and stir to blend. Heat to a simmer and cook for about 20 minutes.

2. Remove from heat and allow to cool slightly. Purée the soup in a blender or food processor and return it to the pot. Heat the rest of the olive oil in a skillet, add the sage, and sauté for a few minutes. Add this mixture to the soup pot; bring it to a simmer and cook for another 20 minutes. To serve, place a slice of bread in each serving bowl and ladle the soup over the top.

Pumpkin and Coconut Cream Soup

Serves 8

2 cups of reduced-sodium, fat-free vegetable broth can be substituted for the 2 cups of water.

6 cups (1¾ pounds) peeled and cubed fresh pumpkin

2 cups water **or** reduced-sodium, fat-free vegetable broth

1 (½-inch) piece fresh ginger, peeled

1 tablespoon chopped lemongrass

2 scallions, finely sliced (white parts only)

2 cups coconut cream, divided

1 teaspoons salt

¼ teaspoon white pepper

Freshly squeezed lime **or** lemon juice

Zest of 1 small lime (very finely shredded)

1. In a large saucepan, combine the pumpkin, water (**or** broth), ginger, and lemongrass. Cover and bring to a boil; reduce the heat to medium-low and simmer until the pumpkin is very tender, about 12 minutes. Add the scallions and cook briefly.
2. Transfer the contents of the saucepan to a blender or food processor and process until the soup is partially puréed. Pour in 1 cup of the coconut cream and process until smooth.
3. Return the purée to the saucepan. Add ½ cup of the remaining coconut cream. Season with salt and pepper, and heat through without allowing the soup to boil. Taste and adjust the seasoning; squeeze in lime or lemon juice to taste.
4. Ladle the soup into bowls. Add the remaining coconut cream to each bowl, forming a swirl on each serving, and garnish with the lime zest.

Baked Fish Chowder

*3 large potatoes, peeled and
    thinly sliced
4 large onions, thinly sliced
2 tablespoons unsalted butter
    plus extra for greasing
Salt and pepper to taste
½ teaspoon celery seed*

*6 cups low-fat milk
2 pounds cod **or** haddock
    fillers, cut into bite-sized
    pieces
¼ cup fresh chopped parsley*

Serves 8

To cut back on
calories, substitute
reduced-fat margarine
for the unsalted
butter.

1. Preheat the oven to 350 degrees. Grease a large casserole or baking
   dish with butter. Arrange half of the potatoes in the dish; then add
   half of the onions. Dot the onion layer with butter and season with
   salt, pepper, and celery seed.
2. Arrange the fish on top of the onions in a single layer, and season
   with salt and pepper. Add the remaining potato, then onion. Dot the
   onion layer with butter and season with salt and pepper. Pour the milk
   over the fish and vegetable mixture.
3. Bake, uncovered, for 1 hour, or until the fish flakes easily and the
   potatoes are tender. Garnish with the parsley, and serve.

Meatless Chili

1 tablespoon olive oil
2 Spanish onions, chopped
1 teaspoon cumin
½ teaspoon cinnamon
4 cloves garlic, minced
1 (35-ounce) can whole tomatoes with purée, drained and liquid reserved
⅓ cup water
1 tablespoon Tabasco sauce
Salt to taste
1 cup bulgur wheat
1 (19-ounce) can kidney beans, drained

1. Heat the oil in a skillet over medium heat for 20 seconds. Add the onions and cook until translucent. Add the cumin, cinnamon, and garlic. Stir, then add the reserved tomato liquid, water, Tabasco, and salt. Cook for 5 minutes.
2. Add the bulgur, stir, and cook for 5 minutes. Chop the tomatoes and add to the skillet. Reduce the heat and simmer for 10 minutes.

Butternut Squash Soup with Apple

1 shallot
1 clove garlic
¼ cup water
3 cups cored, peeled, and cubed butternut squash
3 cups reduced-sodium, fat-free chicken broth
¾ cup apple cider
¼ cup plain nonfat yogurt
½ of an apple

1. Mince the shallot and garlic. Pour the water into a soup pot, and cook them until soft, about 2 minutes. Add the squash and the broth. Bring to a boil, then reduce to a simmer and cook for about 20 minutes.
2. In a blender or food processor, blend the mixture. Add the cider and yogurt and continue blending. Put the soup back into the pot. Dice the apple, leaving the skin on. Reheat on low.

Carrot and Parsnip Soup with Ginger

3 cups shredded carrots
3 cups shredded parsnips
1 (1-inch) piece ginger root
2 cups reduced-sodium, fat-free
   vegetable broth

¾ cup 2 percent milk
1 teaspoon lemon juice
Salt and white pepper

1. Shred the carrots, parsnips, and the peeled ginger root.
2. Using a soup pot, add the carrots, parsnips, ginger, and broth. Bring to a boil, reduce to a simmer, and cook for 25 minutes.
3. Remove from heat and allow to cool slightly. Using a blender or food processor, purée the soup. Add the milk and reheat *almost* to a boil. Add the lemon juice and salt and white pepper to taste.

> **Serves 4**
>
> Chop some fresh chives and add as a garnish to each serving of this soup.

Fennel-Tomato Soup

2 fennel bulbs
4 tomatoes
1 yellow onion
1 tablespoon olive oil

6 cups reduced-sodium, fat-free
   chicken broth
Salt and pepper

1. Cut off the feathery parts of the fennel to use as a garnish. Slice the bulbs into fourths, removing and discarding the cores. Coarsely chop the rest of the fennel. Chop the tomatoes and cut the onion into a fine dice.
2. In a soup pot, heat the oil. Sauté the onion on medium for 3 minutes. Add the chopped fennel and simmer for 10 minutes, stirring often.
3. Add the broth, tomatoes, and salt and pepper to taste if desired. Bring to a boil, reduce to a simmer, and cook for 15 minutes. Garnish with the fennel fronds, and serve.

> **Serves 6**
>
> Whenever possible, prepare vegetables just before using them in a recipe; as soon as they are cut or peeled (exposed to air), vegetables begin to lose their nutrients and flavor.

Eggplant and Carrot Soup

Serves 4

If you don't have a food processor handy, don't panic. The soup can be pureed in a blender to get the same results.

1 eggplant
8 large carrots
2 potatoes
1 stalk celery
4 yellow onions
3 cloves garlic
2 tablespoons parsley
2 tablespoons olive oil

8 cups reduced-sodium, fat-free
    vegetable broth
Salt and pepper
2 teaspoons fresh chopped
    mint (optional)

1. Peel and dice the eggplant. Peel and chop the carrots and the potatoes. Chop the celery and onions. Mince the garlic. Chop the parsley.
2. In a soup pot, heat the oil. Add the onions and garlic, and sauté on medium heat for 5 minutes. Add the eggplant and cook for 10 minutes.
3. Add the remaining vegetables and parsley to the pot, along with the broth. Bring to a boil, then reduce to a simmer and cook for 40 to 45 minutes, adding salt and pepper to taste if desired.
4. Using a blender or food processor, purée the soup. Reheat gently. Chop the mint for garnish, and serve.

Black Bean Vegetarian Chili

2½ cups dried black beans
1 yellow onion
2 stalks celery
1 green bell pepper
1 cup chopped tomatoes
4 cloves garlic
1 tablespoon chopped cilantro
7½ cups water
1 cup (8 ounces) tomato sauce

6 tablespoons tomato paste
2 tablespoons lime juice
2 tablespoons red wine vinegar
1½ teaspoons cumin
1½ teaspoons chili powder

Serves 4

For a different flavor, substitute 2 table-spoons of balsamic vinegar for the 2 tablespoons of red wine vinegar.

1. Soak the beans overnight in cold water to cover, then drain.
2. Chop the onion, celery, green bell pepper, and tomatoes. Finely chop the garlic and cilantro.
3. In a large soup pot, add the beans and the water. Bring to a boil, reduce to a simmer, and cook for 1½ hours.
4. Stir in all the remaining ingredients. Bring the mixture back to a boil, reduce to a simmer, and cook for an additional 30 minutes.

Lentil Soup with Apples

Serves 8–10

Read the label on the apple juice carefully. This recipe calls for a juice with no added sugar.

1½ cups lentils
2 medium leeks
3 stalks celery
1 onion
6 whole cloves
1 tablespoon vegetable oil
6 cups water

2 cups apple juice (with no added sugar)
1 bay leaf
1½ cups diced tart apple

1. Rinse the lentils. Slice the leeks thinly, using only the white and the light green parts. Chop the celery coarsely. Stud the onion with the cloves.
2. In a large saucepan or soup pot, heat the oil on medium. Add the leeks and sauté, stirring often for 3 minutes. Add the water and the apple juice, bringing the mixture to a boil. Add the lentils, celery, whole onion, and bay leaf. Bring the mixture back to a boil, reduce to a simmer, and cook, uncovered, for 45 minutes.
3. Toward the end of the above cooking period, peel and chop the apple. Add it to the mixture and simmer, again uncovered, for 15 more minutes. Discard the celery pieces, whole onion, and bay leaf. Serve.

Quick Soups

Miso Soup

Yields 4 cups

Miso is a paste that is mainly made up of fermented soybeans and salt. All varieties of miso can be used in making miso soup.

6 tablespoons miso paste
(any kind)

4 cups water **or** Dashi
(see recipe on page 4)

½ cup (4 ounces) tofu, cut
into ¼-inch cubes

1 scallion, sliced diagonally
into ½-inch-long pieces

Bring the water (or dashi) *almost* to a boil in a saucepan; do not let it boil. Add the miso paste and tofu pieces. Garnish with slices of scallion.

✳ Prep time: 5 minutes; cooking time: 5 minutes

Chinese Chicken Corn Soup

Serves 4

If all you have on hand is regular canned corn, simply pour the can (including the liquid) into a food processor and chop it up for a few seconds.

✺

3 cups Basic Chicken Broth
(see recipe on page 3)

1 (8¼-ounce) can creamed corn

1 cup skinned, diced, and
cooked chicken

1 tablespoon cornstarch

2 tablespoons cold water

2 egg whites

2 tablespoons finely minced
fresh parsley

1. Combine the broth, corn, and chicken pieces in a large saucepan. Bring mixture to a boil over medium heat, stirring occasionally. Whisk together the cornstarch and the cold water, then add it to the soup. Continue cooking, uncovered, for 3 minutes.
2. Beat the egg whites until foamy; stir into soup. Reduce heat to a simmer and cook until foamy. Ladle soup into individual bowls and garnish with parsley. Serve hot.

✳ Prep time: 15 minutes; cooking time: 15 minutes

Mushroom and Onion Chowder

2 tablespoons mild nut oil
   or butter
½ pound (8 ounces) mushrooms
   (any variety), coarsely
   chopped
1 medium onion, diced
1 cup diced potatoes
1 cup Basic Vegetable Broth
   (see recipe on pages 4)
¼ cup sherry
¼ teaspoon thyme

¼ teaspoon dill
¼ teaspoon ground cloves
2 cups plain yogurt
   (nonfat is fine)
Caraway seeds **or** parsley
   (optional)

> ### Serves 4
>
> If you're running low on vegetable broth, substitute it with either a cup of mushroom broth or a cup of water.
>
> ∾

1. In a soup pot, heat the oil (or butter). Add the mushrooms and onions and sauté for 3 to 4 minutes. Add the potatoes and broth (or water). Bring to a boil, then simmer for 10 to 15 minutes until the potatoes are cooked.
2. Add all the remaining ingredients and heat thoroughly, but do not boil. Garnish with caraway seeds or parsley.

✳ Prep time: 15 minutes; cooking time: 25 minutes

Cauliflower Soup with Coriander

Serves 6

Using half-and-half or whole milk instead of cream will reduce the fat in this recipe without losing the flavor.

2 cups cauliflower florets
2 potatoes
2 onions
4 cloves garlic
1-inch piece fresh ginger root
3 tablespoons oil **or** ghee
   (see page 80)
1 teaspoon ground cumin
2 teaspoon ground coriander
¼ teaspoon ground turmeric

⅓ teaspoon (or more) cayenne
   pepper
8 cups Basic Chicken Broth
   (see recipe on page 3)
1 teaspoon salt
1 cup cream
Salt and pepper to taste

1. Cut the cauliflower into florets. Peel and dice the potatoes into a ½-inch dice. Chop the onions and garlic. Peel and thinly slice the ginger root.
2. In a soup pot, heat the oil. Add the onions, ginger, and garlic, and sauté on medium heat until the onions are golden brown. Add all the spices, stirring for 1 minute longer. Add the potatoes, cauliflower, broth, and salt. Cook for 10 minutes.
3. Remove from heat and allow to cool slightly. Purée the mixture in a blender or food processor. Stir in the cream and add salt and pepper to taste, reheating gently just before serving.

✳ Prep time: 15 minutes; cooking time: 20–25 minutes

Hearty Ground Turkey and Vegetable Soup

1 pound ground turkey
1 small onion, chopped
1 small green pepper, chopped
1 (16-ounce) can green beans
1 (16-ounce) can diced potatoes
1 (16-ounce) can stewed
 tomatoes
1 can tomato soup
Salt and pepper to taste

Brown the turkey in a Dutch oven until cooked through. Add the onion and green pepper. Mix in the green beans, diced potatoes, stewed tomatoes, and the tomato soup. Heat until warmed through, about 15 minutes. Add salt and pepper to taste.

✳ Prep time: 15 minutes; cooking time: 25 minutes

Serves 4

A Dutch oven is a cast iron pot that is useful for slow cooking in an oven. You can pick one up at your nearest kitchen store.

Peanut Butter Soup

3 tablespoons butter
2 tablespoons minced onion
1 tablespoon flour
1 cup peanut butter
Salt and pepper
4 cups Basic Chicken Broth
 (see recipe on page 3)
1 cup heavy whipping cream
1 tablespoon Madeira wine

In a large saucepan, melt the butter over medium-low heat and sauté the onion until soft. Whisk in the flour and cook, stirring constantly, until smooth. Stir in the peanut butter and add the broth. Season to taste with salt and pepper. Cook, stirring, over low heat until thickened and smooth. Add the cream. Just before serving, stir in the Madeira.

✳ Prep time: 15 minutes; cook time: 10 minutes

Serves 4

No need to be choosy with this soup. Plain or crunchy peanut butter can be used.

Pinto Bean Soup

Serves 4

Garnish each serving with a dollop of sour cream.

4 tablespoons butter
¼ cup finely chopped onions
2 tablespoons finely chopped and seeded green bell pepper
2 tomatoes, finely chopped
1 teaspoon finely chopped garlic
1 teaspoon finely chopped fresh cilantro
1 teaspoon red chili powder
1 pinch cayenne pepper

1 tablespoon tomato paste
1 (10-ounce) can cooked pinto beans
4 cups Basic Chicken **or** Beef Broth (see recipes on pages 3 and 2)
Salt and pepper to taste
4 teaspoons sour cream (optional)

1. Melt the butter in a large saucepan over medium heat. Add the onions, green bell peppers, tomatoes, and garlic. Cover the pan with a lid and simmer for 4 minutes.
2. Add the cilantro, red chili powder, cayenne pepper, and tomato paste. Stir the ingredients together and simmer for 3 minutes.
3. Add the pinto beans, broth, and salt and pepper to taste. Bring to a boil and cook vigorously for 4 minutes, or until the beans are heated through.

✳ Prep time: 15 minutes; cooking time: 15 minutes

Tuna Chowder

2 tablespoons butter
3 stalks celery, chopped
1 large onion, chopped
1 large potato, diced
3 tablespoons flour
3 cups milk
*2 (6½-ounce) cans water-
    packed tuna*

*¼ pound (4 ounces) cheddar
    cheese, grated*
1 teaspoon thyme
1 teaspoon dill
Salt and pepper
*¼ cup fresh chopped parsley
    (optional)*

> **Serves 6**
>
> For added color and flavor, garnish each serving with chopped fresh parsley.
>
>

1. In a large soup pot, melt the butter; sauté the celery, onion, and potato until the potato is tender. Whisk in the flour until smooth. Add the milk and blend thoroughly. Cook for 5 minutes, stirring, until the mixture thickens.
2. Add the tuna, cheese, thyme, and dill. Season with salt and pepper to taste. Heat over medium-low for 5 to 10 minutes.

✳ Prep time: 15 minutes; cooking time: 20 minutes

Very Quick Sausage and Vegetable Soup

*2 cups Basic Beef Broth
    (see recipe on page 2)*
*1 (14½-ounce) can Italian stewed
    tomatoes, including liquid*
1½ cups water
*2 cups frozen hash brown
    potatoes*

*1 (10-ounce) package frozen
    mixed vegetables*
*½ pound (8 ounces) smoked
    sausage, sliced*
⅛ teaspoon pepper
Salt to taste
*2 tablespoons grated parmesan
    cheese (optional)*

> **Serves 4**
>
> While the grated parmesan cheese is considered optional for this recipe, it is highly recommended.
>
>

Combine the broth, undrained tomatoes, and water in a large saucepan. Bring to a boil. Stir in the potatoes, vegetables, sausage, pepper, and salt to taste. Return to boiling. Reduce heat and simmer, covered, for 5 to 10 minutes. Sprinkle with cheese when in bowls.

✳ Prep time: 15 minutes; cooking time: 20 minutes

Nigerian Peanut Soup

2 cups water
2 (2-ounce) packets instant chicken broth and seasoning mix
1½ small dried green chili peppers, finely chopped

¼ cup diced and seeded green bell pepper
¼ cup diced onion
3 tablespoons chunky-style peanut butter

1. Heat the water in saucepan; dissolve the broth mix in the water. Add the chili peppers and bring mixture to a boil. Stir in the bell pepper and onion and return to a boil. Reduce heat to low, cover, and simmer until vegetables are tender, about 10 minutes.
2. Reduce heat to lowest setting; add the peanut butter and cook, stirring constantly, until the peanut butter is melted and mixture is well blended.

✳ Prep time: 15 minutes; cooking time: 15 minutes

Spring Asparagus Soup

1 bunch thin spring asparagus
4 cups shrimp broth

Raw peas (optional)
Sour cream (optional)

Chop the asparagus into 1-inch lengths, keeping the tips separate. Bring the broth to a simmer and add all the asparagus *except* for the tips; simmer for 4 minutes. Add the tips and cook 1 additional minute. Pour into bowls and toss in a few raw peas. Top each bowl with a dollop of sour cream.

✳ Prep time: 5 minutes; cooking time: 10 minutes

Cauliflower and Mushroom Soup

1¼ pounds cauliflower
½ pound (8 ounces) cremini
    mushrooms
2 cloves garlic
2 tablespoons olive oil
5 cups water

⅓ cup whole milk
Salt and pepper
4 tablespoons walnut, almond,
    or avocado oil

Serves 6

If you're fresh out of walnut oil, you can substitute it with either almond oil or avocado oil.

1. Cut the cauliflower into florets. Cut the mushrooms into ½-inch slices and mince the garlic.
2. In a soup pot, heat the olive oil on medium. Add the mushrooms and sauté for 5 minutes. Add the garlic and sauté for 1 more minute. Pour in the water and add the cauliflower. Bring to a boil, then reduce to a simmer and cook for 6 more minutes.
3. Remove from heat and allow to cool slightly. In a blender or food processor, purée the mixture. Pour it back into the soup pot over medium heat. Drizzle in the milk and add salt and pepper to taste. Just before serving, garnish each serving bowl with 1–2 teaspoons of the flavored oil.

✳ Prep time: 10 minutes; cooking time: 15 minutes

Flavored Oils

To infuse oil with flavor and complexity, stuff herbs, spices, and garlic cloves into a bottle of it, and steep for at least three days, or up to two weeks or more. Fine olive oil is transformed into a heavenly condiment when perfumed by rosemary, thyme, savory, garlic, peppercorns, dried mushrooms, or truffles. You can also buy infused oils at gourmet stores.

Quick Pea Soup

Serves 4–6

Thaw frozen vegetables before you will use them in a recipe. More than 2 cups of frozen vegetables could cause the food to heat too slowly at the beginning of the cooking process.

ॐ

2 stalks celery
1 medium onion (yellow **or** white)
2 tablespoons butter **or** oil
2 cups Basic Vegetable Broth (see recipe on page 4)
1 (16-ounce) bag frozen baby peas
½ teaspoon garlic powder **or** 2 cloves garlic, minced
White pepper

½ cup milk (any type)
½ teaspoon nutmeg, plus extra for garnish (both optional)
Lemon peel (optional)

1. Chop the celery and onion. In a soup pot, melt the butter on medium heat. Add the celery and onion, sautéing for 2 to 3 minutes. Pour in the broth, peas, garlic, and pepper. Bring to a boil, reduce to a simmer, and cook for 5 minutes.

2. Remove from heat and allow to cool slightly. Using a food processor or blender, purée the mixture. Rewarm it in the soup pot with the milk and nutmeg (if using), stirring constantly for 3 to 5 minutes; do not allow it to boil. Garnish with grated lemon peel and a sprinkling of nutmeg.

✳ Prep time: 10 minutes; cooking time: 15 minutes

Chickpea Soup with Cumin

*3 (15½-ounce) cans chickpeas
  (also called garbanzo
  beans)*
1 tablespoon olive oil
*½ teaspoon garlic powder **or**
  2 cloves garlic, minced*
*2½ cups Basic Chicken Broth
  (see recipe on page 3)*

1 tablespoon cumin
Freshly ground black pepper
2 teaspoons lemon juice

Serves 4

You can substitute 2 cloves of minced garlic for ½ teaspoon of garlic powder. Sauté the garlic for about 3 minutes on a lightly oiled skillet.

---

1. Drain and rinse the chickpeas In a saucepan or soup pot, heat the oil. Slowly add the garlic, chickpeas, broth, cumin, and pepper to taste, stirring. Heat to *near* boiling, then remove from heat and allow to cool slightly.
2. Using a blender or food processor, purée the mixture. Reheat, stirring in the lemon juice just before removing from the heat.

✳ Prep time: 5 minutes; cooking time: 5 minutes

Ethnic Soups

Thai Shrimp Soup

Serves 6–8

Rmember, you can freeze the shrimp shells to make broth for another time.

5 lime leaves
2 tablespoons dried lemongrass
40 raw shrimp in their shells
10 cups water
1 onion
½ pound (8 ounces) small
    button mushrooms
2 tablespoons shrimp paste
2 tablespoons Thai chili

6 tablespoons lemon juice
1 tablespoon Thai fish sauce
    (nam pla)
6 sprigs coriander leaves

1. Soak the lime leaves and the lemongrass in water overnight, or for at least several hours.
2. Peel and devein the shrimp (leave their tails on). Set the shrimp aside. Place the shells, the water, and the onion (cut in half, peel on) in a large saucepan. Bring to a boil and cook over medium-high heat, uncovered, for 15 minutes.
3. Strain the liquid into a soup pot and discard the solids. Drain the lime leaves and lemongrass, discarding the liquid; then add them to the pot. Bring to a boil, reduce to a simmer, and cook for 15 minutes. Add the whole mushrooms and simmer for 1 more minute.
4. In a small bowl, combine the shrimp paste, chili, and lemon juice; add it to the soup pot. Add the fish sauce and the uncooked shrimp. Bring to a boil, reduce to a simmer, and cook for 1 minute. Add the coriander leaves and simmer for 1 additional minute.

Spanish Mussel Soup

1 cup onion
2 cloves garlic
2 cups chopped spinach
1 tomato
½ cup olive oil
½ teaspoon rosemary
½ teaspoon black pepper

½ teaspoon ground coriander
3 pounds of mussels
6½ cups Fish Broth
(see recipe on page 6)

Serves 6–8

This recipe is equally good with virtually any of your favorite shellfish.

1. Chop the onions, garlic, and spinach. Seed and dice the tomato.
2. In a soup pot, heat the olive oil. Sauté the onion and garlic on medium for 3 minutes, then add the spinach, tomato, and rosemary, and stir for 3 more minutes. Stir in the pepper and coriander and take the pot off the heat.
3. Scrub the mussels and remove their beards. In a large pan, bring the fish broth to a boil; add the mussels, cover tightly, and turn off the heat. Check in a few minutes to see if they have been steamed open. Once they have, remove the meat from the mussel shells. Discard the shells. Strain the broth and discard all solids.
4. Add the mussel meat and the strained broth to the vegetables. Bring to a boil, reduce to a simmer, and cook for 5 minute. Remove from heat and allow to cool slightly. Using a blender or food processor, purée the mixture. Reheat and serve.

Vietnamese Crab and Pineapple Soup

1 cooked Dungeness Crab
15 medium-sized raw shrimp
15 medium-sized steamer clams
1 cup cubed fresh pineapple
½ of an onion
4 cloves garlic
½ pound (8 ounces) ripe
    tomatoes
2 scallions
4 sprigs cilantro
5 basil leaves
3 sprigs dill
6 mint leaves
3 tablespoons olive oil

10 cups water
1 stalk lemongrass
3 tablespoons Vietnamese
    fish sauce
2 tablespoons sugar
½ teaspoon chili garlic sauce
    (if you can find it)
Salt
2 tablespoons lime juice
1 pinch of saffron
1 bay leaf

1. Remove the meat from the crab, peel and devein the shrimp (leaving their tails on), and scrub the clamshells. Cut the pineapple into bite-sized chunks. Chop the onion, crush the garlic cloves, and seed and chop the tomatoes. Chop the scallions, cilantro, basil leaves, dill, and mint.

2. Using a soup pot, heat the oil. Add the onion and sauté on medium for 3 minutes. Add the garlic and tomatoes, cooking for 3 more minutes. Add the pineapple, water, and lemongrass, bringing everything to a boil. Reduce to a simmer and cook for 20 minutes.

3. Add the fish sauce, sugar, chili garlic sauce, salt, and lime juice. Bring to a boil. Add the clams in their shells and the crab, cooking for about 5 minutes, until the clams open.

4. Add the shrimp, saffron, cilantro, bay leaf, basil, dill, mint, and scallions. Simmer for 2 to 3 more minutes, until the shrimp turn pink. Discard the bay leaf and lemongrass stalk and serve.

Crab Cioppino Soup

2 cooked Dungeness crab

1 cup onion

1 (28-ounce) can peeled tomatoes, including liquid

3 cloves garlic

3 teaspoons fresh chopped
basil leaves

2 tablespoons olive oil

¼ teaspoon oregano

1 bay leaf

1 cup dry white wine

1 cup Fish Broth (see recipe
on page 6)

Salt

Serves 4

For an alternate flavor
in this soup, substitute
1 cup of Chicken
Broth (page 3) for the
1 cup of Fish Broth.

---

1. Remove the crabmeat from the shells and discard the shells (or freeze them for making broth another day). Chop the onion and the tomatoes, reserving the juice. Mince the garlic and chop the basil leaves.

2. In a soup pot, heat the olive oil. Add the onion, sautéing on medium for 3 minutes. Add the tomatoes and their liquid, oregano, basil, bay leaf, wine, broth, and half of the minced garlic. Bring to a boil, reduce to a simmer, and cook for 30 minutes.

3. Add the rest of the garlic, the crab, and the salt, simmering for 1 to 2 minutes. Discard the bay leaf and serve.

Asian Salmon in the Oven Soup

Serves 6

Garnish each bowl with some of the chopped cilantro, scallions, and sesame seeds.

4 cloves garlic
2 tablespoons ginger root
4 cups shredded cabbage and
   carrots
⅓ cup cilantro
3 scallions
8 cups (2 quarts) clam juice
2 tablespoons tamari **or**
   soy sauce

½ teaspoon ground coriander
1½ pounds salmon fillets
   (about 1 inch thick)
2 teaspoons sesame seeds
   (optional)

1. Preheat oven to 375 degrees. Mince the garlic, peel the ginger, and grate the cabbage and carrots together. Chop the cilantro and scallions.
2. Using a saucepan, stir together the clam juice, tamari (or soy sauce), garlic, ginger, and coriander. Bring to a boil, reduce to a simmer, and cook for 5 minutes. Set aside, covered to keep the mixture warm.
3. In deep baking dish large enough to hold all the ingredients, spread the grated cabbage and carrot mixture in a layer. Place the salmon fillets on top, skin side down. Pour the clam juice broth over the salmon. Loosely cover the baking dish with foil and cook for 18 minutes.
4. With a spatula, transfer the salmon fillets to the centers of the individual serving bowls. Divide the cooked vegetables among the bowls, then the cooking liquid.

German Frankfurter and Lentil Soup

1 ham bone
2 stalks celery
2 carrots
1½ cups green **or** brown dried lentils
8 cups Basic Beef Broth (see recipe on page 2)

1 tablespoon black peppercorns
2 medium onions
6 frankfurters
2 tablespoon butter

1. Crack the ham bone. Chop the celery and carrots.
2. In a soup pot, combine the lentils, beef broth, ham bone, celery, carrots, and peppercorns. Bring to a boil, reduce to a simmer, and cook for 1½ hours. Skim off the impurities every few minutes until no more rises to the top.
3. Remove from heat, discarding the ham bone. Force the mixture through a coarse sieve and discard the solids. Return the strained soup to the pot. Slice the onions thinly. Cut the frankfurters diagonally into ½-inch slices.
4. In a small saucepan, heat the butter. Sauté the onions for 3 minutes on medium, then add the frankfurter slices and cook for another 3 minutes.
5. Add the onion and frankfurter mixture to the soup pot. Return it to heat and simmer for 5 minutes.

Chinese Pork and Pickle Soup

Serves 4

For better flavor, use a good quality dry sherry wine instead of so-called "cooking sherry."

2 pork chops
1 tablespoon sesame oil
1 tablespoon sherry
1 tablespoon dark soy sauce
Pepper
¼ pound (4 ounces) Chinese
   preserved vegetable*

4 cups Basic Chicken Broth
   (see recipe on page 3)
2 scallions

1. Debone the pork chops and trim off the fat (discard the bones and fat). Using a sharp knife, cut the meat into the thinnest slices. In a bowl, toss the meat with the oil, sherry, soy sauce, and pepper, coating all the pieces. Refrigerate for 45 minutes.
2. Pour the sauce off the preserved vegetable, discarding the sauce. Thinly slice the vegetable.
3. Pour the broth in a soup pot. Bring to a boil, reduce to a simmer, and add the meat and the vegetable. Stir to separate the meat slices. Cook for 10 minutes.
4. Finely chop the scallions, including the green parts. Stir in and cook for 1 more minute.

* Look for a jar of any such Chinese version; similar to the hot Korean *Kim Chi*, these are like pickles.

Hungarian Goulash with Sour Cream

1½ pounds beef (chuck or
   blade steak)
2 onions
1 pound tomatoes
1 bouquet garni (see "Bag o'
   Spices" on page 8)
¼ cup oil (**or** lard)
2 tablespoons flour

1 cup dry red wine
1 cup Basic Beef Broth
   (see recipe on page 2)
2 tablespoons Hungarian
   paprika
1 pound potatoes
½ cup sour cream

> **Serves 6**
>
> The word goulash refers to a random mixture. This Hungarian-born dish consists of some sort of meat in a thick, gravylike sauce, seasoned with paprika.
>
>

1. Trim off the excess fat from the meat and cut it into ¾-inch cubes. Slice the onions and seed and dice the tomatoes. Prepare the bouquet garni using your choice of fresh herbs.
2. Preheat oven to 325 degrees. In an oven-ready casserole dish or soup pot, heat the fat. Sauté the meat on medium high until browned on all sides. Remove the meat, setting it aside but reserving the fat in the pot.
3. Add the onions and sauté on medium for 3 minutes. Whisk in the flour and simmer for 2 minutes more. Whisk in ¼ cup of the broth and stir well. Add the rest of the broth, the wine, tomatoes, paprika, and bouquet garni; Bring to a boil. Transfer it to the oven and bake for 1½ hours.
4. Meanwhile, peel and cube the potatoes. Stir them into the oven mixture when the 1½ hours are up. Cook for another 30 minutes. Remove and discard the bouquet garni, stir in the sour cream, and serve.

German Beef and Cabbage Soup

3 pounds beef
1 cup shredded white cabbage
1 onion
2 carrots
1 small turnip
1 medium parsley root
½ of a small celery root
2 tomatoes
3 pounds beef bones

12 cups (3 quarts) beef broth
⅛ pound (2 ounces) beef liver (optional)
5 black peppercorns
Salt and black pepper

1. Wipe the beef off with a damp cloth and leave it whole. Shred the cabbage. Slice the onion, carrots, turnip, and parsley root. Peel and dice the celery root. Cut the tomatoes into quarters.
2. Rinse the beef bones in cold water. Bring a large pot of water to a boil and plunge the bones into it. Once it returns to a boil, drain immediately and rinse the bones in cold water again.
3. In a soup pot, combine the broth, the beef, the beef bones, and all remaining ingredients. Bring to a boil, reduce to a simmer, and cook for 2 hours.
4. Strain and reserve all solid ingredients except for the bones. Chill the broth until the fat layer solidifies and can be removed (several hours or overnight). Remove and discard the fat, then reheat the broth with all the cooked ingredients. Add salt and pepper to taste and serve.

Vietnamese Beef and Red Curry Soup

2 pounds flank steak
16 cups (4 quarts) water
4 star anise
1-inch section of cinnamon stick
8 ounces rice sticks (dried
  noodles, ¼-inch wide)
2 tablespoons peanut oil
2 tablespoons red curry paste
Salt

1 teaspoon sugar
Bean sprouts
1 lime
Fish sauce

> ### Serves 6–8
>
> Garnish by drizzling in
> small amount of fish
> sauce and adding
> some bean sprouts
> and lime wedges to
> each bowl.
>
>

1. Cut the meat into thin, 1½-inch long slices.
2. Place the beef pieces in a large pot with enough water to cover. Bring just to a boil, then drain. Rinse the meat. Place the meat back into the pot with the 4 quarts of fresh water. Add the star anise and the cinnamon stick. Bring to a boil, reduce to a simmer, and cook for 3½ hours.
3. Meanwhile, place the dried noodles in a bowl, covering them with hot water. Set aside.
4. When the meat is ready, heat the oil in a small saucepan. Stir in the curry paste, cooking for a couple of minutes. Add this mixture to the meat mixture. Add salt and the sugar, simmering everything for 20 minutes. Meanwhile, coarsely chop the bean sprouts and cut the lime into thin wedges.
5. Drain the noodles and divide them among individual serving bowls. Pour in the soup.

Caribbean Beef Soup

Serves 12

The pear-shaped chayote is one of the smallest—and sweetest—of the squash varieties.

1½ pounds beef
½ an onion
½ green bell pepper
1 stalk celery
1 teaspoon ginger root
5 cloves garlic
1 chili pepper (any kind)
4 sprigs cilantro
4 tomatoes
3 plantains
1 sweet potato
½ pound butternut squash

3 new potatoes
1 chayote squash
3 ears corn (white if available)
3 tablespoons oil
1 dash cumin
Salt
¼ teaspoon white pepper
⅓ cup dry red wine
16 cups (4 quarts) Basic Beef
   Broth, divided (see recipe
   on page 2)

1. Cut the beef into 1½-inch cubes. Chop the onion, green bell pepper, and celery. Mince the ginger and garlic. Seed and mince the chili. Chop the cilantro and tomatoes. Slice the plantains into ¾-inch pieces. Cut the sweet potato and the butternut squash into 1-inch pieces. Quarter the new potatoes. Core the chayote and dice it into 1-inch pieces. Slice each of the corn ears into 6 pieces.
2. In a soup pot, heat the oil. Add the garlic, beef, and onions, and sauté on medium for 8 minutes. Add the green pepper, celery, ginger, chili pepper, cilantro, cumin, salt, white pepper, wine, tomatoes, and 4 cups of the beef broth. Bring to a boil, reduce to a simmer, and cook for 40 minutes. Add the squashes, potatoes, remaining beef broth, and corn; simmer for 30 to 45 minutes more.

German Beef and Sauerkraut Soup

2 cups diced potato
1 cup chopped yellow onion
½ cup carrots
1 stalk celery
1 clove garlic
2 tablespoons fresh chopped
  flat-leaf parsley
2 tablespoons olive oil
1 pound (16 ounces) beef
  stew meat
1½ cups Basic Beef Broth
  (see recipe on page 2)

1 (14-ounce) can peeled, diced
  tomatoes, including liquid
¾ cup (6 ounces) beer
¼ cup dry red wine
½ cup sauerkraut in juice
1 bay leaf
⅛ teaspoon thyme
¼ teaspoon pepper
1 tablespoon butter
1 tablespoon flour

Serves 4

Look for a dark German beer at your local liquor store. It adds just the right touch in this recipe.

ॐ

---

1. Dice the potatoes. Chop the onion, shred the carrot, and chop the celery. Mince the garlic and chop the parsley.
2. In a soup pot, heat the oil. Add the beef, browning it on all sides on medium–high heat. Pour in the broth. Add all the remaining ingredients *except* the butter and flour. Bring to a boil, reduce to a simmer, and skim off any impurities that rise to the surface. Cover the pot and simmer for 2 hours.
3. Heat the butter in a small pan, then whisk in the flour. Stir it constantly for 3 minutes. Take off heat. Spoon in a little of the soup broth and whisk to a paste; whisk the paste into the soup pot. Simmer, uncovered, for 10 more minutes. Remove bay leaf before serving.

Japanese Chicken Soup

Serves 4

Sake is a Japanese white wine made from rice. When ordered as a beverage, it's usually served hot.

1 large chicken breast
2 large mushroom caps, sliced
1 scallion, sliced
1 teaspoon sake (dry sherry can be substituted)
¾ teaspoon cornstarch
½ teaspoon peanut oil

4 cups Fish Broth (see recipe on page 6)
1 teaspoon soy sauce
½ teaspoon sesame oil

1. Remove the skin and bones from the chicken breast, discarding them. Cut the meat diagonally into 8 strips. Slice the mushroom caps into thin strips. Cut the scallion into thin slices.
2. In a bowl, toss the chicken pieces with the sake and the cornstarch. In a soup pot, quick sauté (on high heat) the chicken strips in the olive oil. Remove the chicken with a slotted spoon and add the broth to the pot; bring to a boil, scraping up any cooked-on bits from the bottom of the pan. Reduce to a simmer and return the chicken strips to the pot; cook for 10 minutes. Add the scallions and mushrooms, simmering for an additional 5 minutes. Stir in the soy sauce and sesame oil, and serve.

Matzo Ball Soup

4 eggs
4 tablespoons olive oil
16½ cups Basic Chicken Broth,
    divided (see recipe on
    page 3)

1 cup matzo meal
Salt and black pepper

> **Serves 6–8**
>
> Moisten your hands with cold water before shaping the chilled matzo mixture into balls.
>
>

1. In a bowl, mix together the eggs, olive oil, ½ cup of the chicken broth, and the matzo meal. Refrigerate for at least 1 hour.
2. In a large pot, bring salted water to boil. Form 28 small matzo balls from the chilled dough. Add them to the boiling water, and simmer for 35 minutes.
3. In a soup pot, bring the remaining broth to a boil. Place several matzo balls in each individual soup bowl. Pour the hot chicken broth over the matzo balls and serve.

What Does "Lightly Salted Water" Really Mean?

Lightly salted water tastes like tears. Thoroughly salted water tastes like seawater. For foods that absorb a lot of water as they cook, like beans or pasta, lightly salted is the way to go, since your aim is to draw out the natural flavors of the food, not to make them "salty." For foods that don't absorb water, such as green vegetables, the point is to use salt's properties of sealing in nutrients, color, and flavor. For that reason, you would salt the water more assertively. Excess salt can easily be washed from those vegetables. Make no mistake, though: Salt is an important part of coaxing the best flavors from your good ingredients.

German Lentil and Bacon Soup

Serves 8–10

You can use diced, cooked ham instead of the ham bone. Simply add about ½–1 cup of meat at the end of step 4.

1 pound (16 ounces) dried
   lentils
12 cups water
1 meaty ham bone
3 onions
4 stalks celery, with leaves
1 bay leaf

½ teaspoon thyme
1 potato
3 carrots
6 strips bacon (commercial soy
   bits can be substituted)
Salt and pepper

1. Rinse the lentils. Put the lentils and water in a large soup pot with the ham bone, 2 of the whole onions, 3 of the whole stalks of celery with their leaves, the bay leaf, and the thyme. As this mixture is coming to a boil, peel and grate the potato and add it to the pot. Bring the mixture completely to a boil, reduce to a simmer, and cook for 3 hours, stirring regularly.

2. When the soup has only about 30 minutes left to cook, thinly slice the carrots. In a small saucepan, cover them with water and simmer them for 15 minutes. Drain and set aside.

3. In a skillet, sauté the bacon on medium heat. Leaving the bacon grease in the pan, transfer the bacon to paper towels to absorb the grease. Coarsely chop the remaining onion and slice the remaining celery. Sauté them in the bacon fat on low heat for 5 minutes, without allowing them to brown. Using a slotted spoon, transfer them to paper towels to drain. Discard the bacon fat.

4. When the mixture in the soup pot is done cooking, reduce the heat to the lowest setting. Remove the whole onion, whole celery, bay leaf, and ham bone from the soup pot; discard everything *except* the ham bone. Cut the meat from the bone and add the meat back into the pot. Stir in the sautéed carrots and celery. Add salt and pepper to taste. Crumble the bacon on top of the soup in a tureen or individual bowls.

French Lentils and Rice Soup

¼ *pound uncooked long-grained*
   rice
4 *carrots*
2 *onions*
1 *small head lettuce*
¼ *pound (4 ounces) dried red*
   lentils
2 *tablespoons butter*

6 *cups Basic Chicken Broth*
   (see recipe on page 3)
⅔ *cup white bread crumbs*
Salt and pepper

Serves 8

About ½ pound of kale or spinach can be used in place of the lettuce. Be aware, however, that this will add a lot more flavor to the final soup.

1. Cook the rice according to the package directions. Drain, rinse under cold water, and drain again. Set aside.
2. Cut the carrots and onions into thin slices. Shred the lettuce. Rinse the lentils.
3. Using a large saucepan or soup pot, heat the butter. Add the carrot and onion pieces and sauté for 3 to 5 minutes on medium heat. Add the lentils and the broth, stirring well. Bring to a boil, reduce to a simmer and cook for 20 minutes.
4. Add the lettuce, bread crumbs, and salt and pepper to taste. Bring to a boil, reduce to a simmer, and cook for 10 minutes.
5. Remove from heat and allow to cool slightly. In a blender or food processor, purée the soup. Reheat it the serving temperature, along with the rice.

Madras Curried Tomato and Lentil Soup

Serves 6–8

If you're having problems finding curry leaves, try substituting 2 tablespoons of ground coriander.

1 pound Italian plum tomatoes
1 tablespoon minced onion
2 teaspoons fresh minced
  garlic
3 cups cooked lentils
1 cup water
1 teaspoon cumin
¼ teaspoon cayenne
Coarse salt
1 tablespoon lemon juice

1 tablespoon ghee
  (see page 80) **or** nut oil
1 teaspoon black mustard
  seeds
8 fresh **or** dried curry leaves
  (kari)

1. Peel and halve the tomatoes. Scoop the pulp and seeds into a blender or food processor and purée. Set aside the purée and the rest of the tomato parts. Mince the onion and garlic.
2. Pour the water into a soup pot. Add the lentils and whisk, to crush some of the cooked lentils. Add the puréed tomato, the cumin, cayenne, onion, garlic, and salt. Bring to a boil, reduce to a simmer, and cook for 10 minutes.
3. Add the lemon juice and the tomato halves. Simmer for 1 more minute. Cover and remove from heat.
4. Using a small saucepan that has a lid, heat the ghee until very hot. Add the mustard seeds gradually (you may need to put the lid on since the seeds may jump out of the pan). Once they stop spattering, add the curry leaves. Turn the heat off. Shake the pan back and forth a few times. Ladle the soup into serving bowls and garnish with the mustard seed mixture.

Indian Kohlrabi, Green Tomato, and Lentil Soup

1⅓ cups tomatoes

1 pound (16 ounces) kohlrabi

½ pound (8 ounces) hard, green unripe tomatoes

1 onion

3 tablespoons fresh chopped coriander

4½ cups cooked yellow lentils

1 tablespoon crushed dry fenugreek leaves

*8 dried **or** fresh curry leaves*

1 tablespoon sambaar powder

1 tablespoon ground coriander

4 tablespoons light sesame oil

1 teaspoon black mustard seeds

1 teaspoon coarse salt

Serves 8

Curry powder can be substituted for the sanbaar powder but it is milder and less authentic.

---

1. Purée the 1⅓ cups of tomatoes. Peel and slice the kohlrabi. Slice the green tomatoes and the onion. Chop the fresh coriander.

2. Combine the cooked lentils with cold water to make a total of 6 cups. Using a soup pot, combine the lentils, the puréed tomatoes, fenugreek leaves, sambaar, and the *ground* coriander. Bring to a boil, reduce to a simmer, and cover; cook for 10 minutes.

3. Add the kohlrabi and simmer for an additional 10 minutes. Add the green tomatoes and onion and simmer for 5 more minutes. Remove from heat.

4. Using a small saucepan with a lid, heat the sesame oil to a high temperature. Add the mustard seeds, using the lid to keep them from popping out, if necessary. When the seeds stop spattering, remove from heat. Stir in the salt and *fresh* chopped coriander. Pour this mixture into the soup pot. Stir well and serve.

Hot and Sour Chinese Soup

Serves 6

This traditional Chinese soup can also be made with chicken or beef.

3 cups Basic Chicken Broth
　(see recipe on page 3)
1 tablespoon soy sauce
4 dried Chinese mushrooms,
　boiled for 15 minutes, then
　cut into strips
1 (6-ounce) can bamboo
　shoots, drained
¼ pound lean pork, cut into
　strips

1 cake tofu, cut into strips
1 teaspoon white pepper
2 tablespoons lemon juice
3 tablespoons cornstarch
3 tablespoons cold water
1 egg, lightly beaten
1 tablespoon sesame oil
2 stalks scallions, chopped

1. In a soup pot, mix together the broth, soy sauce, mushrooms, bamboo shoots, and pork. Bring to a boil; reduce the heat and simmer for 5 minutes. Add the tofu, pepper, and lemon juice; bring to a boil.
2. Whisk together the cornstarch and water until smooth; add it to the soup and boil, stirring constantly, until it thickens slightly. Reduce heat and stir the egg into the broth. Remove the pot from the heat; stir in the sesame oil and sprinkle with scallions.

Beef Bourguignon

¼–½ pound (4–8 ounces)
  bacon chunk with rind
2 tablespoons olive oil
3 pounds raw beef
1 onion
1 carrot
Salt and pepper
2 tablespoons flour
3 cups dry red wine
3–4 cloves garlic

3 cups Basic Beef Broth
  (see recipe on page 2)
2 tablespoons tomato paste
1 pinch of thyme
1 bay leaf
20 pearl onions
1 pound (16 ounces) fresh
  cremini, Portobello, or button
  mushrooms

Serves 6

This is as classic a French dish as bouilla-baisse. Considered a stew, it can easily incorporate a bit more liquid and become a soup.

1. Preheat the oven to 450 degrees. Cut the rind off the bacon, reserving the rind. Slice the bacon meat into strips. Bring 6–8 cups of water to a boil; add the rind and the bacon meat, and simmer for 10 minutes. Drain, discard the liquid and rind, and pat the bacon meat dry.

2. In a large saucepan, warm the olive oil on medium heat. Sauté the bacon meat for 2 minutes to brown it slightly. With a fork, remove the bacon from pan and set it aside.

3. Cut the beef into 2-inch cubes and pat them dry with paper towels. Heat the bacon drippings on medium and sauté the beef, turning it several times to brown it on all sides. Remove the beef and set it aside with the bacon.

4. Slice the onion and carrot. Add them to the same oil to sauté for 4 minutes. Discard the oil, leaving the vegetables in the pan.

5. Using a large stove top- and ovenproof container with a lid, place the bacon and beef in the bottom. Sprinkle on salt, pepper, and the flour, rubbing them into the meats. Without its lid, place the dish in the oven for 4 minutes. Remove, toss the meats slightly and cook for 4 more minutes. Take out of the oven. Reduce oven temperature to 325 degrees.

(continued)

6. Pour the wine and 2 cups of the broth over the meats. Mash the garlic and add it to the mixture, along with the tomato paste and herbs. Place the dish on the top of the stove, bringing it to a boil. Reduce to a simmer. Put the lid on the dish and place it back in the oven for 2½ hours, making sure it simmers very gently.

7. Meanwhile, heat the remaining broth in a saucepan. Simmer the pearl onions gently for 5 minutes. Quarter the mushrooms and add them, cooking the mixture for another 7 minutes. When the meat is ready, strain the casserole and discard most of the liquid, leaving just enough to create the thickness of soup. Skim off any fat. Place the onions and mushrooms on top, rewarm in the oven for 5 minutes, and serve. Discard the bay leaf.

Hungarian Beef Soup

Serves 6

Use leftover beef, cutting it into cubes. If you have raw beef, cut it up more finely, and cook it quite thoroughly before adding it to the other ingredients.

2 onions
4 small potatoes
4 carrots
2 stalks celery
2 small turnips
3 small tomatoes (but not cherry or cocktail ones)
3 tablespoons nut oil

1 teaspoon paprika (Hungarian is best)
1 tablespoon caraway seeds
4 cups Veal Broth (see recipe on page 11)
2 cups cubed cooked beef
1 cup plain yogurt

1. Finely dice the onions, potatoes, carrots, celery, turnips, and tomatoes.

2. In a soup pot, heat the oil. Sauté the onions on medium for 3 minutes, then add all the vegetables, the paprika, and the caraway seeds. Add the broth. Bring to a boil, reduce to a simmer, and cook for 10 minutes. Add the meat and simmer for another 5 minutes. Take it off the heat. Gradually whisk in the yogurt, and serve.

CHAPTER 16
Chilled Soups and Desserts

Chilled Tomato Soup with Guacamole

Serves 4–6

For an alternate flavor, substitute onion salt for the celery salt.

1 leek
1 stalk celery
1 bulb fennel (small)
1 red bell pepper
½ a Spanish onion
15 large beefsteak tomatoes
5 cloves garlic
1 sprig thyme
1 sprig rosemary
3 sprigs parsley
2 sprigs basil
4 dried fennel sticks

1 tablespoon anise seeds
2 teaspoons fennel seeds
1 teaspoon coriander seeds
3 tablespoons olive oil
3 cups water
White pepper
Tabasco sauce
Celery salt (**or** onion salt)
4–6 tablespoons guacamole
4–6 nasturtium flowers
   (optional)

1. Coarsely chop the leek (white part only). Coarsely chop the celery, fennel bulb, red bell pepper (discarding seeds and membranes), and the Spanish onion. Cut each of the tomatoes into 8 pieces. Crush the garlic cloves gently.
2. Prepare 2 bouquet garnis (see "Bag o' Spices" on page 8): In the first bag, combine the thyme, rosemary, parsley, basil, and fennel sticks. In the second one, combine the anise, fennel, and coriander seeds.
3. In a soup pot, heat the olive oil. Add the leek, celery, fennel bulb, red bell pepper, onion, and garlic. Cover, turn the heat very low, and allow to soften for 10 minutes.
4. Add the 2 bouquet garnis, the tomato pieces, and the water. Bring to a boil, reduce to a simmer, and cook for 15 minutes.
5. Remove from heat and allow to cool slightly. Discard the bouquet garnis. Using a blender or food processor, purée the mixture. Season with salt, white pepper, Tabasco sauce, and celery salt to taste. Refrigerate to chill thoroughly.
6. Ladle the soup into individual serving bowls. Garnish each with 1 tablespoon of guacamole and a nasturtium flower.

Avocado Vichyssoise

1¼ pounds new potatoes
4 cups light vegetable broth
   or Basic Chicken Broth
   (see recipe on page 3)
1 lemon
2 avocados

¼ teaspoon cumin **or** curry
   powder
Fresh cilantro (optional)

Serves 6

Two varieties of avocado are available. One type has smooth green skin; the other has darker pebbled-textured skin.

1. Quarter the potatoes. Place them in a large saucepan covered with water. Bring to a boil, reduce to a simmer, and cook for 15 minutes.
2. Meanwhile, chill the chicken broth and peel and coarsely chop the avocados. Juice the lemon and chop the cilantro, reserving some leaves.
3. When the potatoes are cooked, drain them and put the potatoes into a large bowl or soup pot; discard the cooking liquid. Add the avocados, broth, lemon juice, and cumin (or curry). Using a blender or food processor, purée the mixture. Refrigerate to chill thoroughly. Garnish with a few cilantro leaves and serve.

Pitting an Avocado

For both types of avocado, start by cutting through the skin, down to the pit, and scoring the fruit lengthwise. Gripping both halves, give a quick twist to separate one half from the pit, leaving the other half holding that large nut. If you plan to use only half of the avocado, it's best to leave the pit in the unused portion, since it prevents the fruit from turning brown overnight. To remove the pit, hack into the middle of it with the blade of your knife, gripping the fruit in the palm of your other hand; twist the knife clockwise to loosen the pit. It should fall right out of a ripe avocado.

Melon Soup with Almonds

Serves 4

Garnish with the toasted almonds and chopped mint.

1 small, ripe honeydew melon
½ of a jalapeño chili
½ cup lime juice
½ cup plain yogurt
Salt and pepper
½ cup sliced almonds
2 teaspoons water
¼ cup fresh chopped mint

1. Cut the flesh of the melon into ½-inch cubes. Seed and mince the jalapeño.
2. Using a blender or food processor, purée the melon cubes, lime juice, yogurt, and salt and pepper to taste. Refrigerate until thoroughly chilled.
3. Preheat the oven to 325 degrees. Using a baking dish with low sides, combine the sliced almonds with the water and additional salt to taste. Cook for 15 minutes. Allow them to cool. Meanwhile, chop the mint.
4. Ladle the soup into 4 individual soup bowls.

Fruit Soup with Sesame

Serves 6

Garnish with the reserved fruit and the toasted sesame seeds and serve.

2 teaspoons sesame seeds
½ pound (8 ounces) cherries
  *(Queen Anne **or** bing)*
1 pint strawberries
½ pint blackberries
4 plums
¼ cup minced candied ginger
Cinnamon

1. Preheat the oven to 350 degrees. Place the sesame seeds in a single layer in a small baking dish. Toast for 3 to 4 minutes. Remove from heat.
2. Reserve 6 cherries, 3 strawberries (cut in half) and 3 blackberries (cut in half) for a garnish. Pit the plums and cherries and slice into bite-sized pieces. Remove the stems from the strawberries and quarter them. Mince the candied ginger. Purée together all of the fruit (*except* the fruit reserved for garnish).
3. Divide the fruit mixture into the individual soup bowls. Add a faint dash of cinnamon to each bowl.

Swedish Rhubarb Soup

2 pounds fresh rhubarb
2 teaspoons potato starch **or**
   cornstarch
1 cup sugar

6 cups water
Cinnamon (optional)
Raspberries (optional)

1. Trim the rhubarb, peeling some of the stalks if necessary. Cut them into ½-inch pieces.
2. Using a large saucepan, combine the rhubarb pieces, water, and sugar. Simmer for 6 minutes, or until tender, stirring several times. Allow to cool slightly.
3. Whisk in the potato starch (or cornstarch), stirring well until the soup thickens slightly. Chill thoroughly.
4. Ladle into individual soup bowls.

Serves 6

Garnish with a couple of shakes of cinnamon and a few raspberries.

Strawberry Soup

4 cups sliced strawberries
1 banana
1½ cups cubed toasted pound
   cake
1 cup orange juice

1 cup light sour cream
1 tablespoon raspberry **or**
   cherry liqueur
1 ice cube
6 mint sprigs (optional)

1. Preheat oven to 325 degrees. Stem and slice the strawberries. Cut the banana into fourths. Cut the cake into ½-inch cubes and toast.
2. Using a food processor or blender, purée the strawberries, banana, orange juice, sour cream, and liqueur. Pour the mixture into a bowl. Add the ice cube and stir until it melts, chilling the fruit mixture.
3. Ladle the soup into the individual bowls. Garnish with the cake croutons and a sprig of mint.

Serves 6

It's simple to make "cake croutons." Place a single layer of cubed pound cake in the toaster oven. Toast for 5 minutes, turn and toast again briefly.

Cherry Tomato Gazpacho

Serves 2

Top with walnuts and the fresh chopped dill as a garnish.

1 cup diced cucumber
¼ teaspoon pepper
2 tablespoons walnut oil
1 clove garlic, minced
¾ cup cherry tomatoes

1 cup plain yogurt
2 tablespoons fresh chopped
  dill (optional)
Walnuts (optional)

1. Begin ahead of time by peeling and dicing the cucumber and marinating it in the refrigerator (for at least 2 hours) in the pepper, walnut oil, and minced garlic cloves.
2. When the cucumber is done marinating, drain the cucumbers. Add the cherry tomatoes and the yogurt, stirring well. Chop the dill. Pour the soup into serving bowls.

Parade of Summer Vegetables Gazpacho

Serves 6–8

For this summer soup, be sure that you visit your local vegetable stand and buy only the freshest vegetables available.

4 large tomatoes
4 ears corn
1 cup peas
1 cup green beans
4 zucchini

3 summer squash
1 cup broccoli florets
½ cups cooked pasta shells
10 cups V-8 (low-sodium)

1. Chop and seed the tomatoes, husk the corn, shell the peas, and trim the green beans. Cut the zucchini and the summer squash into bite-size chunks. Cut the smallest florets off the broccoli.
2. Steam the broccoli florets for 8 minutes. Steam or roast the corn separately, for about 8 minutes. With a sharp knife, cut the kernels off the cobs.
3. In individual soup bowls, pour the V-8. Divide the raw vegetables equally among the bowls; then divide the corn and pasta. Top each bowl with a few of the florets. Serve.

Scandinavian Fruit Soup

¼ *cup tapioca*
1 cup dried peaches
1 cup prunes
1 cup dried cherries

2 cups raisins **or** *currants*
2 small tart apples
1 cup dried apricots
½ *cup sugar*

1. Using a large soup pot, combine the tapioca, peaches, prunes, cherries, and raisins. Cover with cold water. Bring to a boil.
2. Meanwhile, dice the apples. Add them to the pot, reduce to a simmer, and cook for 20 minutes, stirring often.
3. Add the apricots and the sugar, simmering and stirring often until the tapioca is transparent but not mushy. Add water to reach the desired consistency.

> **Serves 8–10**
>
> Serve hot in mugs or as a cold soup. It keeps well refrigerated or frozen.
>
> ∾

Cucumber Soup

1 large cucumber
2 cups plain yogurt
½ *cup tomato paste*
½ *teaspoon coriander*
1 clove garlic, minced

Black pepper to taste
Fresh mint (optional)

Peel and dice the cucumber and put it in a blender or food processor. Add the rest of the ingredients (*except* the mint) and blend until smooth. Chill in the refrigerator until ready to serve, garnished with fresh mint.

> **Serves 4**
>
> For an added color and flavor, drop a few fresh, cherry tomatoes in each individual bowl before serving.
>
> ∾

Chilled Shrimp and Cucumber Soup

*8 large cucumbers
   (about 2 pounds)*
¼ cup red wine vinegar
1 tablespoon sugar
1 teaspoon salt
*1 pound raw shrimp (the
   smallest you can find)*
2 tablespoons sweet butter
½ cup dry white vermouth
*Salt and freshly ground black
   pepper*

1½ cups cold buttermilk
*¾ cup chopped fresh dill
   (or more to taste), plus
   additional for garnish*

1. Peel and coarsely chop the cucumbers. Toss them with the vinegar, sugar and salt; let stand for 30 minutes.
2. Meanwhile, peel and devein the shrimp. Rinse them and pat them dry. Melt the butter in a small skillet. Add the shrimp, raise the heat, and toss them until they turn pink, 2 to 3 minutes. Remove the shrimp with a slotted spoon and set aside. Add the vermouth to the skillet and boil until it is reduced to a few teaspoonfuls; pour over the shrimp and season with salt and pepper.
3. Drain the cucumbers and transfer them to a food processor fitted with a steel blade. Process briefly, then add the buttermilk and continue to process until smooth. Add the fresh dill to taste and process briefly, about 1 second.
4. Pour the cucumber mixture into a bowl and stir in the shrimp and their liquid; refrigerate, covered, until very cold.

Fresh Cantaloupe and Raspberry Soup

1 ripe cantaloupe
1 cup fresh raspberries, plus 4
  raspberries for garnish
½ cup orange juice

Juice of ½ a lemon
Juice of ½ a lime
4 large fresh mint leaves

Serves 4

Garnish each serving with a mint leaf and a whole raspberry.

1. Cut the cantaloupe in half, clean out the seeds, peel the halves, and cut the flesh into 1-inch pieces. Put the cantaloupe in a blender to create a smooth purée. Pour into a large bowl. Blend the raspberries into a smooth purée. Pour this into a strainer and push the juice and pulp through the strainer into a small bowl in order to remove the seeds. This should yield about ½ cup (repeat with more raspberries if it comes up short).
2. Stir the purées together, then add the juices and stir to blend.

Roasted Vegetable Gazpacho

4 beefsteak tomatoes
2 medium zucchini
1 medium eggplant
2 medium onions
10 cloves garlic
6 tablespoons olive oil

4 cups Roasted Vegetable Broth
  (see recipe on page 8)
¼ cup sherry vinegar
Black pepper
4 slices stale bread
Fresh cilantro (optional)

Serves 6–8

Garnish with the freshly chopped cilantro before serving.

1. Preheat the oven to 400 degrees. Cut the tomatoes and zucchini into large chunks. Peel the eggplant and the onions; cut them into chunks. Peel the garlic cloves, leaving them whole. Toss the vegetables in a bowl with olive oil; place them in a single layer on a roasting pan. Cook for 25 minutes, turning the vegetables over halfway through.
2. Purée the vegetables with the broth and place in a large bowl. Add the sherry vinegar and pepper. Tear the bread into pieces (discard the crusts) and stir them into the mixture. Refrigerate for several hours (or overnight).

Summer Borscht

Serve 4

The prepared beet soup base may be stored in the refrigerator for a few days.

4 medium-sized beets, cleaned
5 cups water
1 pinch of salt
1 tablespoon white vinegar
2 hard-boiled eggs, chopped
2 medium-sized pickling cucumbers, chopped

1 bunch scallions, chopped
4 tablespoons sour cream

1. Boil the beets in the water, unpeeled, for 20 to 25 minutes; remove the beets with a slotted spoon, leaving the water to boil. When the beets are cool enough to handle, peel and grate them; return them to the boiling water. Cook for another 10 to 15 minutes, adding the salt and vinegar. Remove from heat and allow to cool. Refrigerate until thoroughly chilled.
2. Pour the soup into large serving bowls. Add some egg, cucumbers, scallions, and a tablespoon of sour cream to each; mix well and serve.

Cooking Beets—Preserving Nutrition
The flavorful, nutrient-rich juices in beets are water soluble. To lock in the sweetness, color, and food value of these wonderful vegetables, consider cooking them in their skins. When boiling them, put a few drops of red wine vinegar in the water, which also helps seal in the juices. Beets can also be baked whole, like potatoes, then peeled and sliced.

Index

THE EVERYTHING ONE-POT COOKBOOK

By Lisa Rojak

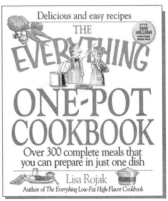

What could be easier than cooking an entire meal using just one pot? One-pot cuisine is characterized by hearty, satisfying dishes that can be prepared using only one of a variety of conventional cooking techniques: a single baking pan, skillet, slow cooker, or conventional stovetop pot. *The Everything® One-Pot Cookbook* features hundreds of exciting recipes that are guaranteed crowd pleasers, with minimal mess. From appetizers to entrees and even desserts, these one-pot meals are quick, simple, and delicious.

Trade paperback, $12.95
1-58062-186-4, 288 pages

OTHER *EVERYTHING*® BOOKS BY ADAMS MEDIA CORPORATION

Everything® **Pregnancy Organizer**
$15.00, 1-58062-336-0

Everything® **Project Management Book**
$12.95, 1-58062-583-5

Everything® **Puppy Book**
$12.95, 1-58062-576-2

Everything® **Quick Meals Cookbook**
$14.95, 1-58062-488-X

Everything® **Resume Book**
$12.95, 1-58062-311-5

Everything® **Romance Book**
$12.95, 1-58062-566-5

Everything® **Running Book**
$12.95, 1-58062-618-1

Everything® **Sailing Book, 2nd Ed.**
$12.95, 1-58062-671-8

Everything® **Saints Book**
$12.95, 1-58062-534-7

Everything® **Scrapbooking Book**
$14.95, 1-58062-729-3

Everything® **Selling Book**
$12.95, 1-58062-319-0

Everything® **Shakespeare Book**
$12.95, 1-58062-591-6

Everything® **Slow Cooker Cookbook**
$14.95, 1-58062-667-X

Everything® **Soup Cookbook**
$14.95, 1-58062-556-8

Everything® **Spells and Charms Book**
$12.95, 1-58062-532-0

Everything® **Start Your Own Business Book**
$12.95, 1-58062-650-5

Everything® **Stress Management Book**
$14.95, 1-58062-578-9

Everything® **Study Book**
$12.95, 1-55850-615-2

Everything® **T'ai Chi and QiGong Book**
$12.95, 1-58062-646-7

Everything® **Tall Tales, Legends, and Outrageous Lies Book**
$12.95, 1-58062-514-2

Everything® **Tarot Book**
$12.95, 1-58062-191-0

Everything® **Thai Cookbook**
$14.95, 1-58062-733-1

Everything® **Time Management Book**
$12.95, 1-58062-492-8

Everything® **Toasts Book**
$12.95, 1-58062-189-9

Everything® **Toddler Book**
$12.95, 1-58062-592-4

Everything® **Total Fitness Book**
$12.95, 1-58062-318-2

Everything® **Trivia Book**
$12.95, 1-58062-143-0

Everything® **Tropical Fish Book**
$12.95, 1-58062-343-3

Everything® **Vegetarian Cookbook**
$12.95, 1-58062-640-8

Everything® **Vitamins, Minerals, and Nutritional Supplements Book**
$12.95, 1-58062-496-0

Everything® **Weather Book**
$14.95, 1-58062-668-8

Everything® **Wedding Book, 2nd Ed.**
$14.95, 1-58062-190-2

Everything® **Wedding Checklist**
$7.95, 1-58062-456-1

Everything® **Wedding Etiquette Book**
$7.95, 1-58062-454-5

Everything® **Wedding Organizer**
$15.00, 1-55850-828-7

Everything® **Wedding Shower Book**
$7.95, 1-58062-188-0

Everything® **Wedding Vows Book**
$7.95, 1-58062-455-3

Everything® **Weddings on a Budget Book**
$9.95, 1-58062-782-X

Everything® **Weight Training Book**
$12.95, 1-58062-593-2

Everything® **Wicca and Witchcraft Book**
$14.95, 1-58062-725-0

Everything® **Wine Book**
$12.95, 1-55850-808-2

Everything® **World War II Book**
$12.95, 1-58062-572-X

Everything® **World's Religions Book**
$12.95, 1-58062-648-3

Everything® **Yoga Book**
$12.95, 1-58062-594-0

*Prices subject to change without notice.

EVERYTHING KIDS' SERIES!

Everything® **Kids' Baseball Book, 2nd Ed.**
$6.95, 1-58062-688-2

Everything® **Kids' Cookbook**
$6.95, 1-58062-658-0

Everything® **Kids' Joke Book**
$6.95, 1-58062-686-6

Everything® **Kids' Mazes Book**
$6.95, 1-58062-558-4

Everything® **Kids' Money Book**
$6.95, 1-58062-685-8

Everything® **Kids' Monsters Book**
$6.95, 1-58062-657-2

Everything® **Kids' Nature Book**
$6.95, 1-58062-684-X

Everything® **Kids' Puzzle Book**
$6.95, 1-58062-687-4

Everything® **Kids' Science Experiments Book**
$6.95, 1-58062-557-6

Everything® **Kids' Soccer Book**
$6.95, 1-58062-642-4

Everything® **Travel Activity Book**
$6.95, 1-58062-641-6

Available wherever books are sold!
To order, call 800-872-5627, or visit us at everything.com

Everything® is a registered trademark of Adams Media Corporation.